We Scholars

We Scholars

Changing the Culture
of the University

DAVID DAMROSCH

Harvard University Press
Cambridge, Massachusetts
London, England
1995

Library of Congress Cataloging-in-Publication Data
Damrosch, David.
We scholars: changing the culture of the
university / David Damrosch.
p.   cm.
Includes bibliographical references and index.
ISBN 0-674-94842-4 (cloth)
ISBN 0-674-94843-2 (paper)
1. Education, Higher—United States—Aims and objectives.
2. Universities and colleges—United States—Faculty.
3. Universities and colleges—United States—Departments.
4. Expertise. 5. Education, Humanistic—United States. 6. United
States—Intellectual life—20th century.   I. Title.
LA227.4.D35   1995
378.73—dc20
94-32442
CIP

To my wife
Lori Fisler Damrosch
closest of colleagues

Acknowledgments

By its very nature, this book is the product of conversation with many of my students, colleagues, and teachers over the years. In particular, the manuscript has benefited from perceptive readings by my brother Leo Damrosch, my colleague Priscilla Wald, my editors Lindsay Waters and Ann Hawthorne, and two readers for Harvard University Press, Roger Abrahams and Theda Skocpol. Recalling valuable conversations with many people, I want to signal especially the impetus provided by discussions with Kenneth Bruffee, Caroline Bynum, Ann Douglas, Hal Freedman, Bruce Greenwald, Jean Howard, Constance Jordan, Dominique Jullien, Steven Marcus, Herb Marks, James Mirollo, and Laura Slatkin. Finally, I am grateful for the chance to observe the very different academic culture in which my wife and her colleagues work at the Columbia Law School. The dedication to this book is meant to suggest this and much, much more.

Contents

The extent and towering structure of the sciences have increased enormously, and therewith also the probability that the philosopher will grow tired even as a learner, or will attach himself somewhere and "specialise": so that he will no longer attain to his elevation, that is to say, to his superspection, his circumspection, and his *despection*. Or he gets aloft too late, when the best of his maturity and strength is past; or when he is impaired, coarsened, and deteriorated, so that his view, his general estimate of things, is no longer of much importance. It is perhaps just the refinement of his intellectual conscience that makes him hesitate and linger on the way; he dreads the temptation to become a dilettante, a millipede, a milleantenna . . . This is in the last instance a question of taste, if it has not really been a question of conscience.

—Friedrich Nietzsche, "We Scholars"

Introduction

Readers of *Jude the Obscure* will remember a character they might prefer to forget: Jude's wizened, stunted son "Father Time," who hangs his siblings and himself late in the novel. Although Hardy presents Father Time as a type of the modern age, "the outcome of new views of life . . . the beginning of the coming universal wish not to live" (331), his readers have generally felt that he was going a bit too far in the creation of this melodramatic child. Yet Hardy erred in this only: his archetype of the modern *youth* has proved to be the type of the modern *scholar*. What academic today can read Father Time's suicide note without a shudder of recognition? "Done because we are too menny." Even as we stifle our impulse to correct the boy's spelling, must we not also repress a fleeting desire to follow his example?

Modern scholarship has been marked, above all, by its astonishing scale and scope; an immense volume of work has been produced, displaying close attention to masses of data and to nuances of texts, and, lately, an intensity of both theoretical and cultural concern. Yet along with this growth in scholarship, and indeed in part because of it, an insecurity of purpose pervades both the humanities and the social sciences, in a struggle for self-definition that reflects an uncertainty as to the larger social value of scholarly work. We must even question the usefulness of the vast accumulation of scholarship to other scholars: our academic fields are strewn with more books and articles than anyone can possibly read, many of them (worse yet) actually worth reading. Are we scholars ourselves, in Father Time's incisive formulation, *too menny?*

The growth of the "towering structure" of scholarship has only accelerated since Nietzsche discussed its effects in 1886. In the essay from which I take my title, he noted the growing pressure toward an exhaustive and exhausting specialization, and he also emphasized the close connection between modern scholarship and modern politics, describing "the declaration of independence of the scientific man" as "one of the subtler after-effects of democratic organization and disorganization" (498). This linkage became especially close in the United States from the 1880s onward, as German scholarly methods took root in the American academic system.

Increasingly consulted—and funded—by government and by civic-minded individuals and foundations, academic experts began to play a prominent role in public policymaking at the turn of the century. As the academic system grew in the ensuing decades, an ever greater proportion of intellectuals of all sorts, from defense strategists to novelists, found a home on a college or university campus. This migration has had ambiguous results in American intellectual life. Extended analysis of public problems has come more and more to be conducted by academics, rather than by the independent intellectuals who had earlier supported themselves by private incomes or by their writing alone. In itself, the movement of intellectual work to a campus base need pose no problem, especially as one result has been a tremendous growth in the sheer numbers of researchers. We now have some 660,000 fulltime college and university faculty, and so we nominally have far more intellectual workers than ever before; and yet it is hard to feel that we have more real *intellectuals*. The shifting of so many resources onto our campuses has come at a price, for modern academic life, as Nietzsche argued, profoundly inhibits the broad consideration of general questions.

A substantial number of people engaged with intellectual issues still work in other locations, in politics and in the media, in think tanks, religious organizations, professional and trade associations, and the research departments of lobbying groups. Yet even these organizations often show a quasi-academic specialization of focus, of expertise, and of perspective. A prime reason for this mimicking of academic habits of thought is the fact that the lobbyists and think-tankers themselves are now likely to be the products of extended academic training. A generation or two ago, committed intellectuals would often have gone to work in journalism or in the public sector immediately upon graduation from college, if they had even bothered to finish college at all. This is no longer the case. More and more intellectuals of all sorts now begin by earning graduate degrees in fields like economics, political science, or history, even if they then make their careers outside academia. Undergraduate curricula as well have become increasingly specialized in the postwar era, and so even before they enter graduate school intellectuals' training is characterized more by specialized inquiry than by the broad perspectives of general education.

To an unprecedented degree, then, American intellectual life today is shaped by the values and habits of mind inculcated during years of specialized undergraduate and graduate training. In his book *The Last Intellectuals* (1987), Russell Jacoby saw this development as signaling the eclipse of genuine intellectual life. Jacoby argued that the basis for public debate has eroded as the contentious, independent, wide-ranging "last intellectuals" of the past generation have been replaced by jargon-writing academic specialists. At the same time, as several other writers have emphasized, the shift of intellectuals into academia set the stage for a new politicization of teaching and scholarship, a development that can be seen positively as fostering an overdue engagement with the real world, or negatively as exposing the current generation of undergraduates to "illiberal education" at the hands of a new corps of "tenured radicals," to recall the titles of widely read books by Dinesh D'Souza and Roger Kimball.

Yet academic specialization is as much a fact of life as the complexity of modern society, and it can hardly just be wished away. For better or for worse, our colleges and universities are the primary locales in which the present generation of intellectuals now works and in which the next generation will be trained. If public debate needs to be revitalized, as many feel, we ought to begin by reconsidering the ways in which we train our future debaters. I propose to examine the structuring of academic work, looking at its history and its present political economy, and to outline a series of fundamental reforms, both in our teaching of students and in the ways we develop and circulate ideas. These reforms are needed not only if we are to gain a better purchase on general public problems, but also if we are to do better in scholarly communication across the lines of differing bodies of knowledge and divergent methods of analysis.

Our present perplexities stem as much from the wealth of specialized inquiry as from the poverty of general discussion. There are still some disciplines in which scholars complain that there are too few workers and too few outlets for publication—Egyptology comes to mind, for instance—but in most fields scholars find themselves increasingly unable to "keep up with," or bear up under, the drifting accumulation of masses of specialized scholarship, across whose surface there play the shifting lights of a vertiginous succession of competing theoretical models. Information theorists sometimes use the analogy of a pot of boiling water: increasing the information coming into a system is like increasing the heat applied to the pot. As the water begins to boil, it circulates in patterns of growing complexity, so as to dissipate the excess energy it is receiving. But a system can multiply its patterns only up to a point: then the patterning breaks down, and the material itself is transformed into some very different form, as when the water turns to steam. The state of fields and subfields in many disciplines seems to be reaching a boiling point; how are we to manage their transformation?

Underlying both scholarly uncertainty and public debate on the current state of academia, and often unseen by the debaters themselves, are deep structural tensions in the modern university. These tensions are the subject of this book.

Too often, in an extension of academic specialization, both the proponents and the critics of academic change have addressed these matters in piecemeal fashion, picking one issue as the essential one that needs to be got right. The core curriculum should, or shouldn't, be revised to include writing by women and ethnic minorities; the methods and perspectives of antihumanist philosophers like Michel Foucault or Jacques Derrida should, or shouldn't, be the basis of teaching and scholarship in general; professors should teach more and write less; then again, competition from abroad dictates that we redouble funds for basic research.

These issues are approached in largely separate ways by people who work from one or another single perspective. Administrators discuss administrative problems, people in literature departments reconstruct the canon, journalists conduct interviews with some of the more newsworthy administrators and professors, and sociologists do statistical analyses of attitudes and trends, but each group of inquirers pays little attention to what the other groups are writing even on the same issues. We need to engage these disparate perspectives more fully with one another, if we are to get beyond the endless rehashing of the latest polemics. Particularly when discussion focuses on questions of the construction and uses of scholarship, the history of ideas has been the usual framework within which the perennial "crisis in the academy" is addressed. Yet equally important are the *institutional* history, and the institutional structures, within which ideas about scholarship have been played out. This is so not only because scholarly ideas necessarily take shape within scholarly institutions, but equally because ideas about scholarly method generally prove to be closely dependent upon ideas about scholarly *community*.

A central theme in the following chapters is that every argument about the material scholars should study, and every argument about the methods to be used, is at the same time an argument about the nature of the community that is to do the studying. If genuine academic reform is to occur, this community needs to be more fully understood, and then creatively reconceived. In bringing together insights from the sociology of education, organizational behavior, and critical theory, I wish to propose a new model of the scholarly community and of its relation to society at large.

We work within departments as well as within disciplines, and our departments in turn are anchored in the large and complex institutions that are our modern colleges and universities. The role of scholarship in the creation or stifling of community is most pronounced in universities, but colleges too share these problems, both because their own faculty are largely university trained and because academic work in colleges too is increasingly being modeled on university-style patterns. In fact the growing dominance of specialization in modern times has contributed to a process of homogenization on college and university campuses alike, where support for certain modes of scholarship too often leads to the devaluation of most other kinds of academic work.

If we wish to combat this homogenization, we need to focus on the deep institutional structures that sustain but also constrain our work. As Mary Douglas has said,

> Institutions systematically direct individual memory and channel our perceptions into forms compatible with the relations they authorize. They fix processes that are essentially dynamic, they hide their influence, and they rouse our emotions to a standardized pitch on standardized issues . . . The solutions they proffer only come from the limited range of their experience. If the institution is one that depends on participation, it will reply to our frantic question: "More participation!" If it is one that depends on authority, it will only reply: "More authority!" Institutions have the pathetic megalomania of the computer whose whole vision of the world is its own program. For us, the hope of intellectual independence is to resist, and the necessary first step in resistance is to discover how the institutional grip is laid upon our mind.   (*How Institutions Think*, 92)

Academic work is institutionally arranged in a patterned isolation of disciplines, and then of specialized fields within disciplines. This patterning is not something inherent in the material; it stems from decisions made a century ago when the American university assumed its modern form. Those decisions reflected political and economic assumptions then current, and although conditions have changed in society at large, our academic structures have remained relatively constant, and the old assumptions built into our institutions continue to have largely unseen but pervasive effects. The result to this day is a heady mix of scholarly alienation and disciplinary nationalism that shape the questions we ask and the ways in which we ask them. These scholarly values in turn foster—and reward—alienation and aggression at all levels of academic life. Little meaningful reform can be achieved until this situation is changed.

On many campuses, and in much of the scholarship produced on them, we see a growing concern to find ways to transcend both the disciplinary isolation and the social disjointedness that pervade academic life. In scholarship, interdisciplinary work is meant to bridge the disciplines, and even specialized work these days often focuses on crosscutting issues like race, class, and gender, seeking to make sense of the relations among the varied social groups now increasingly visible on campus and in the world at large. Too often, though, these efforts are hampered by the archaic hyperindividualism of our prevailing academic ethos. The humanities are particularly wedded to the model of individual scholarly work, but even the social sciences display a pervasive individualism, both in the way work is carried on and in the way society itself is represented. Social science articles that are written by multiple authors are certainly collaborative, but often this collaboration is of a circumscribed sort. The authors are frequently based within a single field, each doing part of the interviewing or statistical analysis for what is fundamentally a project developed from a single perspective by one or two primary authors. As a result, often in the social sciences and almost always in the humanities, interdisciplinary work ends up being folded within the values of individual production. Either it is limited to the relatively modest crossdisciplinary work that a single scholar can do well, or else it degenerates into the shallow globalizations to which individuals are forced if they go beyond their real areas of expertise.

The important issues of race, class, and gender all too readily face this difficulty, or else they are restored to specificity at the substantial price of a renarrowing into one or another identity politics. Identity politics is in fact a sort of social corollary of academic specialization, which is why it has become so popular in our colleges and universities: it readily becomes just a new form of business as usual. As early as 1916, John Dewey observed that the increasing fragmentation of the curriculum reflected "the isolation of social groups and classes" in modern society (*Democracy and Education*, 249). By now we have reached the point at which a sort of biofeedback loop comes into play: a small-group identity literally becomes a scholarly specialty, if one is, say, a Jewish feminist whose field is modern Jewish women's writing. The new emphasis on particular identities can be a great opportunity, at once socially and intellectually, as the academy is no longer closed to all Jews except those like Franz Boas and Lionel Trilling who had forsworn any direct connection to Judaism. But this opportunity also carries with it the danger of a new kind of conformity, as when many programs in women's studies foster a rather strongly (and often similarly) defined political outlook, or when black literary scholars run against the assumption that "of course" their scholarly field is African-American studies.

Neither specialization nor identity politics should be faulted for their convergence, and neither should simply be wished away—an undesirable reaction even if it were possible. There are good reasons why most scholars today are committed specialists, just as there are good reasons why many people now find the old generalizing image of the melting pot to be inadequate. Indeed, these good reasons are often the same reasons, seen respectively in their intellectual and social manifestations. We do specialization and individualism very well in this country, and there is a cultural logic to our fondness for building group identity on the basis of shared individual interests or background. One consequence of our talent for specialization is that we enjoy the best system of higher education in the world. Compared to the centralized, bureaucratic university systems of most other countries, the American academy is in a real sense "the home of the free," and this freedom offers exceptional choices and opportunities for students and faculty alike. At the same time, it must be said that we do *freedom* rather better than we do *home,* and indeed the persistent weakness of community in our country leads to pronounced limitations on the freedom of the less powerful members of our society and its institutions.

Within academia, we need to do better at talking across the lines of specialties and identities, lest the rifts between them deepen and proliferate. The great strength of specialization, as of all kinds of small-group identity, is that those in the group can communicate on the basis of shared understandings and a shared language, whether it be a professional jargon or a social slang. The great difficulty comes when in-groups find that they need to coexist with, and really understand, groups very different from themselves. We should give renewed attention to the ways in which we can bring together differing perspectives and the people who hold them, even as we continue to develop further the strengths of specialized work and individual identity.

In academia as in society at large, our increasing stress on personal and small-group identity has not yet been matched by a commitment to attending to other points of view and learning from them, particularly when those viewpoints differ markedly from our own. Even within a single department we now regularly find not only more and more divergences in positions and approaches but also differences concerning what should count as scholarship at all. In a sense, such disagreement is nothing new, and yet the old academic tensions now seem more problematic than ever, since there genuinely is greater diversity in our departments than there has ever been before, both in terms of the makeup of the student and faculty populations and in terms of the questions being presented for consideration.

When campuses were more socially homogeneous than they now are, scholars could assume a certain collegiality of debate, or at least a certain peaceful coexistence, even given disciplinary rifts such as those between cultural and physical anthropologists or between philologists and New Critics. Equally, the philologists and the New Critics would at least all be studying *texts,* and would not have to contemplate tenure decisions concerning people whose research involves analyzing pornographic films and interviewing sex workers. To date, we have responded poorly to these changes, and the result has been an increase in factionality and coterie behavior. This is as much an intellectual as a social problem, as we thereby lose the real opportunity offered today, to broaden our discussions in a new way.

The increasingly personal character of contemporary debate tends to obscure the degree to which the basic responsibility for our difficulties in communication lies with the institutional structures within which we work, and with the organizational culture that our institutions foster. When campus and public debate alike degenerate into brawls with gloves off, the natural temptation is to start swinging ourselves, or at best to step in with a referee's whistle. Soon, though, the sluggers are at it again, and it may be more to the point to ask ourselves why we have turned the campus into a boxing ring to begin with. In such a setting, it makes only a small difference whether our charges go on to fight with gloves on or off.

For this reason, in the following chapters I emphasize both the ways we train students and the personalities of the professors who do the training. For the better part of a century, we have been selecting for certain kinds of alienation and aggression on campus. We need to reconsider the sorts of academic personality we encourage— and even create—through our extended rituals of training and acculturation. The progressive isolation we enforce on graduate students

favors personalities who have relatively little need for extended intellectual exchange; over time, as such norms have taken hold, people
have self-selected in or out of academia accordingly. "Oh, yes," a
colleague once remarked when I raised this point, "I went to graduate
school because I flunked sandbox."

Over the years, we have built up a system that gives high marks
to people who flunk sandbox; professors who are themselves most
comfortable when working alone have come to assume that their
students should adopt a similar mode of work. The very structuring
of our graduate training emphasizes an increasing isolation, as students go from working in courses to working with a few professors
for their doctoral orals, and then working alone in the library to
complete a dissertation, often under the guidance of a single sponsor.
So natural does this progression seem that we rarely take note of the
cultural adjustment we require students to make in the process. We
make no direct effort to assist them in this change; still less, in many
fields, do we provide for more collaborative modes of advanced work
that might better suit our more intellectually sociable students.

Some students thrive under our essentially medieval model of apprenticeship, whereby the advanced student earns the guidance, and
ideally takes on the perspective, of an honored mentor. Yet all too
often this process fails to work as it should, to judge from the fact
that a surprisingly high number of people never complete their doc-
torate at all, a problem we will examine in detail in the fifth chapter.
Often as many as two-thirds of those who begin a Ph.D. program
fail to complete it, and yet few people seem to feel any responsibility
to improve the situation.

Alarming as they are, high dropout rates are not the only problem.
Equally serious is the situation of someone for whom the mentor-
apprentice system works poorly. All too often, students struggle to
an unhappy conclusion with an unworkable topic—or with an adviser who gives poor advice or no advice at all. Yet the general isolation of graduate training makes this situation seem inevitable, even
if years of people's lives are wasted in the process. While I was in
graduate school, I had a friend who spent five years writing a dissertation on what had at first seemed to be a good idea, one that I believe
was suggested by her sponsor. It was a study of a single particle in a
long-dead language. Somehow this topic began to pale after a couple

of years; worse yet, my friend and her sponsor began to disagree concerning her approach and conclusions. She finally completed the thesis, failed to find a teaching job, and left the profession. I do not know whether her difficulties on the job market stemmed from problems in her argument, from a lack of support for genuinely good work by an unsympathetic sponsor, or simply from a glut of single-particlists on the market that year. But I thought highly of her intelligence, her literary sensitivity, and the depth of her knowledge of a range of ancient Mediterranean cultures, and I cannot help feeling that she was poorly served by the master-apprentice model of doctoral work.

The problem of scholarly isolation is easy to see but difficult to address. My effort is to come at it from a variety of directions. The first chapter sets the stage historically, looking at the rise of modern specialization in the context of late nineteenth-century ideas of nationalism, economics, and individualism. A historical perspective can bring out certain assumptions and processes that were clearer in their inception than they may be now that they have been routinized, operating almost invisibly as part of our daily environment. Above all, a historical perspective can help to demythologize our current practices, reminding us that we do not work either within the timeless community of academic nostalgia or within the stable, steady-state system often presupposed by sociological analysis.

An approach that is both historically grounded and sociological in emphasis can do much to unveil the *political economy* of academic work, the subject of the second chapter. Far from the "organized anarchy" it is often taken to be, academia is more of a quiet plutocracy, masked by nominally democratic procedures. The third chapter explores the psychological consequences of this economy—the sorts of scholarly personality our system fosters, and the ways in which those personalities in turn reinforce our underlying academic political economy. This historical, sociological, and psychological account provides the basis for the ensuing discussion of reform.

Bringing these perspectives together means, first and foremost, resisting one's own *disciplinary inertia*. The Catch-22 here is that a really effective analysis of the problems of specialization requires a transcendence of specialization that can be fully realized only when the argument has been made and its implications carried through in practice. My goal is not to vanquish specialization, which will continue to thrive, as it should, but to describe new modes of interaction whereby, among other possible collaborative efforts, a group of specialists in different fields and disciplines could work together in a sustained way to produce a more effective version of this very book.

The fact is that a cosmopolitan, deracinated mastery of many disciplines by one individual is finally neither possible nor desirable; learning new disciplinary languages takes time, and one's "home" perspective pervasively shapes and even distorts one's grasp of new disciplines. Even so, although a definitive critique of specialization and its attendant principles of isolation and aggression may be impossible in the current era of the dominance of specialization, it is still true that a preliminary discussion of the problem is easier than our disciplinary habits of mind may lead us to think.

Considered as a field of study, academic life is a subject in which every young scholar is forced to develop a kind of expertise while still in graduate school. There is even a danger that people who are moved to write on academic issues have developed such strong opinions, and such a fund of telling experiences, that they may never realize the value of studying the literature *on* academia. A surprising number of recent contributions to debates on scholarship have been written in the mode of a busman's holiday: people who would never think of writing an article in their own field without first reading most of the literature on the subject will produce entire books that reflect only the most cursory attention to the work of specialists in the several fields that include academic life and work within their purview.

At times, a professor-administrator will even renounce reading the literature on principle, lest it tarnish the authenticity of direct experience. Jacques Barzun begins *The American University* by glancing ironically at the enthusiasm with which "well-known educators and anonymous compilers alike are collecting data without cease," and he stresses that "what I offer by way of panoramic view is an interpretation based on experience, rather than a report embodying comparative figures and 'studies'" (ix). At heart, Barzun's objection appears to be that such studies are actually *too* rooted in particular experience: they obscure the deeper truth that "the university is an institution transcending time and geography" (x). I myself will regularly recur to specific examples from my own institution and others I know well, since I wish to emphasize the local contexts that powerfully shape academic work. Yet personal experience alone can perhaps too quickly translate upward into broad generalities about "the idea of the university"; a solid base in the literature on academia helps to keep arguments on their feet. I am living testimony to the fact that a person based in the humanities can read the *Administrative Science Quarterly* and survive. Yet I also retain my own disciplinary fondness for close reading, and in the chapters that follow I periodically look closely at a particular discussion, both because I wish to do justice to the argument being made and because the way an argument is made can be as illuminating as the actual claim that is being defended.

Work along the lines proposed here can help to advance academic debate beyond the mixture of anecdote and innuendo that only reinforces the current polarization of liberals against conservatives. No matter whether an analyst thinks there has been too much change in academia or not enough, it is a rare study that looks closely at the actual workings of the encompassing institutional structures of the academic world. As a result, the exhortations for—or against— change tend to remain vague in content and isolated within the realms of intellectual or personal history. Progressive and conservative reforms alike will be temporary and superficial unless they encompass fundamental changes in the larger framework within which all teaching and research are conducted. In the second half of this book I detail examples of the kinds of reform that I believe are both desirable and manageable, looking first at undergraduate education and then at graduate education, for the ways we train scholars are crucial to any rethinking of the modes and culture of academic work. Finally, I discuss fully developed scholarly interaction, considering a range of collaborative work and the possibilities for bridging the gap between specialized scholarship and general public debate.

None of these discussions is intended to be exhaustive, and the reforms discussed are meant to be representative rather than exclusive. I have conceived of this book as a manifesto, partly because it is inevitably polemical, but also because it is necessarily tentative. I hope to provide a general framework within which we can begin to think more creatively about how we structure our work and how we manage the social relations that are so closely linked to the ways we work. Just because my emphasis is collaborative and institutional, I would emphasize that specific reforms can be worked out only locally, by interested people on actual campuses. At the same time, I try to give enough specific examples of reform to show something of the way in which the perspectives advanced here can work out in practice.

Colleges and universities are not only collections of disciplines; they are also institutions, and organizations, and sets of loosely interlocking cultures—cultures that vary not only by gender and ethnicity but equally by level of study or of academic rank. These different aspects must be studied together if we are to reconstitute the academic community—or, better, to *create* forms of academic community that would be something more than the contradiction in terms that the phrase now represents. At heart, my emphasis is ethical. Alienation and aggression are distasteful grounds for an educational system; further, I wish to argue that they are now also historically outmoded and intellectually counterproductive.

For all the emphasis in many disciplines on such traditional unities as "the West," "the self," and "society," scholarship itself has often been deeply divided, has even constituted itself *by means of* division: an ideology of unity and wholeness has strangely gone hand in hand with a hermeneutics of opposition, clothed in an aura of exile. Scholars are fond of thinking of themselves as laboring in exile from society at large, and they often employ opposition as a prime heuristic device. But not only as a heuristic device (here ethics comes in again): equally as a means of personal and institutional self-aggrandizement, enforcing and reinforcing the interests of senior faculty and large departments against younger and less established scholars and disciplines alike.

In exploring these problems I have somewhat paradoxical goals: as, for example, to convert people away from the wish to convert people; to envision disciplines as not primarily engaged in the production of disciples; to talk against the almost universal tendency of scholars to talk *across* one another rather than *with* one another; to propose a scholarship and teaching practices that can be simultaneously generalizing and specialized; to recover the breadth of the great generalists of the past two generations, while acknowledging, and indeed emphasizing, the loss of the very foundations upon which their work rested. Inspired by earlier synthetic thinkers like Durkheim, Freud, and Dewey, academic generalists like Lionel Trilling and Talcott Parsons ranged widely, writing powerfully synoptic studies of broad social problems. The more resolutely specialized generation that followed them rightly sensed that the earlier generalists had ridden roughshod over inconvenient facts, texts, and social groups. The intellectual and even ethical value of a full commitment to specialization seemed clear for a generation after World War II, but it carried intellectual and ethical costs of its own, costs that are becoming visible today.

The present state of advanced specialization is such that one person cannot master more than a small handful of fields even in a single discipline, still less do really meaningful work across more than two or three. Many questions extend well beyond this range, and those who are tempted to address them often do so at a heavy price: venturing bold speculations in areas they really know little about, paying scant attention or none at all to the scholarship in the fields they traverse. Equally to the point, even questions that can well be addressed within a single field are now often being framed in terms of issues and perspectives suggested in other fields and disciplines. As a result, work within a single field now often has a multidisciplinary penumbra, one that all too readily thickens into a blanket of received ideas, if the specialist who uses them has no deep and current knowledge of the fields in which those ideas developed.

What I have just said is less an indictment than a confession. I spent twenty years, beginning in college, trying to learn everything I needed to know to work on the things I wished to study. The problem was that I was loyal to too many interests, in several ancient and modern literatures, in literary theory, in biblical studies, in history, archaeology, anthropology, and art history. A reasonable enough constellation of interests, but in the advanced state of modern scholarship it is inherently unmanageable, if one wants to be seriously engaged with scholarly work and not simply retrace ground that others have already cultivated. To be a truly multidisciplinary scholar, one would have to be the "ideal reader with an ideal insomnia" whom Joyce desired for *Finnegans Wake*. Gradually, and to my regret, I have learned that I do, sometimes, need to sleep. Worse, my memory simply isn't good enough to hold in mind everything that would be necessary for full-scale multidisciplinary work.

This book is my attempt to ask how and why our academic culture makes it so difficult for us to mitigate such problems by working collaboratively. What would need to change for such work to seem more natural, and what would need to change for scholars simply to *listen* better to one another? Academic debate is too often academic nondebate, dominated by people who give short shrift to opposing views when they acknowledge them at all. Extended discussion is itself a form of collaboration, perhaps the most basic form of all, but it is too often short-circuited by the alienation and aggression built into the very structures of academic life and work. These structures can be changed, but this will take some doing.

Let us begin by defining the object of inquiry: Just what is the modern university? In the pages that follow I explore this question both functionally and historically: the university *is* what its members *do* (it is as much a workplace as a community), and what academics do intimately reflects the conditions under which modern scholarship began to be produced a hundred years ago, conditions that persist in more ways than is commonly realized.

1

Halving It All:
The Triumph of Specialization

Microcosm or Heterocosm?

What is the university? As its name implies, it is a universe of sorts, but it would be a mistake to think of it as a purely *parallel* universe, a microcosm of society at large. Many discussions of academic life and work seem to make just this assumption, either descriptively or prescriptively. College presidents extol their schools' success in training our citizens for the most effective possible participation in social life, while reformers call for the system to perform this task better. The calls to reform come in two varieties: either the university must change in such a way as to take account of new realities, or else the university must cease to be a mere supermarket of ideas, at the mercy of student or faculty whims and enthusiasms. In either view, the university is seen as a kind of mirror, reflecting either what society is or else what it should become.

Both kinds of call for reform arise from particular needs in specific times and places, and even in a single institution there will often be justification for changes in both directions. Modern economic life really does place a higher premium on computer languages than on Latin and Greek (there are computers now in use in my daughter's kindergarten class), and university budgets and staffing levels have changed accordingly in recent decades, often dramatically. Equally, however, if we are uncomfortably aware that ours is a society of mall-strolling consumers with short attention spans, we would prefer that the university not reflect this particular fact about ourselves. So we see efforts to strengthen course requirements, often including core curricula with extensive reading in Greek and Latin literature—in translation, of course.

As necessary as such reforms may often be, their appropriate sphere is usually relatively local: new course requirements or some faculty appointments may meet a given need. Real confusions arise when opposing camps—pragmatists versus idealists, or conservatives versus liberals—try to reform the university as a whole on the basis of one of the mimetic models sketched above, for the university is not truly parallel to society at large, either as it is or as it should be. Rather than a microcosm, it is what Mikhail Bakhtin would call a "heterocosm," or what Clark Kerr more modestly describes as "a partially autonomous subsystem" (*The Uses of the University*, 61). Both expressions point to the fact that the university is a universe obeying its own laws and deriving from its own history, intimately linked to current social realities at some points but bafflingly distant from them at others. This distance confers both independence and stability. A report by the Carnegie Council in 1980 began by asking how many Western institutions have shown real staying power across time. Beginning with 1530, the date of the founding of the Lutheran Church, the authors asked how many institutions that existed then can still be found now. The authors identified sixty-six in all: the Catholic Church, the Lutheran Church, the parliaments of Iceland and of the Isle of Man—and sixty-two universities (*Three Thousand Futures*, 9).

Much of this stability results from the university's ability to change constantly at a local level while varying little in many basic ways, so that contemporary concerns can coexist with very archaic procedures and values. Sedimented levels of history overlay one another, punctuated by igneous extrusions from the deep past. One of the world's chief centers of high-tech research, the American university is also in many ways a holdover from the Middle Ages, complete with an entrenched guild mentality and the indentured servitude of graduate student apprentices and postdoctoral journeymen. If the founding fathers of our country envisioned the American college as the center of rational inquiry in a secular society, as Allan Bloom has emphasized, this Enlightenment paternity is only half the story, for the mother of the university was the medieval Church—a leitmotif of the most important nineteenth-century statement of the principles of the university, Cardinal Newman's *The Idea of the University,* and a theme underlined in Jaroslav Pelikan's recent book of the same title. If you scratch beneath the surface of the contemporary academic entrepreneur, you are likely to find deeply held ecclesiastical beliefs, even monastic attitudes. Graduate training to this day emphasizes ascetic practices of self-discipline and meditative solitude, even though the actual lifestyle of the students' jet-setting sponsors may be rather different. The fact that different levels of belief and practice conflict in many ways does not prevent both from being firmly rooted, and the coexistence of contradictory impulses must be taken into consideration when one contemplates academic reform. The most rational modernization may encounter implacable resistance if it runs afoul of a professorial prerogative first established in the thirteenth century and maintained into the present with a tenacity only increased by the fact that it persists unconsciously and unquestioned.

It is, then, a mistake to suppose that the modern university is purely and simply modern. Old patterns can persist in many types of organization, but universities are almost unique in their degree of independence from year-to-year social change. In our society, only religious structures have an even longer life (priests celebrate Mass wearing the street clothes of first-century Palestine). Among secular institutions, none has the ability of the university to resist change, or to change from purely internal motives, for hundreds of years at a time. Whenever a given aspect of academic life or practice does become the subject of significant social scrutiny, any changes made will generally reflect the social values and constraints then current. Given a breakthrough of pressure from "the real world," typically in an area of social stress, the result will usually be the realignment of some aspect of the university toward contemporary society. Once a given structure is in place, though, it assumes a life of its own. It can persist indefinitely, developing in accordance with the internal logic of the university, but at an ever-increasing distance from society at large.

Language can give us some interesting examples. Having gradually metamorphosed into the modern vernaculars, Latin was preserved in monastic circles and then revived as a lingua franca in the Renaissance, used by diplomats, businessmen, and scholars alike. It became enshrined as the preferred language of scholarship and even of instruction in many universities. Once established, this pattern persisted for hundreds of years, long after no one else—apart from Catholic priests—was still using it. This led to the interesting phenomenon that modern biblical scholarship was conducted largely in Latin when that field of study first arose in Germany during the eighteenth century, even though Latin was the language neither of the biblical authors nor of any modern society—and was not even the language used in church by most of the biblical scholars themselves, who, as they were Protestants, worshipped using Luther's German translation of the Bible. The Bible, at least, is an ancient text, but the sway of Latin extended to the study of later literature as well. Matthew Arnold created a sensation in 1857, when he took the bold step of becoming the first Professor of Poetry at Oxford to lecture in English, a change he made as part of his program to reform education and make it accessible to more people.

The persistence of an archaic mode of speech in the nineteenth century was not simply the result of common agreement for the sake of scholarly convenience: the universities, and even the governments of their countries, enforced it upon their scholars. In 1841, for example, Søren Kierkegaard decided to write his master's thesis in his native Danish rather than in Latin. He was dealing with a technical issue in modern philosophy, a Hegelian treatment of the concept of irony; he very naturally felt that his style and even his argument would be hampered by the need to translate his metaphysical discussions into Latin.

Kierkegaard did write his thesis in Danish. What is remarkable is what he had to go through to do so. To start with, he had to agree to begin his essay with a Latin summary of his arguments, and he still had to conduct the public oral defense of the thesis in Latin. Thus, he had to frame his argument in such a way as to prove that he could just as well have written the thesis in Latin to begin with. Further, his request to use Danish had to be made by a formal written appeal, and this appeal had to be made not to his sponsor, nor to the university administration, but to the king of Denmark himself. In his "humble petition," as he calls it, Kierkegaard says that "I shall permit myself respectfully to call Your Majesty's attention to how difficult, indeed impossible, it would be to discuss this subject exhaustively in the language which has thus far been that of scholarship, not to mention that the free and personal presentation would suffer too much" (*The Concept of Irony*, 350).

The whole business may seem ludicrous now, but Kierkegaard was testing his limits on dangerous ground, and he knew it. King Christian VIII was not known either for an interest in Hegel or for a sense of irony, but he had only recently ascended a none-too-secure throne, and his nine-year reign was largely taken up with resisting calls for political and social liberalization. Although he had been something of a darling of the liberals in his youth twenty years earlier, having stepped into his father's shoes he was taking a dim view of the merits of constitutional democracy. He did go so far as to allow the long-banned parliament of Iceland to resume meeting, but at home in Copenhagen he did his best to keep the lid on liberalization. Then as now, the university had its reformist agitators, and Kierkegaard was using loaded language in pleading for the means to "free and personal" presentation of his material. Signing himself "Your Majesty's most humble and loyal subject," Kierkegaard got what he wanted: a symbolic gesture of defiance, approved by the monarchy itself.

At this distance in time, it may be difficult to realize that for Matthew Arnold to lecture in English, and for Kierkegaard to write in Danish, entailed a loss as well as a gain. On balance, the gain was greater than the loss, particularly since Arnold and Kierkegaard were far from memorable Latinists. Yet a real trade-off had to be accepted, one that we can see most clearly in terms of the issue of community. By moving into the vernacular in the middle of the nineteenth century, scholars made a new commitment to direct engagement with their local and national communities; but they weakened their character as an *international* community. Until the eighteenth century, and in many cases well into the nineteenth, Western scholars not only published but taught and corresponded in Latin, thereby making their results immediately accessible to all other scholars, whatever their location. In contrast, the jet-setting of the modern professor is confined largely to brief appearances at conferences and to employment opportunities elsewhere within one's own linguistic region. Few if any contemporary scholars can match the mobility of Erasmus of Rotterdam in the early 1500s. Erasmus lived and worked in Holland,

England, France, Italy, Belgium, German territories, and Switzerland, writing and lecturing in Latin all the while.

Erasmus himself was well aware that this genuinely international community came at a price: only a few could afford the time and cost to become fluent in Latin. Erasmus became a prime promoter of the translation of the Bible into modern vernacular languages, since only in this way could a full knowledge of the scriptures extend to all nations, to all classes of society—and to both genders, as women were not ordinarily permitted to study classical languages. His defense of this project shows an interesting awareness of the use of Latin as a diplomatic code during his times. As he wrote—in Latin—in the preface to his great edition of the New Testament in 1516,

> Perhaps the state secrets of kings have to be concealed, but Christ wanted his mysteries to be disseminated as widely as possible. I should prefer that all women, even of the lowest rank, should read the evangelists and the epistles of Paul, and I wish these writings were translated into all the languages of the human race, so that they could be read and studied, not just by the Irish and the Scots, but by the Turks as well, and the Saracens . . . I would hope that the farmer might chant a holy text at his plow, the spinner sing it as she sits at her wheel, the traveler ease the tedium of his journey with tales from the scripture. ("Paracelsis," 121)

Erasmus got his wish, although he provided no vernacular translations himself—apparently, according to the editor of this text, "because he did not know any one of them well enough to do it. His 'native' language was Latin" (121n.). Translations of the Bible proliferated in the ensuing years; but only three hundred years later, in the mid-nineteenth century, did the many modern vernaculars supplant Latin as the language of scholarship. The result was a strengthening of the role of the universities within the life of their own nations, but also a weakening of linkages across borders. This nationalizing of scholarly community could be compensated for, of course: new modern language requirements supplemented, and gradually displaced, the traditional requirement of fluency in Latin. A Danish scholar could always write in German and expect to gain a reasonably wide readership. All the same, having made the nationalistic move of switching to the vernacular, universities and their faculty could hardly conduct all their scholarly business in foreign languages, and so inevitably an increasing amount of scholarship—such as Kierkegaard's study of irony—began to be written in languages accessible only to fellow nationals. Even today only a small proportion of scholarly writing is ever translated into other languages, and so scholars working even in one of the "major" scholarly languages now need to be fluent in several foreign languages, instead of Latin alone, in order to follow scholarly developments abroad. Such requirements present no problem in theory, but in practice a new parochialism has emerged, in which untranslated foreign scholarship is relegated to the back burner, either ignored outright or at best surveyed less thoroughly and less thoughtfully than what is available in one's native tongue.

The shift from Latin into a variety of vernaculars can serve as an emblem of what occurred not only across borders but within the universities as well. When C. P. Snow bemoaned, in 1959, the emergence of "the two cultures" of science and humanities in society at large, he was identifying (and simplifying) a separation that had already been under way in academia for the better part of a century. The 1880s and 1890s saw the emergence of a variety of new disciplines within the university, and an increasing development, both in the new and in the older disciplines, of "vernaculars"—their own specialized jargons, closely linked to favored bodies of material, kinds of questions asked, and methods employed. The result is that the very term "university" has come into question as outmoded; already thirty years ago, Clark Kerr suggested replacing it with "multiversity." More and more, the contemporary university has become an ivory tower of Babel.

The growth of specialized languages and methods has enabled the university to encompass more and more aspects of life, to "have it all"—but only by an accelerating process of *halving* it all as well. "Social science" arose, distinct from the natural ones; sociology arose, distinct from anthropology; physical anthropology separated from cultural anthropology; within cultural anthropology itself new subfields, new "schools" of thought, arose, mutated, subdivided again.

What we still often think of as "a community of inquiry" had become, early in the century, largely a *dis*unity of inquiry.

This is the situation in which we still find ourselves today. We need to assess the institutional history of specialization if we are to get beyond the extremes of resignation (*of course* modern knowledge is too complex for us to be able to talk to one another) or nostalgia for some organically unified community. In many ways, the political, social, and economic imperatives of the later nineteenth century continue to inform the contemporary academic world—for better and for worse.

Nationalism, Capitalism, and the Rise of Specialization

The shape of the modern American university was forged during roughly twenty years, from the early 1870s through the mid-1890s. Not only did many of our current disciplines arise or achieve their characteristic shape during this time, but many of the basic bureaucratic mechanisms of modern academic life were instituted as well: the division of academic work into departments, headed by a chair and responsible to a dean; the standardization of course requirements and grading policies; the division of undergraduate work into "majors," "minors," and electives; the institution of the Ph.D. degree and the doctoral dissertation.

This same period was also, and not coincidentally, a period of tremendous expansion in enrollments. Only in the decades 1960–1980 did enrollments grow as much and as quickly. In both cases college enrollments more than tripled in twenty years, from 52,000 to 157,000 in the first period, and then from three and a half million in 1960 to over twelve million in 1980 (Carnegie Council, *Three Thousand Futures*, 103). Such a dramatic increase puts great strains on the organization of academic institutions. When an increase in numbers also involves significant shifts in the wider economy and in the composition of the student body as well—as it did in both of these periods—pressures build for broad change in the general orientation of the university system, its goals and purposes as well as its organizational structure. Much of the current sense of tension and uncertainty in contemporary academic life stems from this fact: as in the mid-1890s, we have just come through a period of dramatic changes in the size and composition of our student body; but unlike in 1895, we have not yet transformed the definition or the structuring of academic work. We are still trying to squeeze our greatly expanded student population into structures designed a hundred years ago, for students of dramatically different backgrounds and expectations; and we are still using the basic academic structures of the Industrial Revolution to prepare our students for the "postindustrial" age.

We cannot address this situation comprehensively by looking only at the local specifics of student life and work, whether they be core curricula, science requirements, admissions criteria, or "hate speech" regulations. Nor, on the other hand, should we go directly to the opposite extreme and attempt a global redefinition of the goals of education. As Michael Cohen and James March have wryly remarked, "Almost any educated person can deliver a lecture entitled 'The Goals of the University.' Almost no one will listen to the lecture voluntarily. For the most part, such lectures and their companion essays are well-intentioned exercises in social rhetoric, with little operational content" (*Leadership and Ambiguity,* 196). It is at an intermediate level of academic life that this operational content may be found: in the *structuring* of courses and other forms of academic work, rather than in the specifics of individual offerings or in the generalities of academics' views of life as a whole, whether those views are politically correct or incorrect. For this reason I wish to focus on the particular question of how the structuring of academic work was affected, and in particular how specialization achieved its dominance, as the nineteenth-century university strove to reorient itself toward its changing population and to address the changing needs of the modern society around it.

Nowadays a B.A. is a requirement for almost any middle-class job, and "everyone" (that is, almost 60 percent of all high school graduates) goes to college. From this vantage point, it may be difficult to realize that in the middle of the nineteenth century, colleges had a largely tangential role in American life. Most people saw no reason to go to college at all: not only farmers (still the majority of the population) but even prospective businessmen ordinarily went directly to work on receiving their high school diplomas, if not sooner. The colleges, few in number and small in size, existed largely to provide a way station for the sons of the wealthy, a four-year domestic equivalent of the traditional European Tour.

Those few youths who went to college spent as little time as possible on their studies, which most of them viewed as a sort of conspiracy to limit their social lives. The students themselves were quite candid about their views, amply illustrated in the testimony of Lyman Bagg, who wrote *Four Years at Yale* soon after his graduation in 1869. The great bulk of his book is devoted to loving descriptions of social clubs, rooming arrangements, and student activities of all sorts. When he finally starts describing curricular issues—on page 542— he follows sixty pages on academics with forty pages detailing the many elaborate methods of cheating devised by students with better things to do than study.

One reads Bagg with a growing sense of astonishment. His opening chapters dwell on the endless machinations of rival societies for freshmen, sophomores, and juniors and on the senior-year secret societies, with their elaborate induction rituals often enacting symbolic scenarios of death and rebirth. These scenes later reach an eerie climax in reality, when an undergraduate stabs a townsman to death in a street brawl. Thereupon the undergraduates barricade themselves in their dormitory, pistols in hand, while a mob of a thousand working-class "townies" uproots the ceremonial cannons from the New Haven Green and attempts to blow up the college. Bagg recounts these events in a tone of amused detachment that only increases the strangeness of his account (505–509). In his pathbreaking *Emergence of the American University,* Laurence Veysey has called Bagg's memoir "one of the most incredible American books of the nineteenth century . . . a monumental curiosity" (453); but the book's strangeness does not stem from Bagg himself, who matter-of-factly reports what he has seen and done. What is hard for even Veysey to believe is just how minimal was the educational impact of Yale College on its students in the 1860s, and how elaborate were the social rituals with which the restless undergraduates filled their time.

This is not to say that the colleges were teaching nothing; the problem is that they were teaching a great deal of material their students had little use for, and teaching it in dreary ways. A student would typically spend half his time in college being drilled in Greek and Latin, with class time largely given over to "recitations," in which one student after another would be called on to translate a few sentences. In addition, students took courses in mathematics, history, logic, theology, and natural science, with instruction in these classes also centered on recitation of facts from textbooks. There would usually be some electives in the later years, in subjects like English and modern languages, but few courses would progress beyond the level of an introductory survey, and students had little opportunity to tailor their program to their individual interests or to do extended or concentrated work in any given area. Today the university is filled with specialists, and a common complaint is that undergraduates are really being taught to become professors, but in the middle of the last century matters were very different indeed. There were few specialists of any sort teaching in the colleges (the same person might have to teach Greek, theology, and history), and if there was any real focus at all to the college curriculum, it could have been said that the students were all being trained to become classicists or ministers, or rather some watered-down combination of both.

Just because the colleges were so divorced from direct social needs, they might perfectly well have continued as they were, small institutions enrolling only a tiny percentage of the late-adolescent population, related tangentially if at all to more concrete forms of training. A B.A. was not needed for a career in law, nor was it required for entrance to seminary. The seeds of expansion toward the modern university were present, but in a highly rudimentary form. In Bagg's day the Yale Law School did, more or less, exist—it had a president, one professor, and three lecturers—but it had only a very loose relation to the college: you could enter the law school directly, without a college degree. If you had happened to get a B.A. first, you got time off for good behavior, a semester's reduction in the two-year law program.

The colleges might have drifted along in this way indefinitely, but in the 1870s reformers in several schools succeeded in reorienting their institutions or in founding new ones (notably Cornell in 1865 and Johns Hopkins in 1876, both underwritten by progressive Quaker businessmen). The reformers began to break the hold of the classics on the college curriculum and to emphasize new disciplines like economics, sociology, and the evolving natural sciences, which could directly address problems of the modern world both in theory and in practice. The college was reconceived as the center of a universe of academic pursuits, and as the necessary threshold to many of the others. These reforms were widely imitated in the 1880s, in public as well as private institutions. For the first time, businessmen began to give significant sums to colleges and universities, and public funds were granted in increasing amounts. This process culminated in 1890, when the land-grant colleges, first established in 1862 as small agricultural schools, were given a new mandate and greatly increased public funding; they began to emphasize academic subjects, and soon to take on all the trappings of university structure and life.

Taken overall, the dramatic increase in the size and complexity of the college and university system during this period can be described as the *industrialization* of academic life and work. The influx of students on many campuses led, in fact, to the importation of bureaucratic and managerial methods from industry. Thus, as Veysey notes, "Assembly-line methods of registration arrived at Harvard in the autumn of 1891, and efficient orange perforated registration cards were introduced there in 1896" (312). If these words bring to mind recollections of long lines at folding tables set up in a humid gymnasium during registration week, this image may suggest something of the continuity between the ultramodern efficiency of the 1890s and business as usual in very recent times.

The industrialization of the university went far beyond people management and the measurement of courses by mathematical units of credit. The subjects of study were themselves reorganized, in a new division of labor mirroring that in industry. College deans and scholars themselves now began to speak of the "production of knowledge," a notable shift from their earlier tendency to see their mission as the preservation of culture. This production, moreover, was to be marked by "efficiency," a term used with approval by academics of many varieties (Veysey, 116–117). The division of intellectual labor entailed the organization—and separation—of branches of knowledge. Disciplines, both old and new, were now defined with increasing distinctness, and they were organized in separate departments. Within a given department, in turn, separate "fields" of study were recognized, and where possible each field received a faculty member of its own. As Gerald Graff has said, "the field-coverage principle made the modern educational machine friction-free . . . making individuals functionally independent in the carrying out of their tasks" (*Professing Literature,* 7).

All this industrial machinery was operated in accordance with sound late-nineteenth-century economic principles. The norms of free-market competition pervaded the system at every level, particularly those of the discipline and the department. Within disciplines, a Darwinian struggle was to obtain, a free competition of ideas with success determined by the consumers in the marketplace (the survival of the most often footnoted). Thomas Haskell has argued that the emerging professions and disciplines were so structured as to reproduce the conflictual struggle for supremacy of capitalist enterprise. Ideas were to be developed and refined through this process of competition, in a manner "strangely reminiscent of the price mechanism in economic markets" ("Professionalism *versus* Capitalism," 211).

In keeping with nineteenth-century norms of political organization, this professional market competition had a decidedly nationalistic cast. Academic departments came to resemble little nation-states, with largely self-contained economies. Foreign trade could profitably be carried on, between departments and with like-minded polities in other universities—that is, with members of one's own discipline elsewhere—but the department had to have its own secure economic base of operations. This required, so far as possible, complete "coverage" of the discipline within the department, and a basic independence from other departments in the university. To this day, the administrators at my own university use a telling phrase to describe cross-registrations between different units of the university: these registrations are called "the balance of trade," as though the Law School and the Political Science Department were really England and France.

The construction of departments on nationalistic lines fostered a tendency to look down on other departments' methods and to ignore their results on related issues. Isolationism could even shade over into jingoism, and the suppression of rivals elsewhere in the university became common, again under the rubric of efficiency: so as to avoid "duplication," faculty in one department were discouraged from teaching material dear to the heart of another department. To give one example of this process in recent times, I vividly recall the negotiations I had to undertake when, as a new assistant professor of comparative literature, I proposed a course entitled "Scripture and

Literature," a subject derived from my dissertation. My department readily agreed, but the college's Committee on Instruction sent the proposal back: the Religion Department had objected to my syllabus. Two thirds of the texts I proposed to teach were scriptural, and they considered that my course too closely resembled a survey of the Bible, which they already offered—even though a good number of my texts were nonbiblical and my own approach was exclusively literary. I was allowed to teach the course only after I agreed to reduce the Bible's representation to a safe quarter of the syllabus.

Such negotiations pass unnoticed in the everyday business of the university, except when some openly political issue is involved, as in the controversy stirred up at San Francisco State University in the fall of 1990, when a professor of political science proposed to teach a course on black politics. This proposal was bitterly opposed by the head of the Black Studies Department, who had similar interests, and who argued that such a course should not be taught by a member of another department—even though the political scientist in question, himself black, had wide knowledge in the area, and even though— or perhaps because?—he wished to pursue a different approach to the subject from that favored by the chair of Black Studies. This case obviously has very different publicity value from the previous one; naturally only the San Francisco State incident was reported in the *New York Times*. The very ordinariness of my own experience is part of the point. But similar principles of disciplinary nationalism are involved in both cases, and a similar combination of open competition within departments and protectionism *between* them, a subtle but insistent pressure toward the monopolization of knowledge.

At the turn of the century, the proliferating division of labor and the semimonopolistic dissemination of the products of that labor were the order of the day. In adopting parallel methods, the universities came to share in the explosive growth of the economy at large. In the context of the times these adaptations seemed natural, even imperative, and they helped create what rapidly became the leading university system in the world. All choices involve trade-offs and compromises of different sorts, and even at the time, as we will see, some unfortunate consequences attended the creation of the new academic structures. On balance, though, the changes made represented an enormous improvement over what had gone before, and our current need to rethink the organization of academic life and work reflects the fact that conditions have changed dramatically over the past ninety years. Our universities are now wealthy enough in many kinds of resources that we can afford to look askance at the Religion Department for discouraging the study of the Bible in a literature course. In a real sense, though, my colleagues in Religion are carrying on (however reflexively) principles that had a certain logic in 1900, when Columbia's full-time faculty numbered eighty-seven instead of the current twenty-five hundred, and the institution's annual budget was only $820,000—a small fraction, even in constant dollars, of the current budget of a billion dollars a year.

By directly addressing the concerns of the modern world, the universities positioned themselves to become a major social resource, a unique forum for research and training in the growing complexities of the modern world—its cultures, its economic and social life, and the increasingly sophisticated exploration and exploitation of nature. Interest groups of all sorts—commercial, scientific, governmental, social-welfare, cultural—began to see the value of working with university-based researchers, and people wishing to pursue careers in all these areas now had reason to seek out higher education as the best means of training for those careers. As this process gathered momentum, the late-nineteenth-century expansion of undergraduate enrollments was followed a generation later by an explosion in graduate enrollments in all fields. The Ph.D. degree, established late in the century in a few schools, soon ceased to be an arcane German import and became a basic road to advanced practice in the humanities, social sciences, and natural sciences alike. While undergraduate enrollments increased tenfold between 1920 and 1970, graduate enrollments increased *fifty*fold, from 15,600 to 826,000 (Blau, *The Organization of Academic Work*, 5).

This great increase in students had an enormous impact in consolidating the role of specialization in academic life. Specialization had been one of several factors contributing to the greater desirability of a university education; now it, in turn, became one of the prime beneficiaries of the increase in enrollments. For the first time, universities had large enough enrollments that they could afford to hire a great many new faculty members, giving them the luxury of hiring ever more specialists in disciplines both old and new, and in the further specialized fields within them. In this hiring pattern, the universities reflected the strongly individualistic tenor of the emerging industrial state. As a recent sociological study puts it, "with the coming of large-scale industrial society, it became more difficult to see work as a contribution to the whole and easier to view it as a segmental, self-interested activity" (Bellah et al., *Habits of the Heart,* 66). This attitude persists especially strongly in academia, as university and even college faculty let their teaching reflect the disparate imperatives of their individual research interests.

At the turn of the century, specialized hiring was still only one of the available options: it would equally have been possible simply to *duplicate* faculty resources, and have fifty people, say, teaching Plato and Aristotle where only one had done so before. This option ran so counter to the dominant logic of expansive specialization that very few institutions chose this route; but a few did, with a faculty comprised largely of generalists comfortable in teaching in many periods and even in various disciplines. Increasingly, though, even small colleges gravitated toward the dominant model of specialized research and specialized teaching. Today only a few obstinate holdouts keep to a broadly generalist model, which by now has something of the status of radical experimentation. St. John's College, for example, has a largely fixed curriculum for its whole student body, with multiyear required sequences in literature, history, philosophy, history of science, mathematics, and Greek. The school's faculty members all have some sort of disciplinary home base, but in principle, and largely in practice, they are all prepared to teach most of the courses offered by the college.

A college like St. John's can be said to continue the older nineteenth-century tradition of the preservation, rather than the creation, of knowledge. This has not, however, been the usual choice. By the turn of the century, even in the humanities and all the more obviously in the natural and social sciences, anyone who wanted to advance knowledge had to specialize in order to do so. What was entirely true of research was increasingly true of teaching too, as many of the subjects in which students wished to prepare themselves—and for which governments and corporations were prepared to provide funding—were becoming specialized as well. Increasingly, the prestige, the enrollments, and the funds flowed toward research-oriented institutions, and even small colleges began more and more to imitate this dominant pattern in their course offerings.

The new graduate programs had to decide how, and even whether, they would guide their students in specialized study. Johns Hopkins, founded originally as an entirely graduate institution, affords an instructive example. At first students were left largely to their own devices in planning their own programs, studying whatever they felt would be useful for their interests, with no particular schedule or requirements at all. With the best will in the world, though, their professors soon began to treat their students in ways comparable to the ways factory managers treated their workers. The transition to a fixed course of study is described with telling industrial metaphors by Ira Remsen, one of the early faculty members:

> At first, we thought it would be sufficient simply to let the students come together and select their courses . . . [But] there was a good deal of indefinite browsing. They would fly from one thing to another . . . And those of us who were charged with the management of affairs concluded that we must take advantage of the degree. We must offer something to keep these students in line. The Ph.D. degree was the next thing after the A.B. degree, and we recognized that we must offer this in order to keep that body of workers in line, and that, in order to secure the results we wanted, it was also necessary to require a piece of research as a requisite for that degree. That is the machinery we used. We thought, at first, that we might avoid it, but we found that we must adopt it. (Quoted in Veysey, 313–314)

Remsen stresses his helplessness to have done things differently, as if to allay a lingering discomfort at having had "to keep that body of workers in line," but he and his colleagues were making a deliberate choice, really a series of choices, in favor of rationalized, organized, measurable progress, a pattern that favored specialized knowledge production rather than a generalist's bovine "browsing."

By the turn of the century, generalists were everywhere on the retreat. They were not lacking in eloquence when they defended general education, but their words fell on deaf ears, for they were attacking fundamental beliefs of their age. Thus in 1894 the Harvard

philosopher George Santayana deplored the alienation of the specialized academic worker as industrial values supplanted the organicism
of an earlier era: "Each man knows the value of his work . . . but he
feels also the relativity of this work and its value without being able
to survey the whole organism of human interests and adjust himself
confidently to the universal life" (quoted in Veysey, 311). The problem was that the specialists Santayana was opposing shared little of
his confidence in the universality of "the universal life." Perhaps too,
the specialists had little taste for "adjusting" themselves to such universal norms even if they could be defined. A culture, even an ethics,
of fierce independence was growing up along with the spread of specialization: while constantly, and even obsessively, judging the work
of their fellow specialists, scholars were increasingly insisting on not
being judged by anyone else.

 This was a dramatic change. The nineteenth-century colleges had
prided themselves on the transmission of widely accepted values, and
college presidents had routinely considered it their duty to fire faculty who adopted controversial views. By the turn of the century, a
decreasing number of presidents (usually of small, sectarian schools)
could afford to do so, at least openly. Faculties everywhere fought
for academic freedom and insisted on the institutional corollary of
life tenure, perhaps by analogy with the freedom from partisan pressure granted by the awarding of lifetime appointments to federal
judges. This freedom was substantial, but it also involved various
kinds of self-restriction, in terms of both the need to seek the approval of one's "peers" and the need to refrain from looking closely
into what people (still thought of as "colleagues") were doing in other
disciplines. The result was a boom in disciplinary discussion, but at
the same time a dampening of debate, and of common purposes,
across the campus. As Santayana later put it, "Did the members of the
Harvard Faculty form an intellectual society? Had they any common
character or influence? I think not . . . I believe there were some
dinner clubs or supper clubs among the elder professors; but I never
heard of any idea or movement springing up among them, or any
literary fashion. It was an anonymous concourse of coral insects,
each secreting one cell, and leaving that fossil legacy to enlarge the
earth" (*Persons and Places*, 397).

 The scholar as polyp. Santayana's image perfectly combines the

principles of endless, accretive growth and simultaneous ossification
that produce both the coral reef and the academic department. It is
a measure of the triumph of specialization that half a century later
Northrop Frye should have adopted the same metaphor to describe
the scholarship of the 1950s. Allowing that scholars must make specific contributions to their fields, he insisted that they must try to
do so with a general view of their discipline in mind: "it is not necessary that the thing they contribute to should be invisible, as the coral
island is invisible to the polyp" (*Anatomy of Criticism*, 12). It is perhaps also a measure of the triumph of specialization that Frye offers
this witty metaphor as his own creation; since Santayana was a philosopher and Frye a literary critic, Frye had no occasion to know
that someone else had invented the metaphor before him.

Paradoxically, the university came to rely on a kind of *willed ignorance* as an essential component of its pursuit of knowledge. Veysey
sums up the problem well:

> Tacitly obeying the need to fail to communicate, each academic
> group normally refrained from too rude or brutal unmasking of
> the rest. And in this manner, without major economic incentives
> and without a genuine sharing of ideals, men labored together
> in what became a diverse but fundamentally stable institution.
>
> The university throve, as it were, on ignorance . . . the univer-
> sity throve on the patterned isolation of its component parts,
> and this isolation required that people continually talk past each
> other, failing to listen to what others were actually saying. This
> lack of comprehension, which safeguards one's privacy and
> one's illusions, doubtless occurs in many groups, but it may be
> of special importance in explaining the otherwise unfathomable
> behavior of a society's most intelligent members.   (337–338)

The defeat of the generalists should not be seen simply as a morality
play of the vanquishing of the guardians of culture by a horde of
soulless technocrats. On the contrary: the specialists carried the day
because they persuaded their public that it was they, and not the
generalists, who were the real champions of cultural values. They
argued that new methods were needed precisely in order to find ways
to hold modern culture together. Factors like the growth of industry

and the parallel growth of cities, fueled by the new waves of immigration from many different cultures, had fundamentally changed the social landscape from the beginning of the nineteenth century, when 96 percent of a more homogeneous population still lived in rural areas. Even the cities were relatively small affairs then, with a definable public culture that could express the "universal life" fondly recalled by Santayana at the century's end.

In a highly interesting essay, "The Erosion of Public Culture," Thomas Bender has argued that the rapid growth of cities during the nineteenth century was the single greatest factor in the breakdown of the traditional sense of a cohesive and coherent society. Manhattan's population, for example, went from 33,000 in 1790 to over 800,000 in 1860, a pattern seen across the country. To cope with this population explosion, cities began to divide their functions spatially and socially, minimizing and channeling contacts between groups. The new universities divided their work, and their populations, similarly, as they both mirrored and fled modern civic life. Ivory towers—or, more precisely, granite and brick neo-Gothic campuses—arose in pastoral settings like Ithaca and Hanover, or else city streets were closed off and gates were erected in Baltimore and New Haven, with the surrounding neighborhoods left to wax, wane, or decay with little influence either on or from the universities in their midst. It is noteworthy that Bender chooses a speech by the founding president of Johns Hopkins, Daniel Coit Gilman, to illustrate the theme of the university as place of refuge from the city. Notwithstanding his own school's location in Baltimore, Gilman praised the university for allowing men of intellect to withdraw from the "turmoil" and "distractions of modern civilization," arguing that the university alone allowed the "cultivation of a spirit of repose necessary for scholarship" (97). "There is a wonderful irony in all of this," Bender concludes,

> and we must not miss it. The social complexity of urban life was embraced by academic social scientists as their special subject. The special capacity of their disciplines made them, so they said, uniquely able to grasp, interpret, and control this new social world. Yet while making this positive claim, they created the university as an intellectual refuge where they could avoid

the city's complexity and disorder in the construction of their
discourse . . . Without this counterweight of urban culture, intellectual life in the United States took on a heavily academic
and relentlessly specialized character . . . producing island-
communities that reduced the common universe of discourse
to an exceedingly limited sphere. (100–101)

This irony is, in fact, double-edged. In some ways, our scholars
have taken refuge in self-enclosed and often self-confirming academic discourses, advancing knowledge in some ultimate sense even
as their own communities stagnate or decay around them; in other
ways, though, specialized academic study has actually reproduced
the proliferating complexity of urban culture and the isolation of
individuals within "the lonely crowd." Our universities, then, stand
in need of reform not only because times have changed but also because we can now see that for all their success, the turn-of-the-
century reformers finally perpetuated many of the problems they
sought to solve. Perhaps they have even contributed to those problems; is it any coincidence that the neighborhoods around so many
campuses seem to be in states of permanent decay? Clark Kerr has
even suggested, with ironic practicality, that this is to the university's
advantage: "An almost ideal location for a modern university is to be
sandwiched between a middle-class district on its way to becoming a
slum and an ultramodern industrial park—so that the students may
live in the one and the faculty consult in the other" (*The Uses of the
University*, 89).

The New Uniformity

The reason the university is a heterocosm rather than a microcosm
of society is that it persistently embodies a profound ambivalence
toward society at large, often and in various ways both opposing it
and mirroring it, even reproducing many of the features it most
wishes to oppose. The university characteristically displays a blend
of engagement and withdrawal, a combination that under the right
circumstances, as at the turn of the century, gives it a valuable purchase from which to survey and assess the wider social scene. Under
altered circumstances, however, it may be necessary to change our

familiar patterns of work. The changing conditions of the past twenty
years share many features with the major changes operating a century
ago: a rapidly expanding university population, a great increase in
the diversity of that population, an egalitarianism as pronounced
since the 1960s as during the 1860s. To see how deeply the solutions
of the university reformers a hundred years ago were woven into the
economic and social texture of their era is to indicate the magnitude
of the stakes at play in our own time. And yet the lesson should
not be that our changed circumstances will somehow automatically
produce a new university system; difficult choices had to be made
then, and new choices must be made now. The response so far to
the latest wave of new and different enrollments has largely been to
adapt simply by going on doing what we've been doing, but on a
larger scale. The tremendous expansion in the university system in
the past thirty years has not yet produced any significant reconstitu-
tion of academic life and work in four-year universities. The major
innovation, the creation of the two-year community colleges, has
served as a safety valve to protect the four-year institutions—and
their faculty—from having to make any fundamental changes in the
way they work. Instead, we find a reflexive attempt to continue old
patterns, with adaptations made only piecemeal and on an ad hoc
basis.

Further, the growth of the four-year university system has generally been accomplished by a simple process of addition: a few new
dorms on campus, and a great proliferation of new campuses, each
mirroring the others. The most striking feature of the many new campuses established in the 1960s and 1970s, in fact, has been the lack
of genuine newness in almost all of them, apart from various short-
lived experiments. As several recent observers have noted, the
growth in the numbers and diversity of the student population in
recent years has not led to an increased diversity in the university
system, but on the contrary has fueled a new uniformity across the
system. Specialized research increasingly sets the tone, even in
schools with a traditionally small role in research. Already twenty
years ago, Harold Hodgkinson noted a dramatic increase during the
1960s in faculty who only did research and taught not at all: by 1968
there were no fewer than eleven thousand such faculty, located in
356 institutions. As Hodgkinson commented, at that time no more

than 40 American universities could claim "to be basic research centers . . . This set of statistics lends support for the idea that there is
a monolithic status system in American higher education, and that
its base is in research and in the 'national reputation,' both for the
person and for the institution, that research (and a rapid increase in
graduate programs) apparently can bring" (*Institutions in Transition,*
17).

Over the years there has been a steady decrease in the proportion
of students enrolled in small colleges, and in private institutions of
any size. In 1950 half of all students went to private institutions; by
1980 only a fifth did. This shift was the result of relative stasis in
private education and explosive growth in the public sector, and
most of this growth occurred on large campuses, favored both by
governmental policy ("efficiency," again) and by student choice—
the diversity of large campuses proves to attract more students than
does the intimacy of small colleges. As a result there was a dramatic
shift in the proportion of large campuses across the country. In 1955
only a quarter of the student body attended schools of over ten thousand students; by 1977 fully half the student body did so.

Two basic changes have followed from these shifts, both of which
carry on the internal logic of the patterns set at the turn of the century: first, there has been an increasing uniformity among institutions; second, there has been a steady weakening of cohesive identity
within them. The large state schools have increasingly adopted the
specialized modes of the major private research institutions, and
these scholarly values have permeated the system as a whole to a
remarkable degree. Smaller schools, even colleges with no graduate
programs of their own, now routinely require all the trappings of
specialized research in their faculty. The Ph.D. degree, for example,
has become a sine qua non of full-time employment. But what is
the Ph.D.? Now that there is widespread use of the M.Phil. degree,
signifying completion of doctoral coursework and examinations, the
Ph.D. degree itself indicates the additional completion of a two- or
three-hundred-page doctoral dissertation on a specialized topic, a
topic ordinarily too focused ever to be directly of value for an undergraduate course. Until very recently smaller, teaching-oriented
schools treated the Ph.D. as optional; indeed, as recently as 1969,
fully a third of all full-time college and university faculty members

still did not hold a Ph.D. (Blau, 27). In the 1970s, the Ph.D. degree became widely regarded as the necessary entry-level degree for college as well as university faculty, even though, in reality, it is tailored for the production of research scholars rather than teachers.

This same shift in values toward research continues after the completion of the Ph.D., in the crucial early years of one's career. To "publish or perish" has become the norm not only at major research institutions but even at many small, undergraduate-oriented schools. Some exceptions do persist, at holdouts like Sarah Lawrence, but research values have become dominant almost everywhere else, and assistant professors at places as theoretically divergent as Mount Holyoke and Queens College are now under an Ivy League–style pressure to publish—even though the majority of their senior colleagues may have themselves published little during their own careers.

The Carnegie Council sums up these changes well: "The diversity of American higher education used to be found between and among institutions with conformity within each of them; now diversity is more often found within institutions, with the institutions in their entirety being more alike. Fewer institutions have their own strong individual personalities" (*Three Thousand Futures*, 22). Taken in purely social terms, the Carnegie Council's characterization is accurate: manifestly, diversity is likely to be the hallmark of a campus with fifteen thousand students and a thousand faculty, divided into a large number of separate schools and programs. The cohesiveness of the community will be further weakened on a purely social level if, as is often the case, many of the newly enrolled students live off campus rather than on.

This diversity needs closer examination, though, from the perspective of scholarship. Even within institutions, the inherent logic of specialization has had a somewhat paradoxical effect, simultaneously weakening scholarly cohesiveness and yet also increasing the underlying intellectual uniformity. The first of these changes is probably the more readily apparent, especially in these days of ever-increasing air travel. It has long been true that an anthropologist at Yale might have more in common with her fellow anthropologists at Berkeley than with any sociologist on the Yale campus; by now, the anthropologist may well *see* her Berkeley colleagues as often as she sees the sociologists across the quad. As I write these words, I have on my

desk the latest issue of the Yale alumni magazine, which reports with
satisfaction two items of interest: the successful conclusion of negotiations with the city of New Haven to close off another campus street
to city traffic; and the addition of jet service from New Haven to
Chicago and points west—a significant boon to the faculty, the magazine informs us, with no hint of irony and no suggestion of the
symbolic connectedness of these two news items.

Scholars have less and less need, or even opportunity, to talk to
people outside their own special field of interest. The proliferation
of faxes and electronic mail will only increase this dispersive tendency; our anthropologist will now hardly have to come into the
office at all, except to hold those few remaining seminars she occasionally teaches, whenever she touches earth between Pago Pago and
Bellagio. Far from discouraging this vanishing act, the universities
actually encourage it, as it enhances their prestige. Less active members of the faculty may grumble at their colleague's unavailability for
routine committee work, and hapless graduate students bemoan their
sponsor's inaccessibility, but they do not protest too much. They all
share in the reflected glory of the peripatetic academic star. Although
the star's own engagement with the institution is likely to be weak,
the star's very presence (if "presence" is not too strong a term to use)
enhances the desirability of the institution all round.

Departmental nationalism has persisted in the structuring of academic work, but things have changed: many professors, and particularly the most original and productive scholars among them, no
longer behave like good citizens, or even like citizens at all. They
are more like resident aliens. Aliens, though, of a rarified and exotic
sort, not to be confused with the migrant workers known as "adjuncts." Departments do actually get something from the current arrangement; to a significant degree, though, everyone also loses in
various ways. I won't dwell on the difficulties caused for the abandoned graduate students, or even on the pressure this system puts
on people to publish whether or not they have something substantial
to say. For it is the peripatetic scholars themselves who lose the most
by current patterns, for by ceasing to have steady engagement with
the work of others on their own home campuses, they are reduced to
doing the sorts of work that can be managed by solitary individuals,
supplemented only by ephemeral and insubstantial contacts with

people elsewhere. Conferences can have a genuine intellectual value, but as they now exist they are a poor substitute for extended collegial interaction.

Given the widely regretted dispersion of attention on (and off) campus, it may seem surprising to suggest that specialization not only increases fragmentation into disjointed subgroups but also breeds uniformity in academic work. Yet this is very much the case. Our universities have always housed a great many sorts of people doing a wide variety of tasks; to the extent that a single standard begins to dominate the others, the result is a real decrease in the diversity of the *forms* of academic work, even as we see a steady growth of one form, namely specialized research. The increase in uniformity on a campus is clearly illustrated by the history of my own department, which has shown first a steady expansion both in numbers and in purposes, and then a steady decrease—in everything but enrollments. As the department grew with the university, it sub-divided into three quite separate entities, each serving a different student population. The center in this departmental triptych was the College faculty, devoted to undergraduate teaching and to generaliz-ing scholarship—home of such luminaries as Lionel Trilling and Mark Van Doren during the middle decades of the century. The grad-uate faculty, largely separate and actually housed in another building, concentrated on specialized scholarship and on graduate teaching; still a third division, again housed elsewhere, was part of the School of General Studies, a continuing-education program for adults. Most faculty members taught largely or even entirely in only one of these divisions, and hiring was carried on fairly independently, with a view toward the quite different needs of the three student populations; tenure decisions similarly reflected different criteria.

The distinct ethos underlying each division is well reflected in the names of the three buildings in which they were housed: the College faculty was in Hamilton Hall, named after Alexander Hamilton, an early graduate of the College; General Studies, long a cash cow for the university, was in Lewisohn Hall, named for a wealthy alumnus; the graduate faculty was in Philosophy Hall, named for an intellectual abstraction. Philosophy is also, of course, the name of a discipline in its own right, now only one occupant among several, but still accorded the quietest and sunniest rooms, farthest from street level, on the seventh floor.

Until recently, indeed, Philosophy Hall was laid out to reflect an ideal hierarchy of disciplines, really a Great Chain of Being. At campus level was the language lab; above it was Linguistics; above Linguistics was French; above French was the Department of English and Comparative Literature; above them all was Philosophy—while *beneath* them all was the Registrar, in the basement. Over the last several years this clear division has broken down: English now has offices on three different floors, Comparative Literature uses offices on the French Department's floor, the language labs have moved elsewhere, and the Linguistics Department has been closed altogether. Even within the English department alone, the old tripartite system has broken down: faculty are no longer recruited for a particular division of the department, but are expected to teach in all. This is not so much a new egalitarianism, though, as the result of a dramatic shift in power toward the graduate school. The General Studies faculty was the first to wither away, and for some time now retiring General Studies professors have been replaced by scholarly specialists. Even the College faculty, with its substantial student base and nostalgic prestige, has largely lost its individual character, although there are still a few diehard senior faculty whose hearts are in undergraduate teaching. By the same token, however, these faculty are generally less well known outside the university than their more actively publishing peers, and as large salaries usually come only in response to offers from outside, most of the College faculty are paid much less than those whose interests center in graduate education.

Even more to the point than the prestige implied by salaries are current hiring and tenure policies, which are weighted almost entirely toward specialized research interests and publication records. As a result, the retiring College faculty are being replaced by young scholarly specialists, who still do half their teaching in the College, but who are well aware that their survival depends on their research. Just since 1980, in fact, the assistant professors' teaching load has decreased substantially, from six courses per year to five and now to four, and in addition paid research leave time has doubled. The writing is on the wall, and the walls are those of Philosophy Hall, to which the entire department has recently moved.

The pressure toward homogeneity is scarcely diminished—and may even be increased—by the quasi-religious nature of our commitment to research. As Kenneth Ruscio has said, "Patterns of work across institutions differ significantly, yet there is only one model for the profession. Depending on the setting, this one model has several different versions. Each sector seems to worship the god of research, but organized religion reflects the local culture. Some are more religious than others, and some allow religion to play a different role in their lives" ("Many Sectors, Many Professions," 344). Our eyes fixed on the holy grail of the discipline, we fail to see the variety of our actual practices, and inevitably this divergence exercises a chilling effect on the variety of what we do.

The problem is not only that research is valued over teaching, but that *graduate-style* research takes priority over other kinds of research. Not long ago, I was asked to evaluate the publications of an assistant professor who was being considered for tenure at an excellent liberal arts college. I praised his writings—thoughtful, essayistic syntheses of debates on modernity in several disciplines—as showing an effective adaptation in prose of the methods that had made him an enormously successful undergraduate teacher. His department chair took this praise as a thinly veiled insult and replied that she would never wish her faculty to be judged by a different standard from that used for university faculty.

My own department's consolidation within the walls of Philosophy can suggest both the problems we now face within academia and something of the potential for improvement. The consolidation of the department was made, at considerable expense in renovation, in the names both of efficiency (fewer support staff would be needed) and of community (faculty would get to see more of one another). I suppose that some cost reduction can be foreseen, if we take the long view. The department has reduced its staff by one secretary, for an annual saving of about twenty thousand dollars; as the renovation cost two million dollars, our heirs will start to see the cost savings in about a hundred years.

Will the desired increase in community emerge any sooner? As the move to Philosophy suggests, there has been an increase in uniformity—most of us are industrious researchers now; but how often do we actually see one another? Many of the active scholars in the department rarely work in their offices; housing the whole department in a single building will not in itself alter the centrifugal tendencies built into the present system. At the same time, simply reversing the course of history is not likely to be a productive solution; nothing would be gained by scattering the faculty across the campus again. Still less would we improve matters by trying to restore the organic harmony of the pre-industrial college. To the extent that such an earlier harmony is not a pure myth, it was achieved at the cost of a social and intellectual homogeneity that few would now wish to replicate. The question is how to go forward from where we are now, rather than to wish we could go backward: how can we fashion genuine community *within* our contemporary specialized, research-based academic world?

The history I have been outlining does not in itself dictate the directions we should choose now, but it can help us in plotting the trajectories of the changes we make. Perhaps most important, we can see the university in its *constructed* nature, a fact that is not fully realized by those who sentimentally assume that the university should be a changeless home for eternal verities. Even pragmatically oriented sociologists of education usually take a purely synchronic view; they treat academia as a steady-state system, as though its norms and structures were inevitable and not amenable to deliberate change.

Changes can indeed be made, but they must take account both of institutional histories and of the real interests of those who now occupy the institutions. Critics outside the university propose sweeping reforms at the drop of a hat: to make the professors stick to the classics and stop teaching twentieth-century thought (Kimball); to pay teachers better than scholars (Anderson); to get rid of adjuncts (Sykes). The problem is not just that these reformers rarely suggest how institutions would pay for their changes, some of which would be very expensive indeed; equally, they rarely show much interest in thinking how the system as a whole would have to change to accommodate their desired reforms. Yet it is a rare reform that can succeed if it runs counter to the interests of the faculty, or what they perceive to be their interests.

University-based reformers are painfully aware of this fact. No administrator of the postwar era was more active in revitalizing the university system than Clark Kerr, chancellor of the University of California during its great period of postwar expansion, and a moving spirit behind the creation of such innovative new campuses as Santa

Cruz and San Diego. His *Uses of the University* testifies to the sense of expansive possibility he felt in the early 1960s as enrollments began to boom and California led the nation in a historic commitment to universal access to higher education. Ten years later, however, in a postscript to a new edition of his book, he wrote that despite the tumult of the late 1960s "it is remarkable not how much has changed but how little has changed on so many campuses in those areas that are under faculty control and where the faculty feels strongly about its control. The more the environment has changed, the more the organized faculty has remained the same. It has been the greatest single point of institutional conservatism in recent times, as it has been historically. Little that it has held dear and that it could control has been allowed to change" (130–131).

Another ten years later, in his postscript to the 1982 edition, Kerr is positively somber: "The three fundamental changes attempted over the past twenty years have largely failed. Academic reform was overwhelmed by faculty conservatism. Efforts to turn the university into a direct instrument for social change were thwarted by institutional autonomy . . . Changes in formal governance have generally made little difference and, when they did, mostly for the worse. All that effort, all that passion, all that turmoil was mostly for naught, but it was also mostly inevitable given the conditions of the times" (180–181). Melancholy words! An awareness of the difficulty of achieving reform makes current observers like William Bowen and Henry Rosovsky conspicuously modest in their proposals—too modest, in fact, if the system needs anything more than fine-tuning. To effect any real change, we must change the ways faculty do business. But how can we reshape the system as a whole? The triumph of specialization inhibits discussion of ways to reconceive the academic community and its work. Indeed, if we take specialization at its word, the task may seem altogether impossible. Derek Bok, Harvard's president during the 1980s, has recently surveyed the process of teaching and learning across the university system, but at the outset he dismisses the subject of scholarship in a single footnote:

Some readers may wonder why anyone would write about universities without discussing research. Since scholarship and scientific discovery are the most distinctive contributions of our

major universities, writing a book without mentioning what
goes on in the library or the laboratory may seem odd, to say
the least. Yet the fact is that almost no one can write comprehensively about research. The issues that really matter are intellectual questions concerning the shifting interests, problems, and
methods that mark the process of scholarly investigation . . .
To write about the deeper questions of research across a wide
spectrum of fields may be a task beyond the capacities of almost
any author.   (*Higher Learning,* 2 n. 1)

Retreating before the bewildering array of specialized subjects and
concerns, Bok discusses teaching in isolation from research. As he
himself suggests, though, teaching is partly a function of research—
as a natural extension of subject matter, as a source for postdoctoral
funding, and most generally as an outgrowth of the preferences and
orientation of the faculty. The faculty members' interests, in fact,
express their *interest,* in the sense of their power to have things as
they wish.

A serious limitation in a book on teaching, the impossibility of
saying anything meaningful about scholarship would be fatal to a
general examination of academic life. Most books on the university
repress this problem and gratefully gravitate to other issues like the
political affiliations of professors or their particular choices for their
great books courses. These are worthy subjects, and both will receive
attention in the chapters to come, but these matters too should be
discussed in awareness of the deeper structuring of academic work.
Derek Bok's discomfort at dealing with scholarship stems precisely
from the fact that he stays at the surface level of individual scholars'
"shifting interests, problems, and methods." At best, such a perspective would yield a descriptive botany, when we need an ecology of
the university. Having described some salient features of its evolution, we can now turn to the present-day workings of the academic
ecosystem.

2

The Academic Economy

Socialism or Capitalism?

Social scientists who try to describe the university soon realize that they cannot get very far on direct analogies with other systems. Universities share elements of a business and of a polity, but they work very differently from either governments or corporations. Some of the differences, though, are more apparent than real. Whereas in theory the scholar pursues truth for its own sake, free of political pressures and of the need to make a profit, in reality the difference is only one of degree. Even in the purest of fields, scholars have constiuents, whom they court and to whom they respond in overt and subtle ways, and the "marketplace of ideas" is indeed a market.

Matters become more complicated when we try to develop the analogy more fully. There are, after all, many kinds of markets, open and closed, centralized and decentralized, socialistic and capitalistic. Then there is the fact that during its long history the university has picked up elements of several different economic modes, even as it diverges from all of them. This does not render economic analogies useless, but we must proceed with care. In the end, however eclectically, the university does indeed display both literal and indirect economic modes of activity as it forges its own internal economy and conducts its relations with the surrounding society.

Appropriately enough, several of the people who have written about the university in recent years have been professional economists, notably Clark Kerr, active in the field of industrial relations before he entered university administration, and Henry Rosovsky, the influential dean of faculty at Harvard during the 1980s. Both writers often frame their discussions in economic terms, and they can provide a valuable point of departure for considering the academic economy. Kerr and Rosovsky use analogies drawn from capitalist economics, speaking approvingly of the ways in which the university reflects the needs of its consumers. Their essentially liberal awareness of the university's debt to market forces is even more strongly underscored by radical critics, many of whom are deeply concerned with economic structures even if they are not economists themselves. Thus in his 1989 *Work Time: English Departments and the Circulation of Cultural Value*, Evan Watkins sees American higher education as alarmingly complicit with modern capitalism, serving the economic imperatives of corporate profit and maintaining a repressive status quo in many ways.

Matters look very different to Martin Anderson, an economist who worked in the Reagan administration and then returned to his position as a fellow at the Hoover Institution at Stanford. In his 1992 book *Impostors in the Temple*, somberly subtitled *American Intellectuals Are Destroying Our Universities and Cheating Our Students of Their Future*, Anderson draws a sharp contrast between academic working conditions and those obtaining for intellectuals in the media. "America's academic intellectuals work in a quasi-socialist state," Anderson says, "while our professional intellectuals, for the most part, work under bare-knuckle capitalism" (14). Whereas writing done for newspapers, magazines, and private think tanks is "an expression of capitalist society," the modern university is "a tiny oasis of quasi-socialism" (15).

Anderson's view thus diverges dramatically from the liberal and radical tendencies either to celebrate or to condemn—but in any case to emphasize—the university's closeness to capitalism. His analogy is particularly intriguing since he hints at a degree of nuance in his term "quasi"-socialist, although he never does spell out in what respect America's professors are living in anything other than a socialist paradise. The essence of Anderson's case is that public intellectuals are closely tied to the structures of the free market. They must sell their ideas to editors and to a broad public, or they are soon out of business. Academic intellectuals, by contrast, enjoy two great buffers against the market, peer review and tenure. Not judged by any outside audience, professors write only for one another, and they accept each other's work for publication, review their friends' work in journals, and serve on panels to give out grants to those same friends. Tenure reinforces this independence from the market; academics keep drawing their paychecks even if hardly anyone ever reads their scholarship.

The contrast Anderson draws between the two spheres of intellectual work is surely overstated, at least to judge from the cover of his own book, prominently decorated with puffs from the coterie of neoconservatives who regularly print and review one another's diatribes against liberalism and multiculturalism, their journals often generously subsidized by like-minded corporations and foundations. But even if we suppose that neither William F. Buckley Jr. nor Hilton Kramer is daily bruised by the bare knuckles of raw capitalism, it remains true that profit motives and the need to please a large audience are notably muted in academia. At the least, these motives operate somewhat differently in the university, in part because the academic economy is deliberately, and often defiantly, unconcerned with turning a direct monetary profit. But even tenured professors have customers and markets, and powerful incentives to supply their customers with acceptable goods.

Part of the difficulty in sorting out the nature of the academic economy lies in the fact that we hold two very different, and partially contradictory, ideas of just what is our essential product. For Anderson, "The primary calling of professors is to teach—the sacred responsibility to impart information and ideas to the young . . . Teaching is what they get paid for, it is how they make their living" (14). Like Charles Sykes in *Profscam,* Anderson is outraged that professors are allowed to spend so much of their time on abstruse scholarship irrelevant to their students' needs. He proposes that the valuing of scholarship over teaching should be corrected by abolishing tenure, increasing teaching loads and cutting back on research time, forcing professors to teach more and write less, and thereby to attend to the needs of their consumers, the students.

The problem with this view is that it misstates the actual structure of the academic economy, at least in the major universities, where teaching is most clearly undervalued. Typically, no more than a third of the total revenue for a research university comes from tuition, and expenditures on teaching similarly account for about a third of the total budget. The other two thirds of income and expenditures relate to what is in fact the university's principal activity: the supplying of information to society at large. This emphasis on the production, rather than the transmission, of knowledge is essentially a postwar phenomenon. The novelty of the new mode of production is still evident in the industrial language of Clark Kerr's preface to *The Uses of the University* in 1963: "The basic reality, for the university, is the widespread recognition that new knowledge is the most important factor in economic and social growth. We are just now perceiving that the university's invisible product, knowledge, may be the most powerful single element in our culture, affecting the rise and fall of professions and even of social classes, of regions and even of nations. Because of this fundamental reality, the university is being called upon to produce knowledge as never before" (vii–viii).

The principal buyers in this market during the past forty years have been governmental agencies and businesses, and universities have reshaped themselves dramatically to meet the constant demand for new research, new knowledge, new approaches to social and scientific problems. In Kerr's view, the declining commitment to undergraduate teaching already clearly visible in 1963 was closely tied to the influence of corporations and in particular of governmental grant policies. In the twenty years from 1940 to 1960, governmental support for higher education, largely in the form of research grants, increased a hundredfold, to $1.5 billion annually; the 1991 *Statistical Abstract of the United States* gives the current figure as about thirty billion dollars per year, about half of which is for basic research (135, 589).

As Kerr notes, "There seems to be a 'point of no return' after which research, consulting, graduate instruction become so absorbing that faculty efforts can no longer be concentrated on undergraduate instruction as they once were. This process has been going on for a long time; federal research funds have intensified it" (65). All the same, even the new professorial entrepreneurs will still have to teach courses regularly, and repeated failure to attract a reasonable number of students can seriously affect a teacher's salary and status. More important, large-scale shifts in student interests have a profound impact over time on staffing levels in different departments. The steady decline in language study and, in the past twenty-five years, in humanities enrollments generally has exerted a powerfully constraining pressure on humanities departments, producing at the same time a windfall for business administration, computer science, and preprofessional programs. Although undergraduates may lose more than they gain by their professors' involvement in research, their own priorities often dovetail with those of the outside funders, particularly since the funds often include scholarship money.

Taken together, research funding and student interest largely shape the market within which professors now work. While an individual professor may have a large degree of freedom in choosing research projects, careful decisions must be made by departments and by schools concerning the ways they reward such research and even the extent to which they permit it to be done. Once tenured, you may be able to work on whatever you please, but a department's ability to hire you in the first place will be very largely determined by the needs and interests of the consumers, both student and federal, and these consumers continue to influence your salary and future mobility thereafter. "An appropriate emblem for the American college might be the traditional open book," Kerr remarks, "but lying on a sales counter" (169).

The most successful entrepreneurs are easy to identify and to satirize, like the literary (and now legal) theorist Stanley Fish, acidly portrayed in the works of Dinesh D'Souza and Roger Kimball, and more lovingly satirized as Morris Zapp in the academic novels of David Lodge. Fish is a colorful character, but we should not focus all our attention on the occasional jet-setting academic star. Nor should we go immediately to the opposite extreme and concentrate on the overall institution, whose behavior may simply be that of an individual entrepreneur writ large. Administrators tend to personify their institution, and they rejoice when their hero gains in the national rankings. Henry Rosovsky writes approvingly of the driving force of the market in the lives of American universities: "We have, quite consciously, opened our institutions to the influence of markets . . . For us, the comforts of Oxford, Cambridge, the University of Tokyo, and the University of Paris do not exist. At all times there is a group of universities clawing their way up the ladder and others

attempting to protect their position at the top. If one believes in competition, as I do, one would stress the benefits of the system" (*The
University*, 225–226). It is easy enough to celebrate the workings of
a market red in tooth and claw when you are managing a winner.
And while theoretically this competition ought to harm as many institutions as it helps, in practice, as canny administrators long ago
discovered, the need "to meet the competition" has proved a very
powerful argument by which to separate both legislators and private
donors from their wallets.

Although the system is structured around isolated individualism,
many of the consequences of this individualism are seen at the intermediate levels of the department and of interdepartmental relations.
This is where things become really interesting. How do you run a
department of self-promoters? How do you get departments to talk
to one another? While Rosovsky is happy enough with marketplace
metaphors to describe both individual scholars and their institutions
as a whole, he does not seem to have found a stable way to account
for what goes on in between, when faculty members have to interact
with one another on campus. At times he falls back on the metaphor
of family life, notably in discussing tenure. Far from Anderson's socialist conspiracy to protect incompetence, tenure for Rosovsky is a
matter of tying the knot: "In my view, tenure carries the implication
of joining an extended family; that is the social contract. Each side
can seek a divorce: the university only in the most extraordinary
circumstances and the professor as easily as a male under Islamic
law. It is not an uneven bargain because the university needs its share
of talented people, and professors trade life-long security and familial
relations for lesser economic rewards" (184). We need not undertake
a full-scale gender analysis of these lines to detect an element of male
fantasizing here; what is relevant for present purposes, though, is
not the image of the long-suffering but hopelessly loyal Alma Mater,
but rather the fantasy that her many mates are all the while cohering
into a close-knit familial group.

No doubt some departments can be described as happy families;
it is my own misfortune that I've never encountered any of them
myself. Assuming that Rosovsky's Harvard is his prime illustration
for his analogy, we can ask how his scholarly family operates. Speak-

ing of his years as dean of faculty (the equivalent of the provost in most schools), Rosovsky first illustrates his family theme by noting the ways in which he would aid faculty members in dealing with personal problems like alcoholism and illness, but he stresses that the analogy of family expresses "a much broader vision; in reality, a state of mind." The state of mind in question is that of the researcher who has dreamed up some new excuse to get away from the classroom: "when special opportunities arose, rules were cheerfully broken or reinterpreted in favor of the individual. A tempting invitation from abroad might mean the need for travel funds or extra leave time; a new research idea could call for seed money; one was always able to approach faculty resources through the dean. Not everyone got what they wanted, but the dean would try to help, while loudly proclaiming that his actions in no ways constituted a precedent" (185). This Harvard family, full of its secure-yet-free Islamic husbands, turns out to have a single father: Rosovsky himself, benevolent despot—only a *primus inter pares,* as he modestly protests a few lines later, but by his own account the prime source for cheerful dispensations from "the rules" that would otherwise enforce a more equal distribution of wealth in the community and a full teaching load for all the faculty.

Aware that his account might admit of such a reading, Rosovsky asks, "Am I, with excessive sentimentality, urging an inordinately paternalistic interpretation?" He answers his question by shifting ground to the safer territory of a family *business:* "Not if one thinks of professors as shareholders without bosses, and not as employees . . . [The dean's] actions are not favors granted from above. Instead, they are investments in the general welfare, and therefore in the high quality of the family enterprise: in those with permanent membership who form one set of owners" (185). Elsewhere Rosovsky speaks of the faculty as a professional partnership, like a law firm, and, more ambivalently, as a private club.

Both are interesting analogies, but his most revealing comparison is to a baseball team: "Although the analogy may make some readers uncomfortable, a faculty can be compared to a baseball team—the university president as owner, the dean as manager, the faculty as players, and students, alumni, etc. as spectators. To have a consistent pennant winner requires money and excellent players. These can be produced by a farm system (junior faculty) or purchased from other teams (superstars)" (230 n. 5). I would imagine that Rosovsky has underestimated the strength of his comparison, which should make a rather *large* number of readers uncomfortable: the junior faculty, for example, all too clearly reminded that they aren't real "players" until they get tenure (as few Harvard junior faculty do); the students, reduced to mere "spectators" along with the alums during homecoming week; the senior faculty, whose joint-stock ownership in the family business has now been taken over by the president; the august university trustees who are supposed to hold the basic fiduciary duty to the university but who have disappeared entirely. No metaphor should be pressed too far, of course, but it is striking how dramatically Rosovsky's own explication of the metaphor alters the terms of the family of scholars, even of the family business.

The real problem with the baseball metaphor, though, is the implication that the faculty are a *team*. Departments do occasionally need to function together, most notably when considering the hiring of another specialist to fill an area no one else is working in, but rarely do scholars actually work together even in their teaching, still less in their research. Certainly Rosovsky himself views the essence of scholarly activity as isolated activity, drilled into students as their graduate education progresses:

> Research is a lonely activity, especially when the location is a library rather than a laboratory. Few experiences in our working life can be more isolating than gathering materials for a dissertation deep in the bowels of some large library. No one can help; no human voice is heard; the only constant is that very special smell of decaying books . . . Loneliness or isolation is particularly strong for graduate students in the humanities and social sciences because cooperative research is discouraged, especially when writing a dissertation: that is intended to be individual work to exhibit one's own capacities. (153–154)

We see a kind of scholarly machismo here, under which the difference between the graduate student disappearing into the library and

Humphrey Bogart walking into the mist at the end of *Casablanca* would be that, unlike Bogart, the student must leave both sweetheart and friends behind.

Rosovsky presents as a state of nature what is in fact a choice, that truly advanced work should be undertaken in isolation and with as little cooperation or assistance from others as possible. "No one can help," he tells us. It would be an unusual ball club whose players operated in this fashion, and in fact no business could long survive such a dissolution of teamwork. But Rosovsky's business analogy itself is remarkably individualistic: "The essence of academic life is the opportunity—indeed, the demand—for continual investment in oneself. It is a unique chance for a lifetime of building and renewing intellectual capital" (161).

Continual investment in oneself: the academic economy in a nutshell. A university department is not so much of a joint-stock corporation after all, but more like a record label whose performers do an occasional concert together to promote their own individual albums. But I exaggerate; although Allan Bloom found that the success of *The Closing of the American Mind* made him "the academic equivalent of a rock star" (*Giants and Dwarfs*, 20), universities are more stable venues than Madison Square Garden, and faculty interactions can be complex and involved. As all satirists of university life know, the university has a politics as well as an economics. Yet even this politics reflects the underlying ethos of the scholarly economy. The hierarchies of academic life resemble the plutocracy of turn-of-the-century economic life, buttressed by an individualistic emphasis that antedates even the Industrial Revolution. Scholars are pieceworkers, each office (or each study back home) a cottage industry in itself.

In baseball terms, we have teams made up of free agents who manage to remain free agents even after they sign on. As Clark Kerr ruefully recognized, the modern university is no longer an organic unity, whether a family or a close-knit corporate body. "It is more a mechanism—a series of processes producing a series of results—a mechanism held together by administrative rules and powered by money . . . I have sometimes thought of it as a series of individual faculty entrepreneurs held together by a common grievance over parking" (20). Yet these entrepreneurs do have to find ways to survive in close quarters for extended periods, and they have to allocate resources for research and responsibilities for teaching. The politics of a lifetime association of free agents is unusual indeed, and merits direct socio-logical discussion.

The Politics of Specialization

While universities and their departments show some of the qualities of businesses, fundamental differences remain in how the individual scholarly worker relates to the organization as a whole. Universities are characterized by what sociologists refer to as remarkably *loose coupling*: to a very large degree, not only research but most activities in the university are carried on by individuals working on their own. To the extent that research is a form of production of knowledge, for example, it can be compared to manufacturing; yet unlike factory workers, the members of an academic department do not ordinarily work together to make their product or even to disseminate it. Team teaching is regarded as an expensive luxury; collaborative writing is rare in the humanities, and collaboration across fields of specializa-tion is relatively rare even in the social sciences.

In a company, moreover, different divisions will ordinarily be in-volved in production, sales, and distribution; there will usually be "tight coupling" within each division, and firmly established proce-dures for coordinating among divisions. In academia, the need for people to work together for these purposes is greatly reduced. As Karl Weick has put it, "linkages among research, service and teaching are presumed to occur *within* the single individual, a presumption found in few other organizations . . . Every other connection that occurs outside a single head is looser, more intermittent, weaker. Multiple actors within universities don't share many variables. And those they do share, are weak" ("Contradictions in a Community of Scholars," 16). Nothing actually prevents scholars from getting together for a little variable-sharing, but nothing actively *encourages* them to do so either.

Furthermore, administrative coordination within and even be-tween departments is often managed by these same scholars, usually on a shifting, ad hoc basis, with the result that the work of the univer-sity is left almost entirely in individual hands. As Weick says, "The extreme degree of individualism found in universities is reinforced because when linking is important, individuals rather than administrative units are supposed to do it. A dean, the senior person in an area, the expert on a topic, the person who has the least status, or the person with extra time [is] chosen for locally idiosyncratic reasons to represent larger interests, which themselves are not homogeneous" (16–17). While a professional administrative staff also exists, it is remarkable how little influence the administration exerts on the intellectual direction of the typical university.

This is most strongly evident to the chief executives who nominally run the show. In their *Leadership and Ambiguity: The American College President,* Michael Cohen and James March record their subjects' frustrations that so much of their time is taken up with trivia and with symbolic ceremonial activities, but the authors take these protestations with a grain of salt: "we believe that the college president has difficulty saying 'no' because much of the time he does not really want to. The latent absurdity of being the executive leader of an organization that does not know what it is doing haunts the presidential role." As a result, college presidents fill their schedules with "frequent reminders of the fact that one *is* the president, the attention to minor things one *can* do" (150). Significantly, when Cohen and March asked college presidents to name a successful president and list the factors behind that person's success, finances and public relations dominated their accounts; fewer than a quarter of the respondents mentioned considerations of educational policy at all (108).

In basic ways, of course, administrations can have a great influence on the shaping of academic work, but in most instances they exercise this influence crudely, through the power of the purse: provosts and vice presidents can approve or withhold tenure lines, and these decisions may, over time, have an effect on a department's character. It is rare, though, that any real effort is made to exert intellectual influence through this process, except in the most general terms, such as to encourage the hiring of more scholarly types; what the scholarship ought to look like is left almost entirely to the departments themselves. More dramatically, an administration may decide to "upgrade" a whole department or to abolish one, but such actions are rare, and when the administration's influence is not drastic, it is usually minimal.

The university, then, bears little resemblance to a bureaucracy; basic policy is rarely set from the top of the organization, or even from the deans and other administrators in "middle management." Even in matters not strictly academic, highly decentralized authority is the norm, its workings either fluid or chaotic, depending on your point of view. Cohen and two colleagues have described decision-making in universities as operating according to a "garbage can" model: issues just keep getting thrown on in, with the weightiest tending to sink out of sight, and only the most insistently recycled or lightest matters receiving any actual attention (Cohen, March, and Olsen, "A Garbage Can Model of Organizational Choice"). Furthermore, the items that do end up on top of the heap tend to get mixed together in unpredictable ways. Thus, "A proposal for construction of a building becomes an arena for concerns about environmental quality. A proposal for bicycle paths becomes an arena for discussion of sexual inequality" (Cohen and March, *Leadership and Ambiguity*, 211).

In part, the ubiquity of garbage-can decisionmaking reflects the habits of mind of the scholars involved; as Hazard Adams has said, "Faculties are, after all, composed largely of people who like problems, perhaps even more than solutions, and even to the point of actively seeking them where they have not been recognized. Indeed, some of these individuals positively dislike solutions, preferring the deeper existential absurdity of the problem itself" (*The Academic Tribes*, 11). Administrative decisions tend to reflect the dominant scholarly ethos, not least because many administrators are themselves current or former scholars. Equally, the tendency for nothing ever to get decided on a campus reflects the extreme diffusion of authority within the system. With little or no direction coming from the top, the university bureaucracy really works as an antibureaucracy, whose ideal is to allow the greatest possible number of individuals to pursue their own private interests with the least possible interaction.

In political terms, it is tempting to think of this system as a form of anarchy. Already in 1950 the president of the University of Chicago, Robert Maynard Hutchins, grumbled that his faculty "prefer anarchy to any form of government" (quoted in Kerr, 31). This was a distressing realization for the strong-minded Hutchins, who personally inclined more toward despotism. More recently Cohen and March, refining the idea, have arrived at the oxymoronic term "organized anarchy." Yet this is an inadequate description, as is the idea of "loose coupling." If we look across the system as a whole, we observe that anarchic loose coupling coexists with striking elements of very tight coupling, even of autocracy. Most obviously, students, the nominal beneficiaries of the enterprise to which they pay such large bills, are often very tightly controlled indeed—not merely in the sense that they must take a certain number of courses, but more particularly in that once they have exercised their right of choice in picking a school and a major, they often have little choice of what to study, or even, in important instances, of whom to study with.

A friend of mine in graduate school, for example, had to take an introduction to her field that was taught by a professor who was widely regarded as the worst teacher in the department. A learned and even charming man personally, a valuable resource on a one-to-one basis, he was a disaster in seminars. He was given this important and required course largely to ensure that he would have some students. This sort of decision is more common than one might think. Frank Lutz discusses a comparable case, in which a professor who habitually taught a section of a required course was allowed to go on doing so, despite students' protests that his grading was substantially harsher than the norm. "Loose coupling," far from operating anarchically, simply worked in the professor's favor: he got to teach what he wanted, the way he wanted to. His students, however, were placed into his section at random, without even the option of taking the course pass/fail, and so were subjected not only to an unpleasant experience but also to lower grade point averages and reduced opportunity to graduate with honors. They were tightly coupled to the course, but also *un*coupled in their inability to influence it in any way. As Lutz says, "universities claiming to be loosely coupled are not loosely coupled at all. They may be tightly coupled in ways that preserve the status quo and protect the investments of power holders. They may be uncoupled, however, in ways that protect the powerful and the status quo of the organized anarchy as a whole" ("Tightening Up Loose Coupling," 667).

What is dramatically true in the case of these unfortunate students is also often true when the interests of powerful faculty members clash with those of people in less powerful fields or departments. Small departments may find that their junior faculty are held to heavier teaching loads than large departments are able to negotiate for themselves, and their graduate students are often funded less well. Similarly, university support for new and innovative programs often lags far behind enrollments. While an administration might sensibly be reluctant to shift resources to an unproven program, imbalances can persist for decades. In most universities, for example, film studies remains the poor stepchild of art history and of the literature departments; most teaching of film courses is done either by poorly paid adjuncts or else as a kind of hobby by people employed in one of the better-established disciplines. Despite the vitality of the film industry in this country, the long-established student interest in the medium, and the growing body of critical and theoretical work on film, few institutions have even begun to give film (still less television!) the degree of representation accorded to modern literature.

At Columbia, although New York is one of the world's centers of television and film production, and although the university houses the third largest professional film school in the country, there is no academic film studies department, and until recently it was impossible even to major in film in Columbia College. Occasional courses were taught by people in literature or in art history, but there was no organized program at all, and only at times a single adjunct instructor whose own principal field was film. A major was finally established a few years ago, but there is no prospect for the foreseeable future that film and video studies will have a department of their own, or even a significant presence in one of the existing departments. The academic freedom of both the art history and the literature departments has been preserved, then, by a quiet refusal to admit a competitor to their ranks.

Even within departments, the same process regularly obtains. Year in and year out, the Americanists in my department labor with staffing levels well below those given to English literature. We have, in fact, almost as many medievalists as Americanists, although the medievalists always have few students and the Americanists always have many. Happily, we have been able to buy the Americanists off for some time with promises of an extra appointment, which they will receive just as soon as the latest budget crunch is over, unless, of course, we are suddenly offered the tempting prospect of hiring some rising star in Beowulf studies. As for the students, we can always go on hiring a few adjunct lecturers to flesh out our undergraduate offerings in American literature. The graduate students should be grateful enough that we have finally abolished the requirement that they learn Anglo-Saxon, the department having recently awakened to the realization that Germanic philology is no longer quite the cutting-edge topic it was when the requirement was instituted, ninety years ago.

Lutz notes that in a recent survey of faculty and administration priorities, "preserving academic freedom" was the top priority of faculty and administration alike, while "preserving the status quo" ranked forty-sixth among the forty-seven categories offered. As Lutz concludes, these pieties mask a more complicated reality: "decisions are often defended in terms of program autonomy and academic freedom, although as often as not they limit the autonomy of other programs and the academic freedom of other, weaker, members of the university community . . . *Tight coupling* occurs when an issue supports the status quo. *Uncoupling* occurs when an issue challenges the status quo" (667–668).

The Range of Ostensible Collegiality

If academic freedom and organizational anarchy often serve as means by which vested interests protect their power, the question remains: just how often is "often"? Clearly, the administrators and faculty in the survey cited by Lutz believe that the status quo is supported only very rarely by their efforts; or, if it is supported, this is only by accident, a chance by-product of the forty-five concerns they hold higher. Now, either they are all simply wrong, through sheer blindness or some kind of doublethink, or else the contention is not a serious one, and the status quo is supported only very rarely after all. No doubt a poll of adjunct faculty would produce significantly different opinions as to their institutions' openness to change, but such a group would perhaps not be entirely objective either. If there is a genuine problem here, how is it that it has remained relatively invisible over the years? Haven't the universities, after all, shown a rather high degree of openness to new fields of inquiry and new approaches? We hear more complaints these days about rampant trendiness than about resistance to change. Isn't it only the aggressively trendy who think there should be even more change going on than there already is?

These questions can best be approached institutionally and historically. There *is* a real problem, and it *does* remain invisible to most people most of the time, essentially for institutional reasons. Vested interests are protected, as Lutz claims, but usually the process operates so quietly that few people notice, and fewer care—usually those whose voice in the university is weakest. At certain historical moments, however, the normal institutional masking mechanisms are put under stress, and the problem can assume both a new visibility and a new urgency. The present time is just such a moment.

Let us begin with the institutional ways in which the problem is ordinarily masked. The university normally responds to pressure for change through one of two basic mechanisms: exclusion and addition. Except in highly controversial cases, the process of exclusion remains almost invisible, as it is nothing other than the reverse side of the process of *inclusion* of new people and ideas. The several rites of certification and passage through which aspiring academics must pass serve as a filter. This filter is always open to new ideas, so long as they are ideas of an acceptable sort. Within the generally given parameters of a given discipline, you will most readily and most successfully pass each stage of the process if you have something new to say, some new perspective to contribute. At the same time that the system seeks to encourage original scholarship, though, it also serves to *acculturate* its students and its untenured faculty alike. The deep paradigms by which the discipline is organized are not only learned but also lived, at a basic level of intellectual identity. The great majority of those who truly question the underlying paradigms are weeded out during the process, usually by their own decision.

Many graduate students, for example, come into our department with an interest in film, yet somehow no one ever ends up writing a dissertation on a film topic—rarely even a chapter of a dissertation. Those few students whose commitment to the area is genuinely passionate sooner or later see that a literature department like ours is no place for them, and they leave. The rest stay; they find a course or two to take and may even include a few films in their orals lists, but imperceptibly their interests shift away, and by the time they come to formulate a dissertation topic, they're back to writing about Jane Austen. To be sure, they've rejected the New Critical approach they were taught in college, but their feminist-deconstructionist dissertation is still a Jane Austen dissertation after all, and in fact it still incorporates New Critical methods of close reading. *Something* has changed, but much has not, if you compare their dissertations with the ones that their sponsors wrote thirty years before.

In this instance, the new has simply been excluded, though not by outright censorship: no departmental regulation actually forbids students to work on film, and a few of the faculty even make something of a hobby of film themselves; but the departmental culture subtly, insistently discourages work in visual rather than verbal narrative art. The vested academic interests (here, my colleagues and I) promote conformity in a seemingly benign way: we don't exclude aspiring film students from our ranks, as the rich might zone the poor out of their neighborhoods; rather, we welcome them with open arms, so long as they become like us. More than that, we even aid them intellectually and financially in adding a new wing onto the Jane Austen mansion. We have preserved the uniformity—let us call it the architectural integrity—of the neighborhood, and its value is even enhanced by the renovation; and all by the most seductive of means.

If change is often dampened in such ways, nevertheless it can also be incorporated; new programs, even new departments are occasionally set up, and over time significant changes do occur in the orientation of a school, as when the Classics Department shrinks and Computer Science expands. Characteristically, however, the university tends to make these changes whenever possible by *choosing not to choose.* This is done simply by retaining the existing fields and adding a new one on. In *Professing Literature,* Gerald Graff has trenchantly described this process as a movement "from rags to riches to routine," showing in detail how a new field of inquiry is usually incorporated by adding one or two new specialists to the department, thereby effectively co-opting the latest trend without fundamentally affecting how the old hands do their own work.

Co-optation works most smoothly when an institution can grow at a slow and steady pace, for it is then that changes can be made without really rocking the boat at all. Too little growth, and change can be made only at the cost of open trade-offs, taking money and positions away from people who already have them. Given the system's decentralization and individualism, both of which aid those already in the system, such changes are very difficult to contemplate, much less to carry through, and they are very rarely made. With too rapid growth, on the other hand, overly visible changes in the balance of power could occur. Existing, vested power groups can indeed have their influence diluted over time, but the system usually achieves this dilution very gradually, slowly enough that the more powerful of the vested group have time insensibly to get used to it, and ideally to retire as well.

The ideal rate of growth can actually be quantified, as it has been in the case of McGill University by a group of sociologists there. In "Strategy Formation in the University Setting," Cynthia Hardy and three colleagues report that throughout the twentieth century McGill's enrollments and budget have grown very consistently at a rate of 3 to 4 percent annually. This pattern of growth could be altered by exceptional external forces (reduced by the Depression, increased by the great numbers of servicemen returning after World War II), but the university soon reverted to its norm. Growth in this country has been slightly faster, at around 5 percent a year, but our universities probably follow the general pattern seen at McGill.

In a witty and apt phrase, Hardy and her colleagues call the 3–4 percent growth rate "the range of ostensible collegiality" (206). Within this range, changes can be made without choices' having to be made. As long as you don't actually have to fire any classics professors, they won't object if you hire one or two more computer scientists; indeed, as collegiality is almost entirely "ostensible" across the gulf separating the sciences from the humanities, the classicists are unlikely even to notice the new hirings, although they may vaguely wonder what that new science building is, as they head for their squash date in the gym. The range of ostensible collegiality permits enough change to accommodate local, individual initiatives, which are the only changes that ordinarily get proposed, given the academic manner of work. These small changes can add up, though only very gradually. As Hardy and her colleagues say, "while the Faculty of Medicine at McGill awards in 1983 the same M.D. degree it did in

1840, the content of that degree has changed completely through countless individual professional decisions, consolidated by occasional collective efforts at program redesign. But the complexity of the collective process encourages change to take place at the individual level, in fact, sometimes in a clandestine manner . . . In summary, universities are paradoxically extremely stable at the broadest level and in a state of perpetual change at the narrowest" (206–207). In Santayana's terms, enough scholarly polyps all growing in the same direction can form a new outgrowth on the reef, but a new layer of polyps will rarely change the underlying structure of the reef as a whole; and it would be a rare polyp that could persuade its companions to reconsider the question of polyphood itself.

This slow and even rate of growth is a product of historical circumstances. It has to be supported by steady increases both in students and in general funding. For the past hundred years we have had the necessary conditions for such growth: an increasing population and an ever-growing percentage of the population going on to college and graduate school; steadily increasing financial support from the government and corporations. Yet these conditions did not obtain before 1880, and they have ceased to obtain now. Every one of the major pillars supporting Hardy's range of ostensible collegiality has eroded in recent years, and there is no prospect of significant growth in any of them in the foreseeable future. Our population growth rate has slowed, and the continuing shift toward the service sector of the economy has brought a stagnation in the number of jobs requiring a college or graduate degree. Governmental and corporate support for university research has leveled off; in many areas it has even fallen, as has federal and state support for students. In response, our colleges and universities have become adept at beating the bushes— and the alumni—for every available source of funds; equally to the point, Columbia, though a private institution, now has a vice president in charge of lobbying the federal and state governments.

We may hope that such methods can keep at least the most aggressive institutions from suffering outright declines in the coming years, but it is generally agreed that even in the best of circumstances most universities will do well just to keep up with inflation, while many others are actually having to curtail their operations. This is an entirely new situation for our universities, which for more than a cen-

tury have never had to face a long-term period of steady-state operation; even the effects of the Depression lasted only a few years. The
current leveling-off is likely to be a much longer-lasting affair and
will entail fundamental changes in the ways we do business.

Most important, it will change the way we manage change itself.
For the first time in memory, new fields and areas of inquiry can be
supported only at the direct expense of existing fields. Change could
simply cease, but this is both undesirable and simply unlikely. Pressure for change will continue to come, as it has in recent years, from
the new arrivals on campus—more women, more minorities, and
also more part-time and adult students than ever before. Equally, the
inherent logic of research will always create impetus for change,
ideally for expansion, as there is always more to learn and to assimilate with each passing decade. How will the university adapt to the
unprecedented situation of a steadily increasing body of knowledge
amid stagnant enrollments, staffing, and funding?

These new conditions have made the politics of specialization a
matter of genuine concern. The organized anarchy of the university
can no longer operate seemingly benignly and largely invisibly, at
one and the same time a free world of scholars all doing their own
work and a congeries of oligarchies, each protecting its own special
interests. Now these two tendencies are coming into open conflict,
and it is my contention that new modes of work and new political
structures are needed, if this conflict is to be worked through produc-
tively rather than destructively. In addition to changes in our modes
of work, we also need to consider the political structures that would
form the framework within which our work is carried on. What
might these political structures look like? Those who hold a mimetic
view of the university will perhaps suppose that, since we live in a
democracy, the university simply embodies its values, perhaps even
epitomizes them: a true meritocracy, a major stepping-stone to social
advancement, a community of equals united in the common pursuit
of truth. Critics like Allan Bloom even seem to think that there is
altogether too much democracy in the university: rock music everywhere, disrespect for aristocratic traditions and elitist values, no standards left anywhere, and so on.

Elements of democracy do, of course, exist in the university, but
they coexist with persistent elements of other sorts as well: autoc-

racy, for example, but also anarchy and even communism. This admixture can confuse those who believe that the university works by purely democratic means. A few years ago the Justice Department went to court to enjoin the Ivy League schools from collaborating to offer the same financial aid packages to common applicants. The schools' policy, which makes perfect sense for the distribution of scarce resources within the academic context, was nothing other than "from each according to their ability, to each according to their need," a classic Marxist principle that the Justice Department mistook for an antitrust violation—a position from which it subsequently retreated after several years of wrangling.

In *The Closing of the American Mind,* Allan Bloom eloquently decries the undemocratic tendencies of the leftist protestors at Cornell and elsewhere in the late 1960s, but he is slow to admit, or perhaps even to realize, the extent to which the protests mirrored the undemocratic structures of the university within which they occurred. Even at the time, some administrators were quite open about this. Consider the famous "Strawberry Statement," uttered by my late colleague Herbert Deane, a political scientist who was serving as vice dean of the Graduate Faculties at Columbia in 1967. He created an outcry when he was quoted in the campus newspaper as saying that "a university is definitely not a democratic institution. When decisions begin to be made democratically around here, I will not be here any longer . . . Whether students vote 'yes' or 'no' on an issue is like telling me they like strawberries" (*Columbia Daily Spectator,* April 24, 1967, p. 1). No democratic transformation ensued, and twenty years later Professor Deane finished out his distinguished career at Columbia, as sardonic—and as devoted to his students—as ever.

Those democratic processes that do exist in the university tend to be those of eighty or a hundred years ago. Who had the vote, for example, in 1890? In principle, any adult male; in practice, thanks to poll taxes, rigged registration procedures, and other means, only a fraction of the white male population, heavily weighted toward the propertied classes. Equally, whom these few voted for was no open question; many contests were decided before the event, via gerrymandering and other less obvious tactics, and almost all candidates were selected from within their parties in the notorious "smoke-filled rooms" of the power brokers.

Is the governance of the university so very different today? There is a body at my university called the Faculty Senate, a product of the pressure for democratization in the late 1960s, but it has been effectively marginalized by the administration, which feeds it limited information and presents it with attractively packaged *faits accomplis*. As a member of this body, I recently served for a year on its Education Committee. In a period of financial retrenchment, with commissions being set up to manage tens of millions of dollars of cuts and to review the missions of all university departments, our committee spent weeks debating the minutest details of a proposed Ph.D. program in nursing—a program which had already been approved, and which in any event was expected to admit only four or five students per year.

Not content with overwhelming the Senate with trivia, the administration has even insinuated itself into the process by which candidates are selected to "run" for "election." Ballots are then duly circulated, along with pious notes exhorting the faculty to exercise their right and duty to vote—but, lo and behold, there are hardly ever more names on the ballot than there are places to be filled. One might follow Anderson in seeing this as another manifestation of socialism, or more precisely of communist pseudodemocracy, but for the fact that it so closely resembles the home-grown methods of turn-of-the-century organizations like Tammany Hall.

Faculty members don't object, since they don't really want to have a say in their own destinies, so long as they are given frequent research leaves by a generous administration. Furthermore, they are unlikely to find the system odd at all, since they run their departments in just the same way. The chair of my department is always "elected," but rarely is there an open contest. The issue is decided in advance by an extended process of politicking and caucusing, in which the wishes of the more powerful tenured faculty almost always prevail. Most of these clubhouse mechanisms have long been superseded within American society—not always changed for the better, but changed nonetheless. Real analogues to university governance must now be sought elsewhere; they could perhaps be assembled from some odd combination of the systems of, say, Monaco and Libya. What we have in academia is not democracy as we know it today, but a plutocracy with a sugar coating of Stalinism.

The Politics of Political Commitment

There remains much that is genuinely democratic in the university; merit is sincerely sought out and rewarded, and individual initiatives have considerable freedom in many areas. And yet, as they now operate, many of the elements of democracy in the system actually work to increase isolation and a lack of accountability. We have long since abandoned the authoritarian model (codified in the eighteenth century in Germany) of a department headed by a single professor, with a clear hierarchy of lesser ranks below. Under that system, the professor would paternalistically control the department, but would also look after its members' interests. In this country, we're all "equal." In many departments, the lower ranks like lecturer have been abolished outright or given over to graduate students, while full-time faculty positions have divided into two basic categories, assistant professors and associate or full professors.

The majority of full-time faculty in a department tend to be tenured professors, many of whom have achieved that rank while still in their thirties. All these venerable souls are equal, at least in theory, but none of them has any real responsibility for anyone else, except temporarily, if they briefly chair the department, or on an individual basis, if they choose to take good care of their favorite graduate students. Assistant professors, meanwhile, find themselves in limbo in this egalitarian system, which either relies heavily on them or excludes them utterly, depending on the vagaries of the mood and the moment. They may find themselves shifting several times a day between the roles of trusted colleagues and of some sort of advanced graduate students who won't go away until they're fired.

Still less equal in this egalitarian system is the lot of the adjunct faculty, whose numbers are steadily growing as our financially pressed universities search for ways to mount their courses without paying high salaries. The adjuncts can be sure of a cordial welcome from the chair, if the chair happens to remember their names, and some white wine at the department party; but they will never be given any influence over departmental policy, or any health benefits, even if they teach two courses per year for ten years running.

Undergraduates are given the democratic choice of a vast curriculum, but they have little or no say in the basic structuring of their work (the shape of major requirements or the content of course offerings), still less in larger decisions such as faculty hiring and promotions. As for graduate students, in most departments a rhetoric of merit coexists with a reality of quiet favoritism. At best, a faculty member will look out for the interests of a few favored advisees, but for years or even decades at a time no one will make any effort to think about the shape of the graduate program as a whole or the funding of the students—the latter being an increasingly serious issue, as administrations across the country are quietly reducing teaching stipends and other forms of support even as the government cuts back drastically on fellowships and loans. All too often, as Frank Lutz says, "organized anarchy is a misnomer, a negation, a convenient term that means no one is accountable" ("Tightening Up Loose Coupling," 656).

Given this lack of accountability, any group in a department that achieves dominance can quietly and unobtrusively reproduce itself, and can even extend its hold over other areas of the department. Both initial hiring decisions and tenure votes in particular are influenced only in part by intrinsic merit; equally important is the established faculty's sense of how well the candidate has been socialized into the dominant norms of the department. Schools normally hire on the basis of national searches, and in many fields a desirable opening will receive two hundred or more applicants from institutions of all sorts all around the country. Yet the schools already well represented among the existing faculty will regularly be the schools from which new recruits are drawn. A 1960 survey of the twelve leading research universities, for example, showed that no fewer than 85 percent of their faculty had received their degrees from the *same* twelve universities (Blau, *The Organization of Academic Work*, 94). If somewhat more schools would now be represented if the survey were made today, this is largely because more schools have made every effort to become clones of the top twelve. Moreover, it is not only a few "top" schools that look largely to one another; many schools of all sorts draw their faculty from a loosely defined group of "peer" schools, similar in outlook and often in regional location as well.

The ability of the in group to replicate itself is particularly clear if one looks at important but "irrelevant" factors like gender, race, and political affiliation. The first two of these categories have received a great deal of attention in recent years, and heated debate continues about the appropriate measures needed to bring about a fuller presence of women and of many ethnic minorities among faculties. The question of political affiliation, though, has not been so widely debated, apart from some broad charges, and some equally strong denials, that the university has been taken over by "tenured radicals." Only recently have several critics begun to assemble any hard evidence of this, and what they have found suggests a heavily liberal (though far from radical) cast to many institutions. Consider the data in Table 1, showing the political registrations of Stanford faculty in several departments. Martin Anderson, who provides these data, is struck not only by the imbalance at his institution but also by his colleagues' lack of interest in it: "The most disturbing part of the left-liberal faculty phenomenon is the reaction of the academic community. There is not the slightest bit of curiosity on the part of most faculty or administrators as to how this massive political bias came to be . . . Every left-liberal professor I have discussed this with

Table 1. Stanford faculty voting registrations, 1987

School or department	Number of professors registered as		
	Democrat	Independent	Republican
Economics	15	1	5
Law School	23	5	8
Philosophy	10	1	2
Education	27	5	3
Political Science	22	2	2
Anthropology	13	1	1
English	27	1	1
History	22	3	1
Sociology	15	2	0
Total	174	21	23

Source: Adapted from Anderson, Impostors in the Temple, 141.

assures me that it is in the natural order of things. Men and women with left-leaning political views just naturally gravitate to the universities" (142, 144). Like most other features of university life, political liberalism is not actually inscribed in the natural order of things; instead, it is the consequence of deep-seated, often unconscious, patterns of behavior fostered by a dominant academic culture. Anderson is right that this is a problem; he is wrong, though, to suppose that it is anything new, or even that it is tied to liberalism as opposed to conservatism. Most of the evils currently blamed on "tenured radicals" were already well established by the late 1950s, well before the protests of the 1960s. From a historical-structural perspective, the current situation is less a new departure than the latest manifestation of business as usual.

During the first half of the century, college and university faculties were typically conservative both politically and culturally. In 1930 a prominent critic, Abraham Flexner, considered it natural to refer to universities as "institutions usually regarded as conservative, frequently even as strongholds of reaction" (*Universities, American, English, German,* 5). In a given period the tendency may be conservative, as in the 1930s, or liberal, as it is now, but the lasting politics of university departments can be seen in the ability of faculties to perpetuate, and to reinforce, the dominant trend of the time.

As the shift from conservatism to liberalism shows, changes do occur; but as in other areas of university life, they occur very slowly, apparently on something more like a fifty-year cycle than the much more rapid shifts by which, for example, Reagan Democrats are born, vote, and then desert the Republican fold a few years later. As these changes take place slowly in the university, at any given time the situation may seem stable, even the natural order of things—or else, as to university critics of all eras, a shockingly entrenched *un*natural order, whether that order is the socialist paradise imagined by Martin Anderson or the equally baneful subservience to business denounced in 1910 by Thorstein Veblen in his *Higher Learning in America.*

The oligarchies and plutocracies that set the tone for most university departments seldom need to enforce the architectural integrity of their discipline by any outright firing of faculty who are too conservative (or too radical) for comfort. More often they enforce the current status quo by making members of unfavored groups feel *un-*

welcome. A poll at Columbia showed that the freshman class that entered the university in 1984 supported Ronald Reagan by the same majority as the electorate at large; but I would be surprised if there have been more than a handful of Republicans among the graduate students in my department during the early 1990s, although these graduate students would be the contemporaries of those freshmen. Perhaps some of the class of 1988 at Columbia and comparable institutions were converted to liberalism by graduation day; equally, it seems that those who were not converted gradually came to feel that a career in English was not for them, and they applied to business or law school, certainly to fields other than my own. Their situation is a little better than that of Jews and blacks in the 1930s, who had to face more overt and firm barriers in many institutions; but conservatives now, like liberals then, are often made to feel unwelcome— even by people who believe themselves to cherish vigorous debate among divergent points of view.

Just because the university is a heterocosm rather than a microcosm of society, there are good reasons why it has not immediately reflected the country's political changes. We may go so far as to congratulate ourselves that, even if we have not managed to introduce the equivalent of universal voting rights on campus, we also have been spared (to some extent) the equivalent of sound-bite politics. All the same, it is time that we began to pay more attention to the overall effects of cumulative patterns of individual decisions, the messages they send to groups of people, and the ways in which kinds of people and kinds of scholarly work are encouraged or suppressed. This is especially important now, as the halting of academic growth means that our old plutocratic methods will no longer work so smoothly: there is no rising tide to lift all boats. If we must adapt, better that we should adapt in democratic directions than try to reinforce either the anarchy or the plutocracy now in the system. Yet democracy must not continue to be an excuse for irresponsibility and a mask for persistent inequities. Given the uniqueness of the university, any adaptation of democratic methods and values must be a translation rather than a direct application, but contemporary democracy, rather than the turn-of-the-century version, is the logical place to begin to look.

The hyperindividualism that characterizes our scholarly ethos contributes directly to the persistence of Tammany Hall politics. When academics pride themselves on working alone, and when they do as little as possible to cultivate working relationships with their colleagues, then the natural way to run a department comes to seem to be a mixture of private patronage and part-time powerbrokering. This assumption is vividly illustrated in a recent exchange between two politically oriented scholars, Frank Lentricchia and William Cain. In his contribution to a volume of essays titled *Criticism and the University*, Cain argues that leftist scholars have been spending too much time debating ideas and too little time working for concrete changes:

> "Politics" must be part of our discourse in the academy, but it threatens at the present time to become yet another route to marginality and isolation, another opportunity for indulging in high-powered rhetoric and avoiding problems in methods of instruction, teaching and research, departmental structure and curricula. And it also threatens, even in the case of a critic as shrewd as Lentricchia, to edge into a kind of intolerance for merely "academic" labor, for work that does not light up the path to "radical social change" in an acceptable fashion. ("English in America Reconsidered," 92–93)

Stung by this charge, Lentricchia replies by reaffirming the importance of writing and conferencing, and by placing on-campus work in a decidedly secondary position. As he does so, he uses language reflecting a Tammany Hall–style view of departmental politics:

> it becomes necessary not to succumb to the ward heeler's version of politics. I allude to Cain's sense that real political work in the university goes on at department meetings, where courses, appointments and curricula are debated and shaped. But this only seems to happen. Cain is putting the cart before the horse. People act at those meetings as they act elsewhere and as a consequence of what they think . . . The job of people like Cain and myself is not to try to convince our colleagues in a meeting that the canon should be opened up. I have never seen anyone of commitment change his or her mind over such weighty ques-

tions in an hour or two . . . What happens at the department
(ward) level of political activity is a consequence, not an origin,
an effect within the political scene, not the scene itself.   ("On
Behalf of Theory," 110)

Lentricchia's reply shows—with breathtaking self-assurance—the
degree to which departmental work is held hostage to the norms of
scholarly isolation. People who do the actual departmental work are
mere "ward heelers," while the real operators work behind the
scenes. Books and conference presentations now take the place of
the old-style politicking whereby votes would be lined up well in
advance of the perfunctory meeting where matters "only seem" to be
decided.

Lentricchia's picture of departmental politics may all too often be
accurate, but from my point of view what he is describing is a *dys-
functional* department, whose members try to dispose of weighty
questions "in an hour or two" so that they can all get back to writing
their essays on the necessity for politically engaged scholarship. Of
course essays and lectures feed importantly into departmental decisionmaking, but they are no substitute for extended debate between
actual people in actual departments. Agreement on ideas should be
strengthened by live discussion, and ideas themselves are only half
the story, if one is really serious about changing canons and curricula: crucial questions remain to be worked out, concerning resources
in a given department, students' and teachers' interests and preparation, and the thorny problems of structuring a yearlong introductory
course and a ten- or twelve-course major.

Collaborative scholarly activity, then, is a matter of departmental
work as well as of scholarship proper, and these forms of work influence one another deeply—negatively if not positively. If a more positive relation between these modes of work is to take hold, it will be
necessary for people to take a greater interest in direct exchange than
they often do now. Such an interest is partly a matter of social expectations, but it is also a question of personality: of the sorts of people
who go into academia and who survive in it, and the ways in which
their personalities are affected in the process. One reason my argument is essentially ethical is that modes of academic work do not float
in some impersonal institutional vacuum, but grow out of patterns of

personal behavior and interaction, and in turn influence that be-havior.

The recent shifts in political affiliation and in gender and ethnicity have only just begun to affect an underlying set of deeply held and relatively constant norms for the scholarly personality. It is the individual scholar who most directly embodies the alienation and aggression endemic in the system as a whole, and it is those individuals who in turn reinforce the system through their hiring decisions, their treatment of students, their departmental activity or inactivity, and their modes of work in teaching and research. What sort of people are our contemporary scholars, and what implications do our changing times have for our long-established habits of scholarly thought and interaction?

3

The Scholar as Exile

The Virtues of Alienation

In arguing that the modern university is built upon alienation and aggression, I do not mean to suggest that this situation is altogether new, or even that it is entirely bad. Scholars who preserve and celebrate the traditions of their culture may be able to display a high degree of social integration, but to the extent that they are called on to improve existing society, they will be more effective in doing so if their outlook is skeptical, detached, dissatisfied with the status quo. "Tradition in itself is a fine thing if it satisfies the soul," as the philosopher and poet Judah Halevi remarked in 1145, "but the perturbed soul prefers research" (*The Kuzari*, 248).

In this sense, the university is a home for perturbed souls, a place where they can work through their sense of unease with society as they find it, constructing alternative visions of society as it has been or as it could be. Personalities of many sorts exist in academia, of course, even including a few pure examples of the extremes typically found in popular representations of academic life, the jet-setting entrepreneurs and the absent-minded antiquarians, drier than the fossils they study. Even the stereotype of the professor as fossil, common in the early decades of the century, reflects an awareness of the scholar as not truly congruent with society at large. To take a description by Virginia Woolf of a group of Oxbridge professors: "Many were in cap and gown; some had tufts of fur on their shoulders; others were wheeled in bath-chairs; others, though not past middle age, seemed creased and crushed into shapes so singular that one was reminded of those giant crabs and crayfish who heave with difficulty across the sand of an aquarium. As I leant against the wall the University seemed a sanctuary in which are preserved rare types which would soon be obsolete if left to fight for existence on the pavement of the Strand" (*A Room of One's Own*, 8).

When the American universities began to address social concerns in the latter decades of the nineteenth century, the passive detachment of the fossil began to be superseded by the more aggressive alienation of the social activist. While social scientists worked to mitigate the problems of poverty and rapid urbanization, humanists strove to raise the cultural and moral standards of the mass of the population, now for the first time becoming visible to the eye of higher education.

A good example of the scholar working to transform society is Charles Eliot Norton, a leading cultural critic of the 1870s and 1880s, friend of Emerson, Carlyle, and Ruskin, historian of art, architecture, and literature, social reformer, and prophet of culture in a wilderness of vulgarity and materialism. Significantly, Norton never took an academic degree beyond the B.A., and after his graduation from Harvard in 1846 he went into business. Over the ensuing decade he wrote articles for several prominent journals, championing reform in housing and public education. From 1857 through 1868 he worked full-time in journalism, first as a founding contributor of the *Atlantic Monthly*, then as coeditor of the *North American Review* and a principal founder of *The Nation* in 1865. The publisher of this last journal described its objectives in an interesting progression from economics and politics to popular education and the dissemination of high culture:

To champion the equal opportunity of the "laboring class at the South," and follow the social progress of the Negro

To provide information on Southern business (capital and labor)

To discuss legal and economic issues with less bias than the daily press

To stress the importance of popular education in the United States

> To spread "true democratic principles in society and govern-
> ment"
> To offer "sound and impartial" literary and art criticism
> (Quoted in Vanderbilt, Charles Eliot Norton, 97–98)

It is notable that in 1865 neither Norton nor most of his contemporaries yet saw any particular need for a link to the colleges or universities, which would soon become prime locales for the "sound and
impartial" study of such questions as the social sciences were born
and the humanities shifted their focus from antiquity to modernity.
But a decade later, in 1874, Norton himself made the shift from professional journalism to academia, becoming a professor of fine arts
at Harvard, where he remained for the rest of his career.

From this new institutional base, he published both scholarly
books and a continuous stream of wide-ranging essays in cultural
criticism for the public journals. His essays typically show a mordant
view of contemporary American life, and during his Harvard years
his writing takes on an increasingly dark and disillusioned tone. In
"The Intellectual Life of America," for example, published in 1888,
Norton begins by noting the country's unprecedented material progress and democratization during the century, but he emphasizes the
negative consequences of these improvements. In Norton's view, the
rise of mass culture had brought material benefits to many at the
cost of spiritual impoverishment to all. Long before the invention of
MTV and of the public opinion poll, he wrote that

> the prevailing conditions tend to diminish that variety of experi-
> ence and of thought, that difference in tradition and conviction,
> that collision of ideas of varied origin, which are requisite to
> progress in high civilization . . . In such a society, public opinion
> exercises a tyrannical authority. Suspicious of independence
> and originality, it establishes a despotism of custom, encourages
> moral timidity, and promotes an essentially servile habit of
> mind. One of the marked and most disastrous features of a soci-
> ety in which such conditions prevail, is that the great body of
> its members are unconscious of the fact of their mental servi-
> tude, and take delight in the despotism in which they have a

form of damning with faint praise—a subtler but scarcely less lasting form of damnation than the old kind, as the unfortunate heretic, snubbed at conferences and turned down for grants, gradually discovers. What remains constant, as Augustine presciently observed, is the scholarly value of *having an enemy,* and not just any enemy but someone very like yourself in every respect except for a pigheaded insistence on misconstruing the plain meaning of the Epistle to the Ephesians and all that it implies. As Augustine notes, Tyconius lacked the sounding-board of an opposed interpreter and therefore felt no need to develop fully his ideas on faith and works, never even attending to Paul's crucial formulation in Ephesians 6:23. The result, we may be sure, was a treatise on faith and grace that, however well intentioned, was regrettably superficial and would not have got Tyconius tenure at any major American university.

Valuable as alienation and aggression can be, however, they rapidly lose their value if they are not genuinely responsive both to the requisites of productive intellectual debate and to the realities of the surrounding social world. Charles Eliot Norton was at his best during the first fifteen years after he assumed the professorship at Harvard: his essays of the later 1870s and the 1880s show an admirable balance of moral passion and shrewd analysis, deeper than the somewhat easy optimism of his earlier days as crusading journalist but also more effective than the essays of his later years, in which Norton's "fastidious retrospective nostalgia" often takes the upper hand. Perhaps by then he had reacted too strongly against the dashing of his early hopes for dramatic reform in housing, in labor practices, and in education; suffused with an orotund melancholy, Norton's late essays are sweeping in their condemnation of modernity. Writing near retirement in the mid-1890s, Norton fears that even the university can no longer serve as a catalyst for change, for it is failing to differentiate itself and its citizens from the society around it: "The hoodlum of the street corner and the rough loafer of the village find their mates among the students of our colleges. The difference between them is only one of circumstance and of degree" ("Some Aspects of Civilization in America," 645). As evidence of campus hooliganism, Norton attacks intercollegiate sports, which he excoriates as riddled with abuses. Not only does widespread unsportsmanlike conduct betray the higher ethical ideals that should prevail within academia; perhaps worse still, Norton is uncomfortably aware that these games may constitute the chief impact of the university upon public life at large: "These evils in the field of sport are all the more dangerous because of the profit which the newspaper press finds in fostering the unhealthy popular excitement concerning these public games. The excessive space devoted to highly colored and extravagant reports of them, totally out of proportion to their real importance, is one of the marked indications of the prevalence of conditions unfavorable to civilization" (646).

This argument is depressingly relevant even today, and yet Norton's sudden and exclusive focus on sports hardly does justice to the rapidly changing scene of higher education in the 1890s. The problem is both intellectual and rhetorical: his discussions are rather foreshortened, and their tone must have cost him the sympathy of readers not already converted to his views. Augustine really *was* surrounded by forces unfavorable to civilization as he knew it—the Visigoths, barbarians and proud of it, who had sacked Rome in 410; the Vandals who besieged Augustine's own city of Hippo as he lay dying in 430—whereas the "glittering barbarism" of Norton's day included genuine social and cultural progress, closely tied to the spread of modern technology and the new leisure culture.

Norton's students increasingly regarded him as a lovable holdover from some distant past. In a commemorative essay written shortly after Norton's death, Henry James expressed a profound debt to his old teacher, but at the same time he ambiguously credited him with living "among pictures and books, drawings and medals, memories and relics and anecdotes, things of a remote but charming reference . . . a stopgap against one's own coveted renewal of the more direct experience" ("An American Art-Scholar," 415). To the day of his death in 1908, Norton refused to introduce electricity, or even gas lights, into his Cambridge house, preferring to use—less glittering?—oil lamps and candles. Alienation is good if it gives an independent purchase for looking at the world and at one's subject; it is counterproductive when it becomes an excuse for an outright retreat from modern life. Similarly, aggression is useful when it stimulates lively debate; uncontrolled, it has the opposite effect, and discussion degenerates into polemics.

Norton can represent both the best impulses and the lurking dangers in the scholarship of the end of the century, as the modern university was taking shape. "Norton came to personify Scholarship itself, both at Harvard and in the rest of the academic world," according to Kermit Vanderbilt (183), and he personified scholarship not only as a writer but also as a personality. The scholars who followed him continued to build universities in exile, and certain personality types proved to thrive particularly well in this environment. At odds with society at large, more and more scholars became ever more comfortable with the values of isolated work, drawing inspiration from a few like-minded souls and effectively ignoring almost everyone else.

As it has evolved within the university, then, academic work has gradually taken on a certain personal coloring as well as a variety of institutional manifestations, and in a real sense the intellectual structure of academic work has followed from the scholarly personality of the faculty. The more scholars came to see themselves as isolated or even self-exiled, the more logical it became to view the Ph.D., with its culminating years of solitary research, as the necessary precondition for university and even college employment. These years of training continued to shape scholars' ongoing work and their expectations when hiring and tenuring the next generation, thereby reinforcing not only the importance of the Ph.D. degree but, equally, a certain set of assumptions about what that degree should entail.

I am not positing any absolute or one-to-one correlation between a scholar's personality and the writing that scholar will produce, but there is a general family resemblance. At some middle range, in between one's private self and one's public teaching and writing, there exists what could be called one's *scholarly personality*, a guiding cast of mind that is partly a predilection for certain issues and approaches, but equally a fondness for a certain mode of work. Just as the typical literature department weeds out or retrains the young person who comes in with an interest in film, so too, however social they may be in general, apprentice scholars learn to select out from their overall personality those qualities that create a successful scholarly personality. Modern scholarship has taken on a markedly introverted cast, at least in terms of its mode of production. However wide the audience reached (or, more often, fantasized), the work is built out of solitude.

Even if they are the best of friends and the most devoted of parents, prospective scholars will most likely succeed in academia if they can construct a highly individualistic scholarly self; those who refuse or who fail to do so are more likely to turn to other careers, being eased out—or simply losing interest or momentum—at one or another stage during the dozen or more years that will elapse between the start of graduate school and the achievement of tenure.

The evolution of the collective personality of departments can be thought of in Darwinian terms as a small-group version of natural selection. It is not that intellectual sociability is consciously discouraged; indeed, if an explicit policy were ever voiced it would probably produce a counterreaction and actually reduce the power of the unexpressed paradigm. Some irremediably sociable people will always survive in the system, of course; but on average, those who crave solitude will do better than their more intellectually sociable classmates in surmounting the solitary hurdles of Ph.D. orals and dissertation, and thereafter in amassing substantial individual publications in the early years of teaching.

Over time a modest average advantage in natural selection can give a group a dominant position, and its self-image can come to seem the portrait of the true scholar, rather than one option among others. Culture, as Michel Foucault would say, has become nature in the eyes of the dominant group—even when, as in some contemporary fast-track humanities and social science departments, the dominant group is composed largely of Foucauldians who pride themselves on seeing through the myths of their culture. Under these circumstances scholars and administrators begin to make a point of leaving each other alone, an approach that comes to be seen purely positively as rising above petty personal concerns, and collegiality ceases to be a significant factor in hiring. Thus we find Henry Rosovsky making a double argument for the superiority of American universities over British ones—really, when it comes down to it, of Harvard over Oxford. On the institutional level, he emphasizes the virtues of the American love of market competition: whereas Oxford has no rivals, even Harvard must compete in the market and struggle to maintain its prestige. After quoting a British scholar who disparages American entrepreneurialism and celebrates the fact that Oxford's freedom from competition breeds "self-composure and dignity," Rosovsky

comments that "excessive calm can lead to the wrong kind of mental freedom; some would call it sleep" (*The University,* 227–228).

Closely tied to this praise of conflict among institutions is an argument about the relative unimportance of personal compatibility *within* American departments: by contrast to British universities, Rosovsky says, we put little emphasis on whether potential recruits are "clubbable" (202). In hiring discussions at Harvard, "one set of questions is in nearly all instances pointedly omitted . . . Is the candidate a nice person? Will he or she be a pleasant and cooperative colleague? To introduce such considerations would almost certainly be considered bad form" (201). As Rosovsky's interesting choice of the Briticism "bad form" suggests, our departments have not so much abandoned British values as adapted them: ours are clubs of the unclubbable, societies of the unsociable. In rejecting the British model Rosovsky lumps together two very different considerations: the largely irrelevant question of whether the candidate is "a nice person," and the separate issue of whether this person will be a cooperative colleague, which ought to be a much more pertinent matter. Once a need for sustained intellectual exchange has been reduced to a somnolent clubbability, the way is clear for the opposite scholarly personality type of aggressive individualism to reign freely, all under the banner of a quite sincere belief that we don't care about personality at all. Ironically too, the myth of unclubbability allows a very real clubbishness to persist without question, in cases in which a department has taken on a dominant political cast, methodological orientation, or gender composition. The faculty may not make an explicit point of reproducing their present image, and yet types who wouldn't fit in are somehow just not invited in to begin with, and are less likely to be asked to stay if they do appear on the scene.

The most widely observed results of the shift toward the norm of the scholar as isolated individual have been the steady erosion of concern for teaching and the increasing rewards given to superstars who avoid every kind of departmental work like the plague. This is only a secondary problem, though, as the firmament can only hold a small number of superstars at any given time, and the great majority of scholars do actually spend most or all of the school year on campus. A less visible but much more pervasive problem stemming from the ideal of scholarly isolation has been the attendant valuing of certain *kinds* of scholarship, and certain kinds of scholarly interaction generally, to the detriment of others.

One might, of course, make the argument that this choice is actually desirable. Just because universities exist at a tangent to society at large, their faculties are likely to be atypical in a variety of ways, and if individual work is actually better in kind than collaborative work, then our exceptional emphasis on isolation would be fully justified. So natural has the present emphasis come to seem, though, that this case is usually not argued at all; it is simply taken for granted, either tacitly assumed or else asserted as a truism. Thus Martin Anderson tells us that "one of the most jealously guarded prerogatives of any writer is authorship—sole authorship. Thinking and writing is a solitary vocation," and from this undebated premise he concludes that scientific papers by several authors are usually mere scams by which ambitious professors can multiply their publication credits (*Impostors in the Temple,* 110–112). Even Jaroslav Pelikan, who emphasizes ideals of civility and community, works within an essentially solitary model of scholarship. Although he anticipates "a rapid increase in the amount of collaborative research" in the coming years, Pelikan gives greater weight to "the need to respect and to cultivate creative solitude." Therefore, he says, "it will always be necessary in the university for us to counsel those students who think that they would like to become scholars to find out early for themselves whether they can bear to be alone as much as a scholar must be alone; for many find that they cannot, and it is just as well for them to learn this fact about themselves, and the earlier the better" (*The Idea of the University,* 63–65). The reason that it is just as well for Pelikan's less solitary students to learn this is that if they do not weed themselves out at an early stage, the weeding will be done for them later on.

How Pleasant the Loneliness Can Be

A vivid illustration of the formation of a scholarly personality can be found in a recent memoir, *In the Company of Scholars,* by Julius Getman. As his title suggests, Getman emphasizes both the personal and the intellectual stakes in life among "the company of scholars" at Indiana, Yale, and Texas during his thirty years as a professor of law. At the same time, Getman's book is no hymn to the status quo, but rather an account of disillusionment:

> I thought that universities provided an opportunity for caring relations, a sense of community, an atmosphere in which ideas were shared and refined, an egalitarian ethic, and a style of life that would permit time for family, friends, and self-expression. The reality, as I discovered, was quite different. The academic world is hierarchical and competitive; achievement is generally ephemeral and difficult to measure. Much that is done in the name of scholarship or teaching makes little contribution because it is removed from reality and the concerns of humanity. Rather than feeling an automatic sense of community, I have often felt alienated. In particular, the desire for success and status has often conflicted with other goals of meaning, community, study, and reflection.   (ix)

Getman writes from his sense of loss: the scholarly community he hoped for is riven by hierarchies, elitism, and the scramble for status. His account is thoughtful and reflective, and he doesn't spare himself in seeking to account for what is wrong with academic life. His discussion is particularly germane as he emphasizes the idea of community, writing on this issue from considerable personal and professional knowledge. He has also maintained a positive sense of intellectual life outside the confines of university campuses. Coming from a working-class background, as a student he had felt uncomfortable with the patrician Bostonian mode in which legal education was cast in the Harvard of his student days. His continuing sense that the academic world is not the be-all and end-all of education is underscored at the very start of his book, which he dedicates to his parents, pointedly praising his mother for teaching him "that pleasure in ideas, intelligence, curiosity about people, love of music, art, and literature do not require formal education" (v). Getman went on to specialize in labor law, and he has written extensively on issues involved in union organizing, while also actively advising both unions and universities, as counsel and as mediator. Who better to envision alternatives to the present system, ways in which alienated academic groups might work to build community in their midst?

What is striking here is the degree to which, for all his distress at
the absence of scholarly community, Getman himself has internal-
ized the norms of scholarly isolation. His account of his intellectual
development shows clearly that he made the transition from student
to scholar precisely by learning to love loneliness, a love that had
by no means been prominent in his personality before. Gregarious
by nature and uninterested in library research, Getman had a mixed
record as a student at Harvard Law School. With some difficulty he
secured an initial teaching position at Indiana University, where he
was soon immersed in the challenges and difficulties of teaching. Yet
teaching would not suffice to gain him a permanent place on the
faculty, and so Getman forced himself to produce a technical piece
of labor law analysis for a law review. To his surprise, a mentor urged
him to rewrite his draft and make it clearer and more personal. The
piece was well received, and for the first time Getman began to think
of himself as a potential scholar.

He began a second article, and his work on it became an experience
of conversion. This process was partly intellectual, a matter of finding
a congenial way to approach issues; it was also, and essentially, social
and psychological. I quote his account at some length, in order to
show the way in which these aspects are intertwined:

> I began work on the article in the spring of 1965. Each afternoon
> after teaching class, I would go to my cubicle in the faculty li-
> brary and work for two or three hours. To my surprise, I enjoyed
> the combination of intellectual effort and social isolation that
> it required. I stopped attending coffee hour, gave up billiards,
> and cut down on my socializing.
>
> Many evenings I went back to the library after dinner. A col-
> league, Val Nolan, and I were generally the only two there. We
> spoke rarely, sometimes working at adjoining cubicles for hours
> without a word being said. But I was conscious of a mutually
> understood scholarly link between us. This was my first realiza-
> tion of how individual an enterprise scholarly writing generally
> is, and how pleasant the loneliness can be, particularly when
> one simultaneously feels a part of a community of scholars . . .
> As a student I hated homework and was well known for being

gregarious. I was an unlikely bet to enjoy scholarship. But in working on my second article, I once spent almost three hours rewriting a single paragraph. As I tore up my latest effort and gazed at the blank yellow pad with anticipation, I discovered that I was enjoying myself. (46)

Scholars rarely talk so personally, and so genuinely, about the experience of becoming a scholar. This passage typifies what is best about Getman's book—his dedication to scholarship, his interest in showing the interaction of intellectual and psychological factors, and also his ability to look back with some irony on his youthful self. Here at last is a scholar who can speak against the triviality and self-seekingness of much scholarship—of many scholars—and yet also emphasize the pleasure of creative scholarship; "this sense of pleasure," he tells us, "has continued throughout my career" (46). I can hope for nothing better for each of my students than that they, too, should experience the excitement that can come from long hours of disciplined study and thought.

Yet I also hope for something *more* for my students. Are the pleasures of loneliness the only real pleasures of scholarship? As necessary as solitude may be, is it always and everywhere sufficient? Unfortunate consequences can follow if we elevate one basic component of scholarly work to an unnatural status as the very essence of scholarship. I cannot escape the feeling that the alienation and lack of community that Getman elsewhere so eloquently decries are themselves intimately bound up with the pleasures of loneliness he celebrates here.

Readers familiar with conversion narratives will notice that Getman's account shows some similarities to the accounts of religious converts, even to the point that he gives up strong drink (coffee) and questionable idle pursuits like billiards. Illumination ("a scholarly vision," 48) comes after long hours of interior striving in the deserted law library, separated from family and from all friends except for a fellow initiate—with whom, more disciplined than Papageno in Sarastro's dungeon, Getman exchanges no words for hours at a time.

This is not to say that creative scholarship should require equally long hours in the pool hall, but the coffee hour may well be another matter. Getman elsewhere paints a lively picture of the faculty lounge, where the coffee was served, as the prime meeting place where faculty members would exchange and test ideas. When he later went to Yale, what he most missed was the greater sense of community to be found both in the faculty lounge and on campus in Bloomington. In contrast to "the social and intellectual isolation of elite institutions generally and of Ivy League schools in particular . . . midwestern and southwestern college campuses offer the possibility of different groups coming together socially, politically, and educationally; in short, community. This experience of community is far different from the great coastal and Ivy League universities, where separation and mutual resentment are the rule" (228–229).

Getman criticizes "coastal" isolation and lack of community, and yet his conversion narrative shows him accepting these very values, while still at Indiana, as the foundation of his own work. It is hardly surprising that even as he praises the idea of people's coming together in a common intellectual enterprise, he must regret that "such experiences are rare and tend to be ephemeral. The majority of academics with whom I have spoken mentioned alienation and disappointment at the absence of community feeling. Several said that relations with colleagues and administrators are the worst feature of academic life" (266).

Getman's emphasis on the isolation of true scholarship is the more surprising given that he himself actually wrote a book with another scholar. He found the collaboration deeply satisfying, at once agreeable and intellectually stimulating: "I enjoyed the partnership with Steve, the endless conversations about research design, the pleasure of editing each other's writing, and the sense of mutual dedication to the study. I enjoyed the junior-partner relationship that developed with our student interviewers, the rehashing of interviews, and the fun of eating meals together in some motel late in the evening, after all the interviews were completed, while we laughed and swapped stories about what we had learned" (60).

Getman in fact holds deeply divided views about the value of scholarly interaction. On the one hand, he prefers the general sense of community to be found in the nation's heartland, but on the other hand, he says he is glad to have begun his career at Indiana rather

than at Yale because his colleagues *left him alone* at Indiana. Speaking
of his early years, he writes,

> Those who began at that time in any but the most prestigious
> schools had a great advantage over young scholars today. We
> could choose topics on the basis of interest and find our own
> scholarly voice without much pressure from senior faculty.
>
> It is all different today. Expectations are much higher. Young
> faculty fresh from graduate schools, clerkships, or fellowships
> are expected to develop sophisticated research agendas before
> they ever meet with a class. At any school that claims to be
> a scholarly institution, colloquia, works-in-progress seminars,
> research leaves, mentors among the senior faculty, and periodic
> reviews of scholarly progress will be present . . . I approve of
> little in the current system other than research leaves, and I am
> even ambivalent about them because they remove young faculty
> prematurely from the classroom.   (47)

Once we have forsworn colloquia, mentoring, sharing of work in
progress, even the coffee hour and the billiard game, how could we
have any intellectual community left?

Even so, we know what Getman means. The superficial discussion
of work in progress that no one has read beforehand, the awkward
colloquium at which questions are perfunctory or devoted to one-
upmanship, the mentoring when the mentor's goal is to clone new
disciples—give us the law library, or even Sarastro's dungeon, anytime! Yet has not Getman taken the worst-case scenarios as the
norm? Or let us even concede that the norm of personal interaction
in departments is pretty poor—that, after all, is one reason why I
have felt it important to write this book. As long as genuine intellectual sociability is discouraged at almost every turn, coffee hours and
colloquia alike will continue all too often to degenerate into yet more
chances for X to one-up Y or—less offensively but just as regrettably—for people simply to talk past one another, the discussion ending before anyone has actually learned anything, with everyone rush-
ing off to something else just when a real conversation is beginning.

The pervasiveness of this sort of scene and its essential unhealthi-
ness help to explain why even a Julius Getman, never happier than

when talking ideas through with his students and friends, would hold to the Sarastro's Dungeon model of scholarly community. Having your colleagues working silently at neighboring desks may actually be preferable to having them talk to you, if they resemble the more aggressive individuals Getman encountered at Indiana: the coffee-hour virtuoso who specializes in puncturing every argument while writing nothing himself; the assistant professors who spend their time heaping contempt on the older generation of scholars, the better to mask their own anxiety as to whether they will have anything worthwhile to say.

These sorts of behavior vitiate the common intellectual life of departments, and they harm even those who practice them. The coffee-hour virtuoso in Getman's account spoke brilliantly for years of the treatise he was going to write on law and physics, intending to show how judges could benefit by adopting scientific methods. Finally he went on leave to Princeton to complete the book; "he came back full of stories about life at Princeton but without a manuscript, and he stopped talking about the great work he was planning to write" (53). Getman assesses this colleague's failure sympathetically but also rigorously:

> His mind didn't naturally turn to questions of physics and law. He was led to law and science by his ambition . . . Truly original scholarship is frightening enough, lonely enough, and difficult enough to make intellectual enjoyment crucial for its successful completion . . . Unfortunately, he did not really believe that what he could do well and enjoyed was worthy of his scholarly focus . . . This doomed him to be the type of academic who scattered his best ideas and deepest visions into the coffee cups of the faculty lounge. I have encountered this personality type at every school at which I have taught.   (54)

Perhaps Getman is right that this colleague should have retreated to more modest projects, ones he could actually have managed on his own. Yet I can't help feeling that an alternative has been silently elided here: that his colleague could have countered the loneliness of scholarship by making it *less lonely*. He could have found a physicist to work with, or a philosopher of science, and they could have

seen what might have resulted from a series of discussions. Maybe
not a book; perhaps one or two suggestive articles would have suf-
ficed, but something genuinely interesting might have emerged. Getman's colleague was intelligent enough, and principled enough, not
to press on to write something superficial—as his book would probably have been, given his lack of grounding in physics; but to judge
from Getman's account, he wasted years of his life working alone on
a project that could better have been undertaken in collaboration.

Even apart from the question of outright collaboration, Getman's
memoir shows how strongly the forces of alienation and aggression
tend to discourage a close and engaged attention to other people's
work, particularly if the other people differ from you in important
ways. We are increasingly attuned to the voices of several groups
who have traditionally been underrepresented in academia, but we
give little thought to the most pervasive of differences within all departments: age. When Getman began his career at Indiana, left alone
by the senior faculty,

> the younger members of the faculty quickly formed their own
> scholarly community. I can still picture a group of us, all in our
> early thirties, sitting around a coffee table, laughing contemptu-
> ously while my young colleague Alan Schwartz read aloud from
> the lead article in the *Harvard Law Review* . . . In our laughter
> was the unstated commitment that we would approach scholar-
> ship differently from our teachers and seniors, that we would
> deal more honorably and respectfully with the underlying real-
> ity on which legal doctrine must be based . . . We were, unfortu-
> nately, as arrogant as those we mocked, dismissing, without any
> real basis, styles of scholarship and modes of discourse we
> thought of as old-fashioned.   (268)

This sort of scholarly community, if it deserves the name, is essentially defensive in nature, a bonding process by which an insecure
subgroup tries to gain a sense of self-worth at the price of learning
from divergent views. The scene Getman paints would have taken
place some thirty years ago, but the process of winnowing by age
has only accelerated since then. At a recent Modern Language Association convention, my friend Tobin Siebers described his discomfiture

that afternoon at a meeting of a committee arranging panels for the next year's convention. The planners were all in their thirties and forties, and Tobin observed that whenever someone proposed the name of a scholar over the age of fifty, the consensus would be that that person's views were already well known, and it would be better to get someone younger with fresher ideas. Directly after this meeting, Tobin met a friend at the bar of the hotel where the convention was taking place; at the booth just behind them, several graduate students were speaking in identical terms of the *forty*-something speakers they had just heard at the current convention.

We seem almost to have returned to the premature burnout of many artists at the *fin de siècle,* parodically typified by Max Beerbohm, who published his collected *Works* in 1896 at the age of twenty-four. In his preface he declared that he was retiring from literary production, leaving the field to "younger men, with months of activity before them" ("Diminuendo," 66). As in the case of dreary colloquia, this pattern feeds on itself. The more earnestly the younger generation tries to establish itself by pushing older generations aside, the more inclined their students feel to try a little of the same thing themselves. Further, the more tightly each group encircles its wagons around a few like-minded (and like-aged) look-alikes, the more probable it is that their work will indeed begin to sound repetitive at an early date. Alienation breeds a defensive aggressiveness; this aggression in turn magnifies the alienation, and the whole unhappy cycle begins again.

A Community of One

Academic aggression is not always anxious and defensive. At the extreme, we find individuals who are aggressive *on principle,* fully at home in their alienation and wishing there were even more aggression around than there is at present. Martin Anderson, for example, several times resorts to enthusiastic military metaphors to describe intellectual activity: "The top guns of today's professional intellectuals are the columnists and editorial writers for our leading newspapers . . . Like F-15 fighter pilots, they swoop and dive and strafe ideas on important issues several times a week" (18–19). Any issues that have survived all this strafing can be mopped up by book-length treatments: "And if the columnists . . . are the F-15 fighter planes of the professional intellectual world, then the writers and editors of the big book publishing houses are the B-52 bombers" (20). Anderson urges academics to emulate these for-profit writers, as if there weren't already enough polemics, and polemicists, flying about in academia.

Anderson's use of these metaphors cannot really be described as an argument as such, as if he felt a need to counter some other view of intellectual life; his formulations are significant because they show the sort of ideal he can take as a given, not even requiring demonstration but simply needing more adherents to live up to it. Writers on academia rarely use such heavily freighted language as Anderson's, and yet the image of the intellectual as a solo flier comports well with the views of scholarship we have seen in Rosovsky, Pelikan, and Getman.

If Anderson differs from them in wishing to see even more aggressive individualism than now exists, there are reasons why it currently might seem salutary not just to assume but actually to emphasize the solitude of scholarly work. In light of the rise of special-interest groups within academia, the aggressive individual can come to seem a needed counterbalance to the aggressive group, whether that group is constituted on the basis of a narrow identity politics or on some more purely intellectual basis for the construction of an in-group with an us-versus-them mentality. This problem was first raised by writers outside academia, whose polemics were not always grounded in any very nuanced sense of contemporary scholarship, but we have more recently begun to see thoughtful discussions by scholars within academia. Julius Getman, for example, has a long and telling chapter, "The Struggle for Change" (130–208), in which he highlights the oversimplifications indulged by both left and right during sharp curricular controversies in Texas in 1990.

A particularly intriguing response to this problem is a 1992 book by David Bromwich, *Politics by Other Means: Higher Education and Group Thinking*. In tones of measured sorrow, Bromwich attacks all those both on the left and on the right who substitute group-think for individual analysis. According to Bromwich, indeed, Reaganite conservatives and tenured radicals have more in common than they would like to suppose, and their real enemy is not the other camp but the independent individual: "the caring groups are really hard as nails: they want to destroy us, each of us, and always for the sake of all" (23). As he has followed these controversies, Bromwich has found that the arguments from both sides have only increased his sense of the need for self-reliant critical thinking. Quoting an assertion by Emerson that "imitation is suicide," he describes this as "a sentiment that used to strike me as exaggerated" (23).

Like the other writers I have been discussing, Bromwich holds to the ideal of the scholar as lone worker in the dark library of the soul, but unlike the others, Bromwich does not take this ideal for granted. He sees it as under siege and in need of defense. As a result, he gives an unusually clear picture of scholarly ideals that are normally simply assumed without much discussion. The essence of scholarship, for Bromwich, is the free and skeptical play of the individual mind in dialogue with other scholars and, more particularly, with great minds of the past. In opposition to true scholarship stand the productions of conformist groups, whether conservative or liberal. Whatever the politics of such a group, Bromwich tells us in his opening paragraph, "The results are always the same. Conceits and dogmas of conformity, some of them cruel, all of them timid, cling to the group when they cannot survive in a less settled company" (ix). Genuine education is a highly individual matter, whereas group thinking is largely an attempt to carry forward politics by other, less legitimate means.

In developing this theme, Bromwich gives particularly full expression to the pronounced individualism characteristic of the modern university, contrasting its virtues with the vices of special-interest intellectual politics. He presents these alternatives in stark terms, and he consistently disputes the idea that there can be a middle road between them. The group-thinkers must be combatted and vanquished, conservatives and radicals alike. "Both cultures are deeply sick, and it would be a good thing to rid ourselves of both" (xi). The tenor of Bromwich's argument can be seen in the epigraph with which his book begins, from Simone Weil: "The intelligence is defeated as soon as the expression of one's thoughts is preceded, explicitly or implicitly, by the little word 'we'" (xviii). Note the absolutes in Weil's formulation: the intelligence is not merely harmed (much less enriched) by an identification with others, it is defeated; this defeat does not occur gradually but "as soon as" the mind begins from a group identity; this "we" need not even be emphasized but needs only hover implicitly behind the thoughts expressed.

Bromwich develops this point of view in a variety of ways, beginning with a highly individualistic reading of Emerson, emphasizing passages in which Emerson calls for the individual to hold out not just against narrow special-interest groups but against society itself. We should, Emerson says, maintain a "good-humored inflexibility then most when the whole cry of voices is on the other side. Else tomorrow a stranger will say with masterly good sense precisely what we have thought and felt all the time, and we shall be forced to take with shame our own opinion from another" (quoted on 22). The quotations from Emerson alternate between a rejection of the dogmas of society as a whole and a refusal of the claims of subgroups within society ("If I know your sect I anticipate your argument," 22); one senses that Emerson does not finally distinguish too closely between these levels of society.

Even Bromwich describes these quotations as exhibiting "an extreme of indifference to public opinion, to the need for common action, or even for occasional collaboration with other persons. But as a counter-statement to the communitarian pieties of our day, it is a good extreme" (23). Clearly, Bromwich himself does not entirely subscribe to the extreme views he advances from Weil and Emerson; after all, there is, in Weil's terms, a "we" implied by Bromwich's very choice to begin his argument by quoting Weil herself, and then Emerson soon thereafter. He is constructing a lineage, a company, of antidogmatic intellectuals, and he wishes to stimulate a common resistance of like-minded contemporary scholars against the bad sort of like-mindedness he opposes. Bromwich does not see a contradiction in this, for he understands tradition itself in highly individualistic terms. As he tells us in his preface, his book is to be "a defense of tradition as a social and personal fact—but personal first last and most" (xiv). His readers, then, should not after all be overcome with Emerson's "shame" at taking their own opinion from another, but should feel strengthened in their resolve to conceive of tradition itself as based in individual rather than group identity, and of knowledge above all as "self-knowledge" (xiv).

I raise this point not to suggest that Bromwich is caught in an unwitting contradiction, but rather to open the question of what kind

of community can be admitted by so resolute and principled an individualist. In Bromwich's book, at first it may seem as though no viable idea of community can be affirmed at all, if one sees small groups
and society as a whole primarily as carriers of received ideas and
simplistic solutions. Here and there, however, glimpses emerge of
the ways in which Bromwich's (anti-)community of scholars ought
to work. Above all, a scholar should maintain dialogue with writers
of past eras. The solitude of the dialogue is reinforced, for Bromwich,
by the fact that he finds few people in other disciplines who seem
to be interested in many of his favorite texts, even when those texts
nominally come under their purview. He asserts that entire fields,
like history and philosophy, have abandoned their roots in classic
earlier historians and philosophers (107), so that "departments of
literature alone are now entrusted with the teaching of humane letters" (187). Finding no meaningful dialogue among these disciplinary communities, Bromwich must discuss a thinker like Hume
largely through an extended personal close reading. He does, however, occasionally leaven his own readings through direct use of an
individual modern scholar's work for which he feels an affinity, and
conversely he also benefits from give-and-take with an unfriendly
critic of his earlier writing. Thus, in a long footnote he expresses his
gratitude to a harsh critic "for correcting my ignorance," and then
goes on calmly to strengthen his argument in light of the information
his critic has brought forward (242–243).

What Bromwich admits is a kind of *minimum* of community,
whose essence is to be found in the uncoerced and intermittent coming together of two individuals in conversation. Actually, one hardly
even needs the second individual, at least in person; Bromwich several times indicates that the most productive conversations are with
earlier writers. At heart an intellectual community is *a community of
one,* oxymoronic though that phrase may sound: "Every community
of art is a community of one that wants to be two (not more). Its
only criterion of truth is 'I see it that way, too.' Its only obligation
is fixed by elective affinity" (226–227). This community will achieve
its fullest form when it extends to include a second person, who may
be a contemporary or a future reader, but in the meanwhile it already
exists as "a community of one."

Recalling the scene of conversion in the Indiana University law library, we can say that we have now reached the point at which Julius Getman might give Val Nolan an offprint of his article. Bromwich's terms would probably even allow for somewhat more interaction, permitting Tamino and Papageno to share their thoughts during the research phase in Sarastro's dungeon—as Sarastro in fact allows them to do to a modest extent, even though he had made them promise not to. Still, Bromwich continues to bar the way out of the dungeon and into the banquet hall where the initiates join the company of Sarastro's brotherhood. Bromwich's scholarly community in its ideal form is the mirror image of the Christian community presented by Mozart in Masonic form, as the Church's minimum is Bromwich's maximum: whereas Jesus promises to be present "whenever two or three are gathered together," for Bromwich the room is already getting pretty crowded by then.

With Bromwich we finally have someone who does not merely assume but tries to prove that solitary intellectual work is inherently better than the ideals of "common action" and "collaboration with other persons," which he clearly feels usually degenerate into "communitarian pieties" (23). He eloquently evokes his community of one that wants to be two, and I would not want to suggest that his is an unworkable ideal. On the contrary: this is how Bromwich himself has found a way to thrive within the company of scholars, and I detail his depiction just because he gives passionate expression to a mode of work and of interaction that has worked for many. What I do wish to dispute is the suggestion that this is the *only* viable mode of work, and that the only alternative must be some Orwellian groupthink.

In one striking passage, Bromwich himself testifies to the desirability of collaborative work across disciplines, but in the very process of elaborating on the idea he slides directly back into a reiteration of the virtues of solitude. He is talking about the need to reconnect kinds of texts that have been made prisoner by separate disciplines:

> For example, it should be possible to read *Leviathan* and *Paradise Lost* in the same class, just as they were once read by the same culture, without having to be taught by a scholar who makes up in a hand-to-mouth fashion a whole history of poetry or of political theory . . . the difficulties themselves suggest a

shared belief that books talk to each other in subtler ways than
the existing map of disciplines can reflect. Everyone hears scraps
of this conversation, but it is hard to find the teacher, in a single
body anyway, who can keep up with what books of such different sorts are saying.   (128)

Bromwich responds to this problem as forthrightly as one could
wish; rather than counseling us, as Getman might, to stick to the
narrower topics a single person can master, Bromwich suggests that
the solution "may lie rather in creating a permanent place for collaborative teaching in the humanities." Further, this is no mere utopian
dream: "There exists now at many institutions, though in an unorga-
nized way, a community that might some day give a vivid character
to teaching and research along these lines" (128), and he gives as
examples the sustained reading of thinkers like Hume now occasionally to be found in English departments, and the presence of moral
philosophy in departments of politics and in law schools.

The three paragraphs Bromwich devotes to this theme are admirable, yet the migration of books across departmental lines is far from
a full collaboration, as at present it is mostly a matter of an individual
reaching across the hall for some books from another department's
bookcase—or its wastebasket, if we can really believe that Hume is
no longer taught in philosophy departments. What would it take to
proceed to genuine collaboration? Given Bromwich's overall emphasis on the individual, it is perhaps not surprising that he does not
develop this idea further. Still, what happens instead is striking: the
idea of collaboration *itself* calls forth one of his most heartfelt testi-
monies to solitary reading and thought. In the paragraph following
his mention of the migration of texts across departmental lines, he
considers parallel possibilities for conversations across time:

It can be a liberating discovery to feel that there are thoughts
one has in common with people who lived, worked, acted, and
suffered a long time in the past. Indeed, many of the strongest
feelings of solidarity for a thinking person are likely to be of
this kind . . . There are, that is to say, kinds of discovery foreign
to one's contemporaries, knowledge that neither a sect nor a
school professes, which one can feel called upon to bring to light

alone. And the only way will sometimes be through a personal reading of the past. Dependence and group-narcissism are the paralysis of genuine scholarship; but scholars, like citizens, to whom that seems a healthy state of things will always invoke *the argument of growing solitude.*   (129–130)

Bromwich then urges us to follow Nietzsche and John Stuart Mill alike in accepting solitude as preferable to conformity to the conventions of "the herd." If we do so, our solitude will be warmed by the books around us: "Traditions . . . offer, in fact, a kind of solitude, and a kind of company" (130).

The movement of this passage is the same that we have earlier seen in Jaroslav Pelikan: a sincere assertion of the need for collaborative work somehow leads immediately not to a discussion of how this might be carried on but instead precisely to a warm evocation of the virtues of solitude. My goal is not to deny those virtues but to loosen their lock hold on scholarly work. It should not need to be the case that minds as thoughtful as Pelikan's and Bromwich's should suddenly short-circuit when the idea of collaborative work presents itself. It should be possible to see more kinds of scholarly work, and more productive scholarly interactions, than are now commonly found.

Twenty years ago Lionel Trilling concluded *Sincerity and Authenticity*—delivered, fittingly, as the Charles Eliot Norton lectures at Harvard—by criticizing the contemporary love of alienation for its own sake:

> many among us find it gratifying to entertain the thought that alienation is to be overcome only by the completeness of alienation, and that alienation completed is not a deprivation or deficiency but a potency. Perhaps exactly because the thought is assented to so facilely, so without what used to be called seriousness, it might seem that no expression of disaffection from the social existence was ever so desperate as this eagerness to say that authenticity of personal being is achieved through an ultimate isolateness and through the power that this is presumed to bring.   (171)

Trilling is here opposing the efforts of R. D. Laing and Michel Foucault to see certain forms of madness as expressions of health, as resistance to the coercive homogenizing force of modern society. In Trilling's view, echoing Freud's *Civilization and Its Discontents,* society at large cannot afford to indulge untrammeled individualism; for better or for worse, a sane society requires people to adapt to one another's needs and concerns. To apply Trilling's argument here, it ought to be possible to strike a better balance than to face a choice between a breathless postmodern communal pietism and an archaic late-Romantic individualism.

I have no wish to claim that the scholarly norms I have been describing always and everywhere carry the day, although they certainly pervade the published debates. No doubt there are campuses on which genuine community exists, and I know of a few fields in which scholars are more concerned to work together than to upstage each other; but I believe that such campuses and such fields are the exception rather than the norm. My reading in the literature on the university has reinforced this belief. The sociologists and administrators who wax eloquent on "the scholarly community" tend to become distressingly vague as they do so, while their more specific colleagues usually portray an environment dominated by a highly aggressive individualism. Hazard Adams, a professor with ample administrative experience at both the departmental and the university level, is not untypical in making a virtue of such aggression, although he is unusual in his frankness, and also in his zeal in carrying out his own views. He begins his book *The Academic Tribes* by asserting, "My position can be described as Heraclitean. It was Heraclitus who said Homer was mistaken when he prayed for the disappearance of strife from the universe. He did not know he was praying for its destruction" (15). As his imagery makes clear, Adams regards our contemporary academic culture as the very nature of things. But more than this: he sets his personal experiences against the entire body of literature on academic administration, which he rules out of court without even having read it: "I have read as little scholarship in the fields of educational and organizational theory as is conceivable, given my academic experience . . . I proceed with a skepticism about them that I hope only gradually sinks into ill temper" (ix). Adams' presentation is witty and often trenchant, and yet his observations would benefit from being set within the larger contexts that the literature can provide. It should not be necessary to uphold the integrity of one's individual experience at the cost of refusing on principle to read the scholarship on one's own subject.

All too often, scholars quietly do what Adams and Bromwich do openly, ignoring or dismissing entire fields and approaches that would seem relevant if only they weren't either intellectually bankrupt or ideologically suspect. In this way, an extreme individualism may come to resemble the exaggerated collectivism it believes itself to oppose. Is the wholesale denigration of Dead White Males really different in kind from a refusal to see anything of value in the works of Live French Theorists? When fidelity to one's own perspective produces a desire to brick up whole corridors in the library, we may need to become as wary of individual-think as of the group-think whose press has been so poor in recent years.

The sociologists who discuss behavioral patterns among academics speak quite directly about the unusual—or even deviant—nature of the contemporary academic personality. Thus, Michael Cohen and James March describe academic modes of decisionmaking as "pathological"; but this is not a criticism, for they simply see such pathologies as the norms of an abnormal world: "measured against a conventional normative model of rational choice, the garbage can process does seem pathological, but such standards are not really appropriate since the process occurs precisely when the preconditions of more 'normal' rational models are not met" (*Leadership and Ambiguity*, 91). Seeking an analogy to campus patterns of interaction, another sociologist refers matter-of-factly to prisons: "There are strong pressures in a prison that promote the formation of militant interest groups. On the inside the sharp cleavages between the prisoners and their captors make conflict the normal state of affairs. Powerful groups form on every side to fight for privileges and favors. On the outside there are strong sentiments about the prison and numerous community groups try to influence its operation" (Baldridge, *Power and Conflict in the University*, 17).

If Foucault had made the prison analogy just quoted, we might be inclined to see the passage as satiric overstatement, but Victor Baldridge is little given to satire and stays close to his data. Similarly Karl Weick, in a brief summary of the dominant academic culture:

"Prevailing themes within this culture include academic freedom, the lonely inquirer, anomie as a necessary cost of doing business, intrinsic motivation as the highest good, heterogeneity as strength, originality as virtue, team research as enemy, creativity favored over synthesis and replication, and the necessity for great men rather than great groups" ("Contradictions in a Community of Scholars," 28). Clearly, there are positive elements in this list; what is less clear is the necessary connection of *all* the listed items. Perhaps we need no longer insist that heterogeneity and originality can be achieved only through loneliness, anomie, and hostility to team research.

To return to the historical frame outlined in the first chapter, we may say that the contemporary scholarly personality is an elaborated holdover from the new professional personality created by the rising professions at the turn of the century. As Thomas Haskell, the great historian of professionalism, puts it:

> Most of all, a truly persuasive professional community would have to draw upon all the emotional energies of its members ... The rigorous demands of such a community on its individual members would be evident in its native genre, the monograph, with its burden of footnotes calculated to demonstrate wide acquaintance with fellow-workers, to leave a trail for followers, to acknowledge debts, declare loyalties, display alliances, cover flanks, condemn errors, harass deviants, and otherwise to restrain idiosyncrasy and invigorate community life. What would be classed as obsessive name-dropping and paranoid defensiveness in a natural community is normal in the communications of professional inquirers. (*The Emergence of Professional Social Science,* 236)

Haskell is describing professional norms as formulated a hundred years ago, but in many respects professional life in society at large has moved beyond those norms since then. People work more closely together in law firms, for example, or in architectural firms, than they now do in many university departments. The norms of alienation and aggression still enshrined in the university are the products not of nature but of cultural choices, and archaic ones at that. This culture can be changed if necessary—if, as I believe, more and more topics would benefit from sustained discussion among people with different expertise and perspectives, while relatively fewer topics are still best worked through by single scholars meditating on their favorite authors. We should not remain content with a state of affairs that leads sociologists to compare universities as a matter of course to prisons and mental asylums; we will do better to improve relations with our soulmates—or cellmates—in our own institutions.

4

General Education in the Age of Specialization

Tenured Radicals or Tenured Specialists?

Undergraduate education must be the prime arena for any reform in academic culture, both as an area in which academics do a substantial portion of their work and as the venue in which future scholars are usually first brought to do extended work within academic disciplines. Having argued for the need to consider academic issues not only in disciplinary terms but also historically and institutionally, I would now like to offer a case in point. Few aspects of undergraduate life and work have inspired more controversy in recent years than the debates over the curriculum, often centered on core curricula and great books courses. These courses have come under pressure for change from political activists, and ensuing reforms at Stanford and elsewhere were attacked during the 1980s by traditionalists such as Dinesh D'Souza and William Bennett. Underlying both sorts of pressure is a larger and longer tale, the story of the decline of general education, that last bastion of generalism, of which a healthy core curriculum should be the centerpiece.

These debates have been lively, even heated, but they have often focused on the specifics of the books to be taught. I would argue that equal attention must be given to the underlying structure of how the works are taught to begin with. To study the fate of the contemporary core curriculum is to see how deeply the intellectual imperatives of scholarly specialization have infused even the construction of general education for beginning undergraduates. Progressives have not begun to press their reforms far enough, merely promoting some changes in titles while leaving intact the divided labor of turn-of-the-century capitalism embodied in the ethos of academic specialization. At the same time, the defenders of "the great tradition" have not begun to be traditional enough, reflexively defending a secular humanist tradition as it was codified fifty years ago without seriously trying to consider what the tradition should actually look like in the light of contemporary scholarly understanding.

Too often both sides take absolutist positions, as though our intellectual traditions must either form an invariant and unquestionable unity or else be a specious fiction serving the corrupt self-interest of an elite few. Any canon is indeed a construct; particularly in the extremely selective form of a two-semester course, any representation of "the" tradition of Western literature or social thought is bound to leave out important texts, ideas, movements. Yet this does not mean that a necessarily artificial construction of the canon has no value. The real problem is that at the present time the core itself is largely hollow. Debates over particular inclusions or exclusions often amount to little more than the replacement of a few deck chairs as general education continues slowly, majestically, to sink out of sight.

The sad story of general education over the past several decades is the subject of the most eloquent recent defense of the traditional core curriculum, Allan Bloom's best-selling *The Closing of the American Mind* of 1987. In arguing passionately that the American university has lost the battle for its students' hearts and minds, Bloom stresses that the decline of the traditional great books on campus is a leading symptom of the broader decay of general education, considered as training in enlightened conversation about matters of common concern. Unfettered by the narrow concerns of specialized work, general education was meant to be the basis for genuine community in an otherwise diverse student and faculty population, and the basis for national unity at large.

Bloom sees that the triumph of specialization in academic work was fatal to this ideal, as fewer and fewer faculty remained interested in such general discussions, or even minimally competent at carrying them out.

> The problem of the whole is urgently indicated by the very existence of the specialties, but it is never systematically posed. The

net effect of the student's encounter with the college catalogue
is bewilderment and very often demoralization . . . Most professors are specialists, concerned only with their own fields, interested in the advancement of those fields in their own terms, or
in their own personal advancement in a world where all the
rewards are on the side of professional distinction . . . So the
student must navigate among a collection of carnival barkers,
each trying to lure him into a particular sideshow.   (338)

The most basic threat to general education, then, comes not from
tenured radicals but from tenured *specialists*. Genuine radicals are
actually rare on campus; but almost everyone, progressive or conservative, is now a specialist. The norms of specialization so dominate
the academic ethos that a meaningful defense of general education is
rare indeed; when offered, it usually falls on deaf ears. Bloom himself,
holding the line against change in the 1960s, had no success at all,
perhaps because his arguments at that time had no affirmative content:

During the sixties I sat on various committees at Cornell and
continuously and futilely voted against dropping one requirement after the next. The old core curriculum—according to
which every student in the college had to take a smattering of
courses in the major divisions of knowledge—was abandoned.
One professor of comparative literature—an assiduous importer
of the latest Paris fashions—explained that these requirements
taught little, really did not introduce students to the various
disciplines, and bored them. I admitted this to be true. He then
expressed surprise at my unwillingness to give them up. It was
because they were, I said, a threadbare reminiscence of the
unity of knowledge and provided an obstinate little hint that
there are some things one must know about if one is to be educated. You don't replace something with nothing. Of course,
that was exactly what the educational reform of the sixties was
doing.   (320)

It is little wonder that he lost those votes. Having admitted the devastating criticisms of his opponent (Paul de Man?), Bloom could offer

nothing more compelling than a view of the core as "a threadbare reminiscence," "an obstinate little hint." *The Closing of the American Mind* can be seen as Bloom's attempt, twenty-five years later, finally to find a winning argument in defense of general education.

How well does he succeed? His book is a heartfelt plea ·for the tradition as he sees it, but he leaves the concept of tradition itself strangely unexamined. He assumes without question that the great books tradition, however lamentably disfavored, is at least a stable and clearly identifiable entity, closely reflected in the courses taught at Chicago and several other schools during the past fifty years. It is here that a historical and institutional perspective can be brought to bear to test this idea. How far have the great books courses of the past generation, and their accompanying anthologies, given a persuasive and accurate representation of the Western literary tradition? Why have they taken certain forms and not others?

The Closing of the American Bible

The modern great books course stems from experiments in general education during the 1920s and 1930s, particularly at Harvard, at Columbia, and at Bloom's alma mater, Chicago; many subsequent courses elsewhere have built on the pioneering courses at these institutions. A detailed examination of these courses would take a volume in itself, but for present purposes certain tendencies can be brought out by asking two somewhat pointed questions. The first of these questions relates to the history of ideas and also, less obviously, to the problem of identity politics: Is the Bible a Great Book? The second question is institutional in nature: Whose interests are served by the creation and maintenance of great books courses? A look at the local history of the core curriculum at my own institution suggests some interesting answers, answers with important implications for the future of such programs.

To begin with the first question: Is the Bible a Great Book? Of course it is—or rather, it should be, but the fact is that the Bible has not been given any substantial place in most core courses and anthologies. How could this distortion of our literary and cultural heritage have come to pass? To be sure, the Bible has always been *represented* in great books courses, and understandably so: who could be more dead, more white (if not in fact, certainly in the traditional Western reception), and more male than the authors of the Law and the Prophets? What could be more canonical than the collection that inaugurated the concept of canonicity itself?

Current discussions of our cultural canon defend or denounce the focus of the typical great books course on European masterworks, but both a proponent of "the great tradition" like Bloom and also most of his critics assume that such courses do at least accurately reflect the European tradition. Even campus iconography often presents the basic mission of the university as the preservation and exploration of our Western cultural heritage, with a definable set of the modern great thinkers resting on the shoulders of the ancients. My own university gives a good example: at the center of the central Columbia campus lies Butler Library, its facade decorated with two series of names, one ancient Mediterranean and one modern American. In a gesture of particular respect to antiquity, the American names stand at the ancients' feet rather than upon their shoulders: Jefferson, Emerson, and their peers are inscribed over the doorway, while high above and in larger letters, atop Doric columns fronting the main reading room, are the names of the great ancients: Homer, Herodotus, Sophocles, Plato, Aristotle, Demosthenes, Cicero, and Vergil.

What happened to the Bible? Both the New Testament and the Hebrew Bible have been passed over. At least the central campus contains Saint Paul's Chapel, so that a New Testament writer has a building named after him, a privilege otherwise accorded only to famous campus figures or wealthy alumni. Even Paul has been losing ground, though; his chapel is next to the original Low Library, iconographically suggesting a balance of reason and inspiration; but Paul stayed put, now rather out of the way, when the new and more imposing Butler Library was built in 1934 and Low Library became home to the central administration. Even granting Paul a certain pride of place between the president's office and the former lunatic asylum that now houses the Maison Française, the implication is clearly that the Bible is an object of worship rather than of actual study.

This iconography finds pedagogical expression in the core curriculum, which represents antiquity largely through Greece and, to a lesser extent, Rome, with only brief attention paid to the biblical tradition and none to the other ancient Mediterranean cultures. Columbia's case is by no means exceptional. The most widely used anthology for the past thirty years has been the *Norton Anthology of World Literature;* it is now appearing in a new, multicultural edition, but in its first six editions it defined "world" literature as classical and later European literature. The editor for the ancient material, the classicist Bernard Knox, devoted 900 pages to Greek and Roman literature, as against seventy-seven for the Bible.

Thus the unified great tradition of European literature as presented over the past several decades has enshrined a Hellenistic polemic against Hebraism, and although Christianity inevitably infuses the later tradition as a whole, the Hebrew Bible in particular has languished in almost total eclipse. At Columbia it has not even been presented as an independent text in proper chronological order, as are all the other texts in the course, but has been moved up to mid-year in the literature survey, a simple preface to the New Testament, read after Vergil rather than with contemporaries like Homer, Sophocles, and Plato.

I suppose that the original structure of the course, as of Knox's Norton selections under the general editorship of Maynard Mack, resulted from some alliance of secular humanism with a liberal Christianity that felt no need to insist too strongly on its already pervasive presence. Perhaps too, at Columbia, where a Jew had virtually no chance of getting tenure in the 1930s, institutional inertia suffices to explain why no one has tried to rethink the treatment of the Hebrew Bible even now that the university has a substantial Jewish population, both student and faculty—including, in recent years, the president, the provost, the vice president for Arts and Sciences, the dean of the College, and the chair of the English Department, all at the same time.

Equally, though, the very conception of the course is hostile to any serious treatment of the Bible; a genuine engagement with biblical conceptions not only of God but of history and of ethnic identity would require a very different structuring of the course and would tend toward very different purposes. To examine the purposes that have governed great books courses over the past generation, we can return to Allan Bloom. Bloom's discussion is particularly germane as he speaks directly of his own Jewish background and emphasizes the centrality of the Bible in his grandparents' lives. The Bible served as the center of a truly living general education, linking scholarship to life in community, and he argues that there is no meaningful alternative to such a great book–based education:

> I am not saying anything so trite as that life is fuller when people have myths to live by. I mean rather that a life based on the Book is closer to the real nature of things. Without the great revelations, epics and philosophies as part of our natural vision, there is nothing to see out there, and eventually little left inside. The Bible is not the only means to furnish a mind, but without a book of similar gravity, read with the gravity of a potential believer, it will remain unfurnished.   (60)

Given this evocation of the role of the Bible in his grandparents' life, it is striking to find that Bloom himself excludes the Bible from his ideal program of study: his discussions center on Plato and Aristotle, and then on to Machiavelli, Hobbes, Locke, Rousseau, and Nietzsche. Not only does he make no direct use of biblical traditions; he does not even include them when he defines the roots of Western culture. As many passages indicate, he sees Western culture as having a single source, and that source is Greece: "Moments of great transformation have started with refreshment at the Greek source, its inspiration slaking a burning thirst. An overwhelming sense that something is missing is the serious motive for authentic, therefore careful and exhaustive, recovery of what has been lost. Greece provides the assurance that there was something better than what is" (304).

Bloom's stress on this tradition is counterpointed against university life as he has seen it evolve during his teaching career. As a number of his reviewers noted, the emotional core of Bloom's book is the chapter called "The Sixties," in which he describes with disgust and horror the assaults on academic freedom and, as he saw it, on reason itself during the campus protests of the late 1960s. The students' faddism, narcissism, and self-righteousness were, in Bloom's view, fueled by resentment against elitism of all sorts, in particular the higher traditions expressed in the great books. Unfortunately for the students, their lack of cultural perspective rendered their very ideas for reform superficial, "an exercise in egalitarian self-satisfaction that wiped out the elements of the university curriculum that did not flatter our peculiar passions or tastes of the moment" (320).

Bloom focuses on the classical tradition as his model for high culture, and excludes the Bible, because he sees religion as a prime cause of irrational mob behavior. His Enlightenment is a secular movement based on Greek reason and rejecting superstition and extremism (terms he often associates closely). Furthermore, religion is also the hallmark of ethnic particularism, the great threat to the unity and peace of the polity. The ethnic identity that worked for Bloom's grandparents neither can nor should be preserved today: a search for one's roots is either a trivial matter of dress and cuisine, or it is religious, in which case it is destructive: "This attempt to preserve old cultures in the New World is superficial because it ignores the fact that real differences among men are based on real differences in fundamental beliefs about good and evil, about what is highest, about God. Differences in dress or food are either of no interest or are secondary expressions of deeper beliefs. The 'ethnic' differences we see in the United States are but decaying reminiscences of old differences that caused our ancestors to kill one another" (192–193).

It is somewhat ironic that Bloom has been admired by so many conservative readers, who usually place religious belief high among their valued traditions, when the underlying message of his book is a frontal assault on the value and the viability of religion itself. Perhaps many readers lingered over Bloom's vivid denunciations of adolescent sex, drugs, and rock and roll in his early chapters, and never reached passages such as the following: "We reject by the fact of our [persistently religious] categories the rationalism that is the basis of our way of life, without having anything to substitute for it . . . the religious essence has gradually become a thin, putrid gas spread out through our whole atmosphere" (215).

Western culture, then, is not unified after all, but is the site of a sustained battle between two traditions: the great tradition of philosophy, reason, science, and personal liberty against the not-so-great tradition of religion, irrationality, prejudice, and factionalism. Presumably Bloom would allow that the founding texts of this second tradition should occasionally be studied but should not have any prominence in the core of the humanities. Bloom even argues that the Bible would not want to be admitted to the club anyway: "To include it in the humanities is already a blasphemy, a denial of its own claims" (374).

It would, of course, be possible to argue against the need to relegate religious texts to the sidelines of human inquiry, whether for their own sakes or for ours. Institutionally as well, the university can perhaps better be seen in symbiosis with religion rather than in opposition to it, a perspective recently advanced eloquently and with a wealth of historical examples by Jaroslav Pelikan in *The Idea of the University: A Reexamination*. We could even ask whether Bloom has provided an alternative to religion or only another religion, a mysticism of reason, concerned, like religion proper, with "the souls of today's students," as his subtitle puts it. Bloom's undergraduate experience at Chicago was "the revelation of a community"; "In a nation founded on reason, the university was the temple of the regime" (245). As for the dangers of religious strife, can we be so sure that Bloom's ideal universities, existing for the sake of the theoretical few and in opposition to the excesses of modern democracy (251–252, 260), are inherently less factional locales than the churches Robespierre turned into Temples of Reason?

The full weight of Bloom's argument does not, however, rest on his rather Manichaean cultural history. While his militant secularism has presumably not been the key to his widespread success, his readers have probably been responding more directly to his insistence on education as the road to personal autonomy, to freedom from the "accidents" of one's background and of history itself. Certainly this is the message stressed by Saul Bellow, whose foreword to Bloom's book shows clearly that the great books tradition is in fact an antitradition, a means of escape from a constraining Jewish ethnicity and the modest prospects of an immigrants' child:

> as a Midwesterner, the son of immigrant parents, I recognized at an early age that I was called upon to decide for myself to what extent my Jewish origins, my surroundings (the accidental circumstances of Chicago), my schooling, were to be allowed to determine the course of my life. I did not intend to be wholly dependent on history and culture. Full dependency must mean that I was done for . . . I couldn't say why I would not allow

myself to become the product of an *environment*. But gainful-
ness, utility, prudence, business, had no hold on me. My mother
wanted me to be a fiddler or, failing that, a rabbi. I had my
choice between playing dinner music at the Palmer House or
presiding over a synagogue.   (13)

The danger for Bellow, then, was not civil war but a dreary life of
doing dinner music at a posh hotel. The biblical tradition in itself,
while available to him, no longer held the attraction it had had for
his parents and for Bloom's grandparents, and literature provided the
way out: "In traditional orthodox families small boys were taught to
translate *Genesis* and *Exodus,* so I might easily have gone on to the
rabbinate if the great world, the world of the streets, had not been
so seductive. Besides, a life of pious observance was not for me. Anyway, I had begun at an early age to read widely, and I was quickly
carried away from the ancient religion" (14).

Great books courses have commonly been intended to provide a
way out of ethnic particularism, the opening up of a wider, more
common world, often closely identified with mainstream American
culture, or at times defined (as by Bloom) as a better-than-American
cosmopolitanism. From this point of view, the Hebrew Bible comes
under the same cloud as do contemporary minority voices when arguments are made for their inclusion in core curricula. On this perspective, the Bible should simply be excluded, or else it should be
included on the same basis as, and along with, works like *I, Rigoberta
Menchu,* the Guatemalan peasant activist's autobiography now assigned in Stanford's core curriculum and the subject of a sarcastic
chapter in Dinesh D'Souza's *Illiberal Education.* I won't dwell on the
latter alternative, partly because it could so readily be done, particularly now that Menchu (*pace* D'Souza) has won the Nobel Peace
Prize. If, that is, one wants a course devoted to contemporary social
issues and their roots, it is easy enough to imagine a very effective
pairing of, say, Exodus with *I, Rigoberta,* ideally to be read in tandem
with the Mayan *Popol Vuh,* as Guatemalan social activism is intimately bound up with syncretistic religious thought and practice.

For the present argument, more important than the specifics of
curricular choices are the underlying educational issues raised by the
question of the Bible's status. Taken seriously—even as a cultural

document, not as an article of faith—the Hebrew Bible in particular would undermine Bloom's defenses against his twin enemies of academic specialization and ethnic particularism. The Bible's unique form resists any generic universalizing and requires some degree of specialized attention, and yet at the same time its universalizing *message* is precisely one long polemic on behalf of ethnic particularity. The Israelites' trajectory is in fact the opposite of Bloom's own: they flee cosmopolitan Egypt and recover their ethnic independence, always having to resist the temptation to assimilate to one or another of the older and more powerful cultures around them.

The Hebrew writers have little tolerance for the sort of philosophical "great conversation" to which great books courses usually aspire. It is not so easy to imagine a writer like Ezekiel the way Bloom envisions Plato, as a sort of Iron Age Fred Friendly, assembling his PBS panelists for a symposium on *The Symposium*. To take seriously the perspectives of Jeremiah and of the Priestly writers would entail treating the Bible as something other than a prelude to Dante. It would mean, for instance, assigning substantial portions of the laws, not just the vivid narratives which humanities courses and anthologies take to be the real story but which were preserved precisely to frame and ground the Law. To teach Genesis without Exodus, as is often done, would be like assigning the portions of Matthew's gospel that describe Jesus' miracles while leaving out his actual teachings. This is not to say that only orthodox or fundamentalist readers can make sense of the text or derive valuable lessons from it. Read with attention to its cultural context and to its complex interplay of genres, the Hebrew Bible can give a more capacious understanding than can Plato alone of the possible relations of ideas to events. To do this, though, requires some verbal or written instruction from someone who understands that context and that interplay, and the effect would probably be to complicate any unified idea of "the Western tradition."

Further depth would also be given to the Hellenic readings. Classicists were often prone in the past to give an essentially secular reading of ancient Greece; this situation has changed substantially in recent years, but the change hasn't shown up in most great books courses. If Aristotle, for example, values reason over revelation, this optic is hardly the best one with which to understand Euripides, and even Homer suffers in a secularist reading. Similarly, a dehistoricized mode of reading may not be the best way to introduce the Greek dramatists, and even the philosophers' philosophical ideas may be placed in a more dynamic relation to Greek religion and history. In a text like *The Symposium,* the Athenian wars may not be mere accidents above which the symposiasts rise, as Bloom claims: "in these terrible political circumstances, their abandon to the joy of nature proved the viability of what is best in man, independent of accidents, of circumstance" (381). The problems of tyranny and treachery, of maintaining group identity amid internal and external struggles, might better be seen as the very ground of the discussion of love, meant to be fully in the reader's mind as the future traitor Alcibiades staggers into the party. Perhaps even (or especially) the ideal order of *The Republic* can be seen in relation to Plato's culture and his times and tested against them.

To do so would deprive Plato of a certain special status above the common human condition, a change that Bloom would see as destroying the whole point of reading him: "If there are many cultures, unsolicited by one perfect or complete culture in which man is man, simply—without prefix such as Greek, Chinese, Christian, Buddhist (i.e., if Plato's *Republic,* outlining the one best regime, is simply a myth, a work of Plato's imagination), then the very word 'man' is a paradox" (203). Ironically, in view of Bloom's hostility to religion, this is a religious vision of a mystical unity above history—and a Christian vision at that, not a Jewish one: the Platonic republic will be Bloom's version of the City of God, not of Zion. Now Bloom must defend Plato against the inner fear of all true believers: what if the sacred text is, after all, a myth? I would argue that *The Republic* is both more mythical and more historical than Bloom wishes to admit. The Bible can be used in core courses not to mystify further the great books tradition but quite the contrary, to demythologize Plato.

The challenge now facing core courses and introductory surveys of many sorts is to do a better job of particularizing their material without sacrificing all unity to the multiplicity of events and cultural contexts. It is reasonable enough to say that there is such a thing as the Western tradition, meaning a general cultural heritage common to much of Western Europe, a heritage that via England has been the greatest influence in the formation of American culture. It is another matter, though, to say that this heritage must itself be seen in a purely unitary fashion. Neither antiquity, Western Europe, nor even the British Isles can be adequately represented as organic unities, as has often been done in the past. It is no improvement, though, to adopt a Bloomian dualism in which the Greek tradition is diametrically opposed to the biblical traditions. From the time of Matthew Arnold, the opposition of Hebraism to Hellenism has devolved into the virtual exclusion of the former, both by Bloom and in the *Norton Anthology*, with its twelve-to-one ratio of Classics to Bible selections. Jacques Derrida is surely too pessimistic in his claim that binary oppositions always favor one term over the other, covertly serving the interests of those in power, but this is indeed what has happened in this instance.

This sort of suppressive unity is a problem not just in the representation of the tradition as a whole but equally in the case of individual national cultures. Consider the enormously popular *Norton Anthology of English Literature*. Its two volumes provide a wealth of material—some five thousand pages in all—yet this material is heavily weighted toward a very specific idea of what it means to be English. This bias is shown as early as the map printed inside the front cover, "A Literary Map of England." Although the second volume includes a number of major Irish writers (Wilde, Yeats, Shaw, Joyce), the "literary map" shows only England, Scotland, and Wales, indicating topography, county lines, and major cities; Ireland is left off the map altogether.

The situation is the reverse with Wales, fully represented on the map but largely erased from the table of contents. Dylan Thomas gets a few pages in the second volume, but a student would have no way even to guess that Wales produced one of the great bodies of medieval lyric in the eleventh through fifteenth centuries. True, these poets were writing in Welsh rather than English, but the anthology makes considerable room for translations from Anglo-Saxon and even includes translations from Latin. Great Welsh and Irish texts like the *Mabinogion* and the *Tain* are similarly excluded, despite their persisting influence on later writers such as Yeats. A few Irish writers who wrote in English are admitted as honorary Englishmen—reasonably enough for Oscar Wilde, who made his career in London, but hardly for the anti-British Yeats and Joyce. The anthology, then, promotes an artificially unified idea of "England," including Wales but not Welsh and turning Irishmen into Englishmen. Anglo-Saxon is advanced as the true parent of English literature, even though both Welsh and Irish—and not Anglo-Saxon—continue in use as spoken and literary languages to this day.

Both in the Europe-based core curriculum and in the more confined space of the literature of the British Isles, we see similar problems of national unity against ethnic particularity, social analogues of the scholarly tension between generalization and specialization. To come down solidly on the side of unity had a certain social logic when the campus was thought of as a major manifestation of the melting pot, and this social logic had an intellectual and institutional base when there was a significant proportion of generalists on campus. In the early years of the modern great books courses, their broadly construed European tradition was welcomed by many teachers as a relief from the increasing fragmentation of the humanities by discipline and of literary study by nation. Thus Lionel Trilling wrote in the 1950s about his experience at Columbia twenty years earlier: "I was a member of the first instructional staff of the Humanities course and I can recall my feelings about the smallness of the English representation: I was glad of it. I was delighted by the range and sweep of what was before me. It made all of English literature seem rather confined, rather local" ("English Literature and American Education," 373).

On his way to becoming the first Jew ever to receive tenure in the Columbia English department, Trilling welcomed the release from even the localism of English studies. There is nothing unreasonable about this perspective today, although not everyone would now embrace it, some wishing to retain a stronger local identity, whether ethnic or American, others preferring on the other hand to embrace a multiculturalism ranging beyond Europe. Interestingly, Trilling condemns this latter view in the same article: "As for the World Literature courses, in their implied rejection of the especial value of the cultures that lie nearest to us and that are traditional with us, in their affirmation of the equal value of *all* cultures, there is an implied denial of the actuality, of the force and value, of *any* culture" (379).

What has changed is not the viability of Trilling's solution in cultural terms but the close fit that could still exist in his day between such a cultural perspective and a parallel scholarly method. In his writing as in his teaching, Trilling was a generalist, ranging easily and widely over modern culture. If his essays on Freud, on Marx, and on the liberal imagination are more focused than the timeless great conversation of the core courses, the difference is one of degree rather than one of kind. All his life, Trilling was a devoted member of the College faculty at Columbia, then still the heart of the university. His ideal reader was "the general reader," and even in his own time he was exceptional in maintaining a general outlook from within an academic base. The triumph of specialization during the past several decades has almost entirely eliminated such figures from the university, which is why Bloom felt so lonely during most of his career. The clock cannot be turned back sixty years, even if that were desirable; what is likely to be more constructive is to ask how, if at all, something resembling the ideal of general education can be restored in the age of specialization.

Tenured Specialists and the Core

We can approach an answer by asking our second pointed question, the institutional one: Whose interest is served by the current anachronisms? The major interest groups in this instance are four: students, alumni, administrators, and faculty. This fourth group in turn needs to be thought of in four subcategories: advanced graduate students who receive appointments to teach sections of the core courses, assistant professors who teach in the core, tenured faculty who teach in the core, and tenured faculty who don't. Of these groups, students, alumni, and administrators all have relatively straightforward relations to the core. Most students like it, in part because those who are opposed to core curricula on principle would generally not choose to come to a place like Columbia, in which the core dominates the first two years of study. The core courses are inherently exciting: intensive seminars devoted to great books, well chosen for accessibility and dramatic interest. Given a good teacher and some lively students, they can hardly go wrong. Any course, whatever its chosen texts or methods of analysis, will do well if it gives students the chance to read entire works from the masterpieces of the European tradition,

with or without direct inclusion of modern texts highlighting contemporary social issues. The students are exposed to wonderful
books; they gain invaluable practice in reading; and the seminar format and the papers they write enable them to develop analytic skills,
verbal ability, and, ideally, a taste for intellectual give-and-take. Further, the common core, taken by all students in the college, provides
a base of shared knowledge, a series of points of reference, and builds
esprit de corps. For these same reasons, the alumni generally remain
strong supporters of the core, and return in large numbers on Dean's
Day to hear favorite professors discourse once again on Plato and
Shakespeare. Alumni enthusiasm, in turn, means that the college administrators are absolutely thrilled with the core.

What students and alumni are not in a position to assess are the
relative merits of one kind of core program versus another, either as
experiences in themselves or as preparation for later study. Administrators may not be personally unequipped to develop opinions on
the subject, but institutionally they are rarely concerned to do so,
so long as their student and alumni constituents are happy. It is the
faculty who are ultimately responsible for the shape and content of
the core curriculum, and here is where the puzzle arises. If, as I have
been arguing, few if any of my colleagues are still Trilling-style generalists, why have our specialists not been troubled by the widening
gulf between their own work and the generalism of the core?

Ordinarily, after all, people like to teach material they know well
and are directly interested in; normally a specialist in Victorian poetry will teach Victorian poetry and Victorian prose or, now and then,
for a real stretch, a course that goes back to Romanticism or forward to modernism. It would rarely if ever happen, however, that
a Victorianist in a large department would teach, say, a course
in Shakespeare. Even supposing the receipt of a research grant by
the department's Shakespearean—or, in Columbia's case, all five
Shakespeareans—the department would hire an adjunct or let the
course go untaught rather than consider asking the Victorianist to
do it. Still less would our Victorianist teach a course on ancient Greek
literature, and if such an idea were proposed, any self-respecting classics department would appeal to the administration to block this in-
cursion into its area of expertise.

Yet an exception is made for the core, even at Columbia, which considers the core not as window dressing but as the very foundation of the undergraduate experience. But what happens when a Victorianist teaches the "Literature Humanities" core course, in which there may not be a single work of Victorian literature, and barely two or three English texts at all? Suddenly our specialist becomes an amateur for a day, and this amateurism extends not only to what is taught but even, and relatedly, to *how* it is taught. In a course that devotes, say, a week to *Faust* with no other text from Germany and perhaps only one other eighteenth-century text of any sort, it is simply not possible to teach the work in its historical and cultural context. Nor, given the speed at which the course covers material, can one even perform a serious close reading of the whole. In this respect, the course is a last vestige of the kind of impressionistic general reflection that was otherwise supplanted by the institutionalization of the New Criticism in the 1940s and 1950s. The story is often retold on campus of the apocryphal sophomore who asked his instructor which translation of Shakespeare he should buy. Lionel Trilling saw the positive, cosmopolitan side of this emphasis on foreign language traditions, but for a New Critic this would be uncomfortable ground. Anyone who believes, as the New Critics did, in the essential role of close textual scrutiny, in "the heresy of paraphrase," tends to have a corollary sense of the blasphemy of translation. Most of the movements that have followed the New Critics have retained their emphasis on close reading, often adding new requirements for sensitivity to historical context, thereby making the dehistoricized core courses doubly unsatisfactory.

Thus there is a fundamental divergence between how core courses operate and how their teachers otherwise carry on business. This basic structural problem exists regardless of whether the texts to be taught are Greek elegies and medieval romances or Chinese poems and Afro-Brazilian song lyrics. Our Victorianist will not normally have any real professional competence, as such competence is now ordinarily measured, in *any* of these areas—still less in a dozen different periods and national traditions. What remains as the actual content of the "Great Conversation" constructed by the core courses? When I asked an alumnus, a former student of Trilling's, how he would describe Trilling's core classes, he replied, "It was shooting the breeze—of a very high order, naturally; but still, shooting the breeze."

With the growth of specialization, only a decreasing minority continued to feel genuinely at home teaching the course. Trilling himself, for all his warmth toward Literature Humanities, never taught it after the early 1940s. He remained sympathetic to the ideal of general education, but once he got tenure he himself began to shift his contributions to the core toward a more local field of knowledge, namely the nineteenth and early twentieth centuries in England, France, and Germany. Together with Jacques Barzun he founded a course centered on those countries in that period. This course was a sort of cross between the broad generalism of the basic humanities course and more fully specialized surveys, since it still ranged across several literatures and disciplines, but within a period of only a century and a half.

By then his graduate students were writing quite focused dissertations, solidly grounded in the nineteenth century and clearly centered on literature proper. Steven Marcus, for example, wrote his dissertation under Trilling on a single author, Dickens; hired as an assistant professor in 1957 (the year Trilling was writing his encomium of Humanities), Marcus then taught Humanities for three years. He was expecting to continue teaching the course, but he bowed to his department's request (or thinly veiled command) to teach instead the undergraduate survey of nineteenth-century literature. Thirty-five years later, still meaning to return to teaching Humanities one day, he has yet to find time to do it.

Beneath the surface differences between supporters and opponents of the core curriculum is the institutional and intellectual reality that scholars have come to feel that specialized courses are the logical way to organize knowledge, and such courses have become departments' first priority even for undergraduates. Whether a radical postcolonialist refuses to teach Literature Humanities on principle or a supporter of the core simply cannot fit it in, the net result is the same: few tenured faculty are choosing to teach the course.

Why, then, hasn't the course been abolished outright, or fundamentally changed so as to reflect the ways people actually think and work today? Is this not a strange exception to the rule that the senior faculty's interests always prevail in the long run? The answer lies in the smooth workings of the university's cozy combination of democracy and plutocracy. The tenured faculty have, by and large, ceased to care very much about the College at all; the exaltation of specialized work has increased the focus of interest on the graduate program, well reflected in the department's consolidation into Philosophy Hall. As the plutocrats they—we—are, the tenured faculty have bought their way out of service, in much the way landed gentry once arranged for farmhands to fulfill their military obligations for them. The core is now taught mostly by graduate students and assistant professors. Henry Rosovsky has remarked that the term "assistant professor" is a misnomer, as untenured faculty do not actually assist anyone; they are simply people "who receive low pay and little secretarial help, while performing the same tasks as full professors" (*The University*, 171). In this instance, though, we see a lingering truth to the term: assistant professors assist their tenured "colleagues" by enabling them to *avoid* teaching with them in the core.

Both the School of General Studies and the College still regret and even resent the loss of their distinct divisions of the English Department, but the defeat of General Studies was so complete that no one any longer feels compelled to do more than express a vague regret and mount a minimum of courses; the College, however, still retains strong alumni support, as well as a very sizable enrollment base. The college deans must be given some assurances that teaching ability is still highly valued, even though it no longer figures in hiring decisions or tenure reviews. While the offices vacated by the consolidation of the English Department can always be used by overflow staff from admissions and financial aid, it is hard to avoid a sense that Hamilton Hall, the chief College building, is no longer the intellectual center it once was. In this context, the tenured faculty support the core warmly, a warmth not dampened by any need actually to teach in it themselves; the core essentially serves as a smoke screen to cover their own disappearance into Philosophy Hall.

A few senior professors, none below the age of sixty, remain committed to the core and still teach in it regularly, giving a certain built-in continuity to the program. Staffing the course is no real problem, as younger people can be found, or forced, to teach it. For graduate students, teaching a real literature course is both more fun and a better credential than doing freshman composition, composition lying even further than the core from the palace of scholarly wisdom. For beginning assistant professors, teaching in the core is simply presented as a condition of employment. Further, assistant professors are given a term of leave after three years of teaching the course, in recognition of the fact that the course is more burdensome to prepare than more familiar material, and more of a distraction from one's scholarly work. But the very fact that most of the teachers are the young and restless untenured faculty and advanced graduate students raises the question why those teaching the course have not been moved to change it more dramatically than by the recent additions of Sappho and Virginia Woolf. After all, these people are even more committed specialists than their teachers were; indeed, since all their teachers were specialists, they really have never known anything else.

Here is where democracy comes in. Far from being fixed on high, the Humanities syllabus is revised annually—by the people who are teaching it that year. This is a stroke of genius. Consider how much work it would take to prepare Homer, Sophocles, Thucydides, Paul, Augustine, Dante, Shakespeare, Goethe, Woolf, and a dozen more such authors. Even leaving aside actually learning anything about any of them, it is an enormous task simply to read the books and come up with something—anything—to say about them for four hours, especially if, as for many new teachers, you have never yourself studied half the texts you are now supposed to teach. All this while struggling to write a dissertation or to complete the first book.

Having done all that work, and having had the class go pretty well after all, how prepared would anyone be to contemplate changing half the syllabus in a single year? And if the change involved rethinking the whole structure of the course, so as to require spending next summer studying medieval culture instead of writing your next chapter, wouldn't your heart sink? Thus the democratic ideal of allowing current teachers to decide on any changes to the syllabus works strongly to support the existing syllabus, as only in the most extraordinary circumstances would people who have just got some sort of handle on all that material contemplate any significant revisions to the syllabus.

Even so, substantial change might occur over time; but here the plutocracy comes in again. The lower-ranked instructors are too transient, and too busy with their other work, ever to organize much in the way of sustained change. Graduate students teach the course for only two years or so; even untenured faculty often manage to stop teaching the course regularly after their first three years. The only faculty with any real commitment to the course are the few loyal senior faculty, who will turn out in force if any significant change is proposed, and whom in any event neither the graduate students nor the untenured faculty are in any position to challenge in a basic way. Just because the younger people are such committed specialists, they don't finally have their hearts in the course, and will save their energy for areas of more direct concern, such as angling for the graduate seminars they would like to teach. For most scholars today, teaching is another version of that "investment in oneself" of which Rosovsky speaks, but general education is an investment of dubious value, since it doesn't lead to the payoff of knowledge in depth and the attendant possibility of publication.

The status quo is further reinforced by the way the plutocrats have set up the democratic discussion: by asking what should be taught in Humanities next year, we avoid the larger issue of whether literature, social thought, art, and music should continue to be taught in separate courses. These subjects were originally intended to be taught together, and a powerful scholarly case for doing so was made by Daniel Bell as long ago as 1966, in *The Reforming of General Education,* a study commissioned by the dean of Columbia College and neglected by everyone on campus from that time forward. As Lionel Trilling sadly noted a few years later, his specialist colleagues simply weren't *interested* in discussing questions of general education: "From my long experience of the College, I can recall no meetings on an educational topic that were so poorly attended and so lacking in vivacity as those in which the report was considered. If I remember correctly, these meetings led to no action whatever, not even to the resolve to look further into the matter. Through some persuasion of the *Zeitgeist,* the majority of the faculty were no longer concerned with general education in the large and honorific meaning of the phrase" ("The Uncertain Future of the Humanistic Ideal," 166).

Under such conditions, the younger faculty see no reason to rethink these issues, and they are also disinclined to favor any change that seems to lead even farther away from their areas of expertise. Just because the younger people are committed specialists, they are usually deeply aware of what it means to approach a subject from a specialist's perspective. The problem is not only one of preparation time; a genuinely interdisciplinary course would be so far beyond any one person's competence that it could not be made to work under the present structure of the course. So people make do with the status quo, especially as none of the specialists really cares enough about the course to devote the time and energy needed to lay the groundwork and build consensus for any structural change.

Now the structure of the core courses is the seminar, pure and simple. An experience of togetherness for the students in class, of course, but from the teacher's perspective another case of isolated activity. No core courses are team taught, apart from an honors colloquium for a few seniors; none of the basic core courses even has weekly lectures given by specialists; all involve a single teacher, the texts, and the students, in fifty parallel sections—a last holdout of the mass duplication of labor that was otherwise forgone in favor of creating and filling ever more fields of specialization. As the current academic culture discourages people from questioning the norms of isolated individualism, new instructors feel grateful at least to have a weekly faculty lunch at which an old hand shares teaching tips on the week's text. But no one makes any serious effort to consider any form of collaborative teaching, which might make it possible to bring materials together in more varied ways, or ways more responsive to the genuine perspectives of the various relevant disciplines of literary study, philosophy, and history, not to mention other disciplines if Literature Humanities were ever to be combined with any of the other core courses. "Literature Humanities" itself, indeed, is not the course's official name but rather an all-too-accurate student renaming of "Humanities A," in theory an interdisciplinary course. In fact, it is so largely dominated by teachers from literature departments, and hence by literary selections, that even Plato and Descartes, along with the Bible, become closely assimilated to literature. Thus the course combines the rootlessness of unspecialized work with the limited perspective of a single disciplinary outlook.

Perhaps, though, this is a necessary compromise? How could anyone genuinely prepare to teach Humanities from an active knowledge of the fields involved, really knowing something about literature, philosophy, religion, and social thought in antiquity, the Middle Ages, the Renaissance, and modernity? Allan Bloom actually did this, or approximated it, moving from a base in political science to Chica-

go's interdisciplinary "Committee on Social Thought" and publishing
in the process on Plato, Shakespeare, and Rousseau, among others.
He was, however, a dying breed, as he himself emphasized, since he
was first and foremost a teacher. His previous books, mostly edited
translations, were really adjuncts to his teaching, as was *The Closing
of the American Mind,* dedicated "To My Students." The problem here,
the reason he was part of a dying breed, is partly practical: it is increasingly difficult even to be hired, still less to achieve tenure, as a
teacher who is not equally or even principally a scholar. But this
difficulty reflects a genuine intellectual problem: it is no longer responsible to float among several fields, a Jack of many trades but a
master of none. Those who still do so are likely to be continually
reinventing wheels, treading back over well-worn paths, lagging ten
or twenty years behind the current state of discussion. It is all very
well to decry the narrowness of specialization, but anyone who has
once felt the excitement of clarifying and deepening scholarly debate
is likely to be reluctant to give up that quest and will feel vaguely,
or acutely, dishonest in making ill-founded pronouncements on unfamiliar material, even for an audience of sympathetic sophomores.

Just because the norm of academic work is so isolated, moreover,
one gravitates to community wherever one can find it; and such community as exists is to be found largely among like-minded specialists
in one's own field. It is rare today to find, on small campuses or
large, an Oxford-style common room where the dons gather of an
afternoon to take tea and discuss issues of general intellectual interest. This point was brought home to me several years ago when I
served as an outside examiner for honors students at a prestigious
liberal arts college, famous for its brilliant and creative students and
for its faculty's commitment both to teaching and to research. When
I told my host that I envied his belonging to such a close-knit English
department, he replied, "Well, not so close-knit; I *see* my colleagues
maybe two hundred times a year, but we never really *talk* about anything." As the only specialist in his field at his college, he finds better
opportunities for genuine interchange off campus, at conferences of
fellow Americanists.

So what is to be done? Recent reforms have altered some of the items
on core syllabi or have attempted new configurations of existing

courses. Such realignments are likely to mark an improvement over the inertial drift that normally characterizes undergraduate curricula, yet too often they fall short of a true reworking of the overall intellectual economy. An interesting contrast to Columbia can be found in the new core curriculum developed at Harvard during the early 1980s. Whereas fifty years earlier Columbia's core "solved" the problem of specialization largely by wishing it away, Harvard's more recent effort began from an awareness of the dominance of specialization in the modern research university. Rather than have everyone within an overall discipline teach sections of the same course, Harvard allows its faculty to adapt one of their specialized offerings to fit under one of the core's rubrics.

The Harvard core curriculum aggregates a wide range of courses under six general headings: Literature and Arts; Science; History; Social Analysis; Foreign Cultures; and Moral Reasoning. Students are to take one or two courses under each heading. Faculty who wish to have a course listed among eligible courses must persuade a standing committee that the course is suited to an audience of nonmajors, and that it emphasizes general modes of analysis as much as specific content. At a major research university, getting senior faculty to orient some of their courses to nonmajors at all must be regarded as an achievement. Derek Bok begins a thoughtful chapter on undergraduate education by recalling the advice a fellow university president gave him, shortly after his appointment to the Harvard presidency: to abolish Harvard College altogether. "I decided to play for time," Bok says. " 'That's an unusual thought,' I responded brightly. 'Why do you suggest it?' " His companion replied that this move would "clearly acknowledge that teaching undergraduates has become an anachronism in the modern university"; professors should be freed to do their research and to train graduate students, without wasting their time teaching undergraduates (*Higher Learning*, 35).

Many of Bok's faculty probably shared this view, and so Bok and Rosovsky had their work cut out for them. They did succeed in persuading their colleagues to think broadly about the goals of undergraduate education; the resulting core program aims to introduce students to the modes of reasoning and the kinds of problems that engage researchers in the humanities, the social sciences, and the natural sciences. As Bok rightly says, "a faculty that has made a considered choice of *some* common philosophy is vastly better off than one that struggles along with no philosophy at all" (45). At the same time, though, the actual embodiment of this common philosophy turned out to be a somewhat uneasy amalgam of heterogeneous courses, some of them genuinely new and broad in scope, others ("The Russian Revolution," "Rembrandt and His Contemporaries") hardly if at all distinguishable from the sort of undergraduate course a specialist would ordinarily propose while writing a book on the Russian Revolution or on Rembrandt.

Bok himself favors broader reforms than have been put in place at his own institution. He notes that a number of small colleges have had greater success in mobilizing faculty collaboration in changing *how* students are taught as well as *what* thay are taught. "Curricular debates," he concludes, "only involve the arrangement and re-arrangement of individual courses and do not touch upon the ways in which professors organize their material, teach their classes, and examine their students. Hence, the fascination with curriculum, so typical of American undergraduate education, protects traditional faculty prerogatives at the cost of diverting attention away from the kinds of inquiry and discussion that are most likely to improve the process of learning" (71). As both Harvard's and Columbia's exam-ples suggest, progressive ideas need to be matched by a correspond-ing *mode of work* if they are to achieve their full effect.

Collaborative Learning and Professorial Authority

The ideal of general education is sound: to give students a broad introduction to the study of cultural traditions and social thought, at a time when they are not yet treated like protograduate students, as majors often are. From this point of view, core courses are idealistic constructions, institutionally as well as intellectually, but they should also begin from the realities of the surrounding academic cul-ture. General education can once again become a meaningful concept only if it is carried forward in light of the realities of contemporary intellectual and socioeconomic life, and not in nostalgic admiration for the scholarly ideals of half a century ago—or in unconscious imitation of the mercantile practices of fifty years before that.

Although I disagree with Allan Bloom's vision of the core, he is right to say that it is wrong to replace something with nothing. The mere abandonment of requirements is no better than their blanket reinstatement, and campuswide discussion is needed in order to determine how best to proceed on a given campus. My personal preference would be for a double-credit course organized into units of five or six weeks, collaboratively taught, with some units based in a period and place such as Renaissance Florence, others organized thematically; some basic secondary materials should be given to students to ground their reading of the primary texts. But any option developed through conversation and consensus, taking both history and current conditions into account, will be an improvement over the normal situation of an unreflective perpetuation of half-abandoned ideals.

As long as faculties are populated largely or entirely with specialists, programs of general education ignore this fact at their peril. Ways must be found to integrate specialized knowledge with general education, and in the process to interest tenured faculty in the project sufficiently to gain their active involvement. Team teaching, mixtures of seminars and lectures, seminars taught sequentially by several knowledgeable people, faculty colloquia to explore new areas of use to students but also potentially of interest to the faculty themselves—there are many modes of work that can be considered.

Above all, such reforms will require that faculty members talk extensively with one another. Of particular importance is increased contact across the levels of tenured faculty, untenured faculty, and advanced graduate students, groups that rarely have substantial intellectual exchange outside their own fields of specialization. Further, a real commitment to general education will require departments to reconceive their needs, or rather their "needs," since most departmental imperatives are self-generated, even mythical (although myths have real power when enough people either believe in them or find it easiest to behave as though they do). If greater resources are devoted to core courses, something else must give, quite possibly the number of advanced, specialized offerings, and almost certainly the senior faculty's ability to do most of the latter while the untenured people do most of the core. The senior faculty, the hidden plutocracy, must be brought to distribute some of their wealth, either by administrative fiat (a crude method) or (if possible) voluntarily;

they are much more likely to do so if they can develop courses that serve the purposes of general education while also suiting, and ideally extending, their own interests. A middle ground needs to be found between amateurism on the one hand and, on the other, the mere grouping of specialized offerings under a few general rubrics.

Colleges around the country are in fact experimenting with ways to reach such a middle ground. In particular, the very form of undergraduate courses is now being opened up in a variety of ways. Collaborative teaching need not imply only the expensive method of having two instructors jointly do an entire course; many other options are possible. Courses in different areas that share some overlap can meet periodically in joint sessions to discuss their varying approaches to common texts and issues. Alternatively, as Faith Gabelnick and several colleagues argue in their book *Learning Communities*, several courses that treat related themes can be integrated with one another. They can still be taught separately, but the instructors coordinate their syllabi in advance, and the courses are scheduled so as not to conflict with one another; the cluster of courses is then advertised as a recommended sequence, and students are invited to take the full cluster if possible.

In this way, each course can retain the integrity of its instructor's disciplinary approach and particular interests, and at the same time the teachers and the students can view each course in a context provided by the others. The courses can thus work in synergy together, rather than either simply duplicating one another or, conversely, tearing apart a general theme through atomized presentations. Gerald Graff discusses these and several other initiatives in the final chapter of his *Beyond the Culture Wars,* noting that systemic changes are far more important than local revisions to individual syllabi. As he says, if we are tiring of course catalogues that look like cafeteria counters, we should worry less about the menus and think more about redesigning the cafeteria (118–119).

Much can be accomplished through different forms of collaborative teaching and through the coordination and integration of courses. Much more also needs to be done to foster a greater emphasis on collaborative learning. The students can be involved in the process of gaining a special foothold in one or another aspect of the material and bringing this knowledge to the class as a whole. For students to become interested in active modes of learning, they need to be shown that their input really influences the substance of the course. Such an effect is unlikely to be achieved unless teachers, for their part, can begin to rethink their stance as figures of authority, as Kenneth Bruffee proposes in his recent book *Collaborative Learning: Higher Education, Interdependence, and the Authority of Knowledge.* They should not simply abandon that authority, but conceive and use it in an open and flexible way.

Bruffee admirably combines concrete practical suggestions with a broad theoretical discussion of changing conceptions of the nature of knowledge. He argues that knowledge has too often been regarded essentially as a collection of facts to be transmitted by the teacher; this limited understanding underlies the fact that most undergraduate education "has little use for collaboration, does not teach it, distrusts it, and often penalizes it" (2). Bruffee follows the anthropologist Clifford Geertz and the antifoundationalist philosopher Richard Rorty in stressing that education is only secondarily a matter of amassing information; primarily, it is a process of acculturation into an interpretive community. Properly understood, a liberal education should be seen as "the identification and negotiation of community boundaries" (135), not least of which are the boundaries between the overlapping interpretive communities students bring to a new subject and the new disciplinary community their teacher represents to them, and for them.

Treating the students as something more than passive consumers is, in fact, the best way to increase their interest and involvement in the course. The teacher's authority would now rest less in an encyclopedic "mastery" of the subject than in a fuller membership in a disciplinary community, a membership marked by active engagement with debate concerning the boundaries of the community itself. This engagement would ideally lessen the tendency for teachers to preach *ex cathedra,* and the equally regrettable tendency for students to gravitate toward teachers who do preach authoritative doctrine.

The authoritarian model of professorship is becoming more and more questionable, given the growing variety of approaches and viewpoints within so many disciplines, but it has long been a rather mixed blessing in academic life. In a fascinating study of two rival midcentury scholars, Donald Campbell has given a clear example of the problems that can result when students equate tendentiousness with truth. Campbell studied students' very different responses to the teaching styles of two behavioral psychologists of the 1940s and 1950s, Edward Tolman and D. P. Spence, in order to explore what he calls "the social system vehicle" that carries scientific knowledge. Writing in the late 1970s, he observed that Tolman's theories had proved more influential over time than his rival Spence's theories. During the 1940s and 1950s, though, both were prominent writers and teachers, and Campbell is struck that only Spence, and not Tolman, produced a significant number of disciples who carried on his ideas—even though Tolman's theories would eventually win out, with little help from his own students.

Campbell traces this disparity in influence to a pronounced difference in the two theorists' teaching styles. Interviewing former students of each professor, Campbell and a colleague found that Tolman made a point of stressing the tentative nature of his views and of encouraging his students to go their own way; Spence, by contrast, presented his ideas as the whole truth and nothing but the truth, and his students often took him at his word and followed his lead. The difference in their approaches is strikingly evident in Table 2, which summarizes their students' views of them. Campbell suggests that Tolman would have done better if he had behaved more like

Table 2. Traits on which Spence and Tolman differed (percentages)

Trait	Spence	Tolman
Convinced of value of own systematic position	98	46
Took himself seriously	98	32
Expected strong commitment to his approach from me	98	4
Authoritarian	88	0
Aggressive	84	4
Strong-willed	96	36
Accepted criticism well	13	86
Allowed me autonomy in choice of research problems	26	96
Open-minded	6	100
Humorous	28	96

Source: Campbell, "A Tribal Model," 191.

Spence, emphasizing and even exaggerating his belief in his own ideas:

An openly expressed overconfidence in the excellence of his theory might have been necessary to communicate to his students enough conviction in its correctness to sustain their Tolmanian faith when they were at other universities and found themselves surrounded by nonbelievers. In this light, ratings in Table 2 may be taken as evidence of a default on the tribal leadership role on Tolman's part and of leadership attributes of Spence's that may help explain the remarkable loyalty of Spence's students to his theory long after they left his campus. ("A Tribal Model," 190)

I read this story differently, even if Campbell's conclusion has a certain logic in view of the academic culture of the 1950s—and, too often, of the present as well. What we most need is to reconceive our campus culture so as to give greater play to open-minded, non-authoritarian, unaggressive thinkers like Tolman, rather than promoting the further spread of "tribal" patterns of belief—language that in fact reflects a rather one-sided understanding both of tribal politics and of the historical varieties of religious authority.

To engage students in a different sort of authority structure requires, of course, that they too be willing to make the necessary effort to take an active role in their courses. Such a commitment might have been difficult to assume in the past, when the majority of students were more interested in their extracurricular life than in their studies per se. In her excellent historical and sociological study *Campus Life: Undergraduate Cultures from the End of the Eighteenth Century to the Present*, Helen Lefkowitz Horowitz argues that students have traditionally divided themselves into three groups, whom she labels the collegians, the outsiders, and the rebels. A division of this kind cuts across divisions of race, gender, and region and helps us to think about each group's particular needs, both those that should be encouraged and those that should be resisted. In Horowitz' view, the largest group has always been the collegians, uninterested in ideas as such and concerned chiefly with forming adult social networks, having an enjoyable experience, and moving on into the work world. This group was probably perfectly satisfied to sit back in lecture classes and have information given to them, or at most to engage in some "shooting the breeze of a high order" in their seminars; the challenge would be to interest them in something more substantial.

The major change that Horowitz finds in recent years is that, for the first time in our history, the collegians have begun to work for grades, previously a matter of concern mostly to the outsiders. The collegians still care little for learning as such, but they see the need for a strong transcript as they apply to professional schools. Horowitz herself is not encouraged by this shift, which often results in a querulous search simply to please the professor. Even so, if for the first time the majority of undergraduates are now actually *trying* to please their professors, we finally have the necessary precondition for genuinely engaging them. Students may respond well to efforts to harness their budding professionalism and make it less grim.

Of particular interest for the present argument is Horowitz' observation that collegians and rebels have traditionally been uninterested in scholarship, while the likeliest people to become genuinely excited by scholarly ideas have been the outsiders—people who, for reasons of class or personality, just could not fit in with the group, though without rejecting academic values as the rebels tend to do (*Campus Life*, 15). Outsiders, then, are likeliest to self-select as candidates for graduate study or to win their professors' favor and encouragement to go on. Thus the differing undergraduate cultures exist in symbiosis with scholarly culture, and perhaps undergraduate curricula have silently adapted accordingly over the years. The loyal and generous alumni who so fondly recall the core courses as the best part of their experience may well be Horowitz' collegians, while the tenured professors who leave the core to the assistant professors may well have been the collegians' outsider classmates, currently joined as well by some of the less rebellious rebels.

If we can think seriously and systematically both about collaborative teaching and about collaborative learning, we can begin to create a more vital relation between scholarship and undergraduate education, breaking down the old divisions of labor: the division whereby tenured faculty do their specialized work while the untenured people pick up the pieces; the division whereby sociable undergraduates are given quiet messages that they should be heading off to business school, leaving the academic field for the current outsiders who become the protégés of the last generation's outsiders. Of course such a division is far from watertight, but an initial set of expectations certainly circulates among undergraduates, and studies like Horowitz' provide much food for thought if we wonder who does and who does not decide to become a scholar. In turning now to the topic of graduate education, we will explore the ways in which such "outsiderly" expectations are strongly reinforced in the ways we train our new scholars.

5

The Culture of
Graduate Education

The Ph.D.: Octopus or Squid?

Any fundamental reform in scholarly work must be built around substantial changes in graduate education. It is the several years of graduate school that most decisively shape the developing intellectual personality of new scholars as they move from the more general education of college into full professional activity. It is then that habits of mind are learned and reinforced, then that the choices made by the profession begin to seem natural. Yet the structure of graduate education has remained stable since the triumph of the Ph.D. at the turn of the century. What would it take to achieve a meaningful and lasting series of reforms? The history of the modern university repeatedly shows that changes can occur when faculties perceive them as in their interest, while conversely any reform that is not in the interest of the faculty will wither on the vine. Nowhere is this more true than of graduate education, which has come to be guided almost entirely by individual departments, and largely by individual faculty members in the case of advanced students, often with only minimal oversight even from the department. No exhortations to change will have any effect on graduate education if the faculty do not wish to make the change.

To take one example, the Ph.D. dissertation has been lambasted repeatedly ever since William James satirized "The Ph.D. Octopus" in 1903, when the degree was only just beginning to flex its tentacles in this country. Yet recurrent attacks on the irrelevance of narrowly specialized and turgidly written theses have in no way affected the degree, whose requirements have persisted throughout the century, since faculty have preferred the dissertation as the best way to guide, to control, and to initiate their advanced students. As a result, the importance of the dissertation has steadily increased, as has the length of time to degree. In a recent article, Theodore Ziolkowski has suggested that James's image of the octopus is too mild: "for the contemporary situation the generally small, timid octopus, which tends to confine itself mainly to coastal waters, provides an image less compelling than another cephalopod: the large, aggressive, and highly mobile squid with two prehensile arms in addition to its eight grasping tentacles." Indeed, "the taste for squid is spreading, to the extent that some of the rarer academic varieties are virtually being pursued with drift nets" ("The Ph.D. Squid," 182–183).

Faculty interest is half the story, while institutional inertia plays an important supporting role. The Ph.D. degree was only one option among many when it was first introduced, and its form was freely variable, but the mold has solidified and even rigidified since then. At the turn of the century, the monograph genuinely seemed the best alternative to merely dilettantish or journalistic exercises. Now that the degree is almost universally required for entry into the profession, we really have no choice but to retain it, even if some of us no longer find that it suits our interests or our students' needs. We could afford to give up the degree, or to abolish the dissertation, only if everyone else agreed to do so at the same time. Given the unusually decentralized nature of the American system, there is simply no way for this to happen.

Yet at the same time, it is the genius of the university that you can change virtually every *aspect* of the Ph.D., just so long as you still award a degree of that name. This characteristic of our varied and entrepreneurial system was already clear at the turn of the century, when L. Frank Baum's Wizard of Oz gave the scarecrow a brain by presenting him with a diploma.* Intractable in some ways, the

---

* In some sly way, Baum's book dovetails nicely with the educational situation of his day. Even the Wizard's sole degree requirement—that the candidates bring him the Wicked Witch's broom—can be compared to the new fieldwork whereby scholars were to gain both knowledge and self-improvement (a heart, courage) while helping to solve a pressing social problem. The entire Land of Oz is a kind of outlandish land-grant university, to whose lush fields Dorothy comes from her dusty family farm, gaining admission to the central campus by an oral examination at the gate. In a nice touch in the movie version, this test is administered by a gatekeeper who is none other than the Professor—as the Wizard calls himself in Kansas—in disguise.

system is remarkably open to revolution from within, so long as scholars can be persuaded that their work will benefit.

The chief obstacle to structural reform in the system is the fact that most of the people now in it are products of that system. By the very fact of their having done well in it, it has come to seem natural. I have argued for the importance of history in showing the constructedness of what is apparently natural, but it must also be kept in mind that the story of the university has usually been told by the victors. Barzun and Rosovsky spend much more time telling us how senior scholars are appointed to their universities than detailing what happens to the many assistant professors who are quietly let go. Those who leave for other professions rarely write about their experiences, and even the authors of the occasional disgruntled memoir are usually still ensconced within the system they deplore and may share more of its values than they suppose.

The flaws in history as written by the victors are easier to see when the educational system is not one's own. The drawbacks of the traditional British public schools, for example, are well enough known to us that we are likely to question any account that speaks only of the ways in which caning is good for the character. To take one example, in *Profession of English* G. B. Harrison has given a highly positive account of the British system in which he had been trained before coming to this country. He describes education there in terms of a steady onward and upward march, whereby the confused thirteen-year-old recruit undergoes a series of strengthening rites of passage until his eventual arrival at the upper echelons of school life. Thus: "At the next step in his progress, he is promoted to house prefect. This stage is a severe test of character and personality . . . If he survives this test period successfully, he is promoted to school prefect and becomes one of the aristocracy of the school . . . The final peak of a boy's ambition is to be head of the school. He is a glorious being, almost as important as a regimental sergeant major" (32–33).

Rhetorically, Harrison has invited us to see ourselves as that glorious being, whose experience is the epitome of school life. He says nothing, however, of those who survive this test period in less than glorious fashion—the first-former, say, who isn't good at sports or who doesn't enjoy the regimental life. What is most striking to an outsider, though, is a regrettable fact that Harrison notes only in passing: after mentioning some drawbacks in the British model, he adds that

a third disadvantage of the system (seldom expressed or realized) is its wastefulness. Only one in three of those who enter a school stay for the full course of five or six years. Those who leave at sixteen . . . have endured all the disadvantages of a public school and received few of the benefits of a good secondary education; for it is in the last two years—between sixteen and eighteen—that a boy becomes prefect, member of the Sixth Form, the cricket eleven and the football fifteen or sergeant in the Officers Training Corps, whereby he learns certain lessons in study, man management, self-discipline, co-operation and loyalty to an institution. (39)

It is hard to imagine a more devastating indictment of a deeply flawed educational system than its loss of two thirds of its candidates along the way. These losses, moreover, occur before the students have got the real benefits the system is meant to provide. And yet Harrison describes this wastage as little discussed and even as seldom *realized*. We may be tempted to feel thankful that we Americans are not prisoners of such a hidebound, wasteful system, one we would certainly never accept ourselves—but an unfortunate fact intrudes: a disturbingly similar wastage is commonly found in our own Ph.D. programs.

Over the years there has been surprisingly little sustained analysis of this problem, but we now have the benefit of a major study conducted by William Bowen and Neil Rudenstine and several associates, *In Pursuit of the Ph.D.* In their preface, they testify to the difficulty they have had in obtaining answers "to even the most elementary questions concerning graduate education. For example, no one has been able to say with confidence what proportion of students who enter doctoral programs eventually earn doctorates" (xv). It is to the great credit of Bowen and Rudenstine that they have found at least a partial answer to this and to a host of other questions, and any contemporary analysis of graduate education must begin from their discussion and from the wealth of data they have assembled.

The chief difficulty they found in trying to gather information is

the almost complete lack of any central record keeping, either nationally or even within individual universities. Records of graduate programs are usually kept in the different departments, often in only a
haphazard way; in particular, students who fail to complete a program ordinarily drop out of the department's historical consciousness. Centralized registrars can always call up a given student's record and may be able to reconstruct total enrollments, but often their
masses of data have not been stored in any way that permits any
deeper analysis.

Given these problems, Bowen and Rudenstine decided to look
closely at a few fields: English, history, political science, economics,
mathematics, and physics. They concentrated their research on ten
universities: Berkeley, Chicago, Columbia, Cornell, Harvard, Michigan, the University of North Carolina at Chapel Hill, Princeton, Stanford, and Yale. They caution that the experiences of these universities
cannot simply be extrapolated to all other schools, but certainly their
data are highly suggestive. The average completion rate they found
for all six fields at these leading institutions was only 56.6 percent;
this average included math and physics, whose completion rates were
substantially higher than those in the other fields (212). Similar results obtain if one looks at the best students across the country. One
way to do this is to examine the records of students who have received nationally awarded fellowships. A study of Woodrow Wilson
fellows who began their study in the 1960s showed completion rates
of 55 percent in the social sciences and 50 percent in the humanities;
National Defense Education Act fellowship recipients in the same
period had a 56.2 percent completion rate in humanities and a 57.5
percent completion rate in the social sciences (211).

Given the absence of solid information for most students, we can
take these figures as only generally representative, but it is still apparent that even the best schools, and the best students in general,
achieve completion rates of little better than 50 percent in the humanities and social sciences. Presumably, weaker programs have
poorer overall rates than these. Even the smaller programs at the best
schools, which enjoy the powerful combination of excellent students,
good funding, and low student-to-faculty ratios, manage to graduate
barely 60 percent of their entering Ph.D. candidates in the humanities and social sciences, while the larger programs studied by Bowen

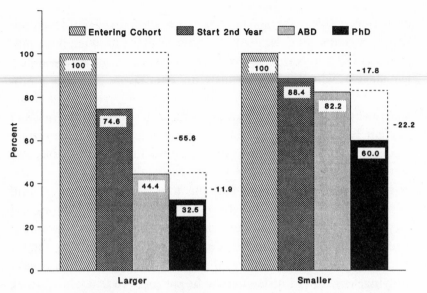

Attrition by stage and scale of graduate program, 1972–1976 entering cohort. Larger programs: Columbia University, the University of California at Berkeley, and the University of Chicago; smaller programs: Cornell, Harvard, Princeton, and Stanford (Source: Bowen and Rudenstine 1992, 154).

and Rudenstine showed only a 32.5 percent rate of completion (154). Thus Berkeley, Chicago, and Columbia show completion rates of one third, the very rate given by Harrison for the British public schools.

Statistics, of course, need to be interpreted and put in context; it would be a mistake, for example, to suppose that the 32.5 percent completion rate tells a single story. In the large programs, some of the loss comes at the end of the M.A. program, in part because the larger schools often limit advancement after the M.A. Yet even the small programs, which ordinarily do not forcibly weed students out, show a significant drop after the first year. Further, Bowen and Rudenstine's data show that large and small schools alike lose students at *each* stage of the process, often in large numbers. The accompanying graph shows their tables for the fields of English, history, and political science. Large programs lose (or turn away) a quarter of their students after the M.A., but even small programs lose an eighth; large programs then lose another 30 percent—that is, 40 percent of the M.A. survivors—during the M.Phil. period, while small programs do better at this stage, losing just a few students. Then large and small programs alike lose over a quarter of their surviving post-orals students (27 percent) before completion of the dissertation—a very late stage at which to lose so many more students.

Students can, of course, benefit from some period of graduate study even if they go on into a different profession, but the fields of English, history, and political science are not ones in which a vibrant job market for M.A.s is forcibly drawing students away from the completion of their Ph.D. In my own experience, almost all students who enter our M.A./Ph.D. program are planning an academic career, and in most cases they assume that they will complete the Ph.D. even if they think they may seek employment outside academia thereafter. The great majority of the losses reflected in the preceding figures come from a student's failure to thrive in the program or from a growing sense of dissatisfaction on the part of a student who is doing well. If the very best programs in the country can regularly lose anywhere from 40 percent to 60 percent of their students, something is wrong.

These low completion rates are all the more disturbing if we compare graduate programs with professional schools. Law schools and medical schools, for example, achieve completion rates as high as 98 percent—yet it would be hard to argue that their programs are easier, or inherently more congenial, than graduate programs in fields like English and history. If anything, the disparity should be in the opposite direction, particularly if we consider that graduate students ought to have a better idea of just what they are getting into than do many beginning law and medical students. After all, most graduate students have majored in the field in which they enroll for graduate study, so that after a dozen or more courses they can be supposed to have a fairly clear picture of academic study in their field of choice. Indeed, they may even have taken several graduate courses while still undergraduates. Few prelaw and premed students will have achieved a comparable familiarity with the kinds of courses and other work expected of law and medical students.

Law and medical students do have the advantage of a far healthier job market, but this fact can account for only part of the difference. In general, students concerned about the job market in fields like literature and history will simply go to law or business school to begin with; those who do enter graduate programs, especially if they are on fellowship, usually seem prepared to take their chances on the job market later on. The job market may well help to explain why so many law students stay in school, but it hardly explains why so many graduate students drop out.

No one approach or set of recommendations can expect to erase a dropout rate of 40 percent and more, but no reforms in graduate education are worth contemplating unless they give promise of making at least some improvement in the present situation. Bowen and Rudenstine's study offers a variety of recommendations, but these are geared chiefly toward helping the present system work more smoothly: streamlining requirements, improving funding, and generally reducing the time to degree. My own belief is that more substantial changes are needed. These changes will involve modifications to program requirements, but such reforms must accompany more basic shifts in the entire culture of graduate education.

The dropout rate is not the only or even the most serious problem from the point of view of concern for scholarly excellence. To the extent that we are overproducing Ph.D.s, a greater completion rate would mean only more superbly educated cab drivers. Yet we should not rest content with this observation. First, it seems likely that a wave of retirements during the next decade will result in an increased need for new Ph.D.s in many fields, a view strongly supported by William Bowen and Julie Ann Sosa's study, *Prospects for Faculty in the Arts and Sciences* (1989). Equally, from my point of view, the current culture limits the range and ultimately the quality of scholarly work in its tendency to weed out certain *kinds* of people in general. My claim, broadly speaking, is that we ought to have two kinds of scholars where now we have only one: if we now discourage most of the really intellectually sociable candidates, then we are left with that fraction of the population who are naturally less sociable. An analogy can be made to coeducation. When several all-male Ivy League schools were finally considering the admission of women twenty-five years ago, opponents of coeducation sometimes claimed that the general quality of the freshman class would remain unchanged, if one assumed a fixed class size. Against this view, it was rightly replied that allowing women to apply would potentially double the applicant pool, and that taking the top 10 percent of the women and the top 10 percent of the men who applied would indeed produce a better class than if one took the top 20 percent of the men and none of the women.

To the extent that intellectually sociable people never go to graduate school or never complete it, we are similarly lessening the overall quality of the resulting pool of new Ph.D.s. Solitary scholars can be fully as interesting and valuable as more sociable scholars would be, but if those who enter and complete graduate programs tend to be solitary workers, then we are likely to end up with a higher proportion of merely competent perseverers entering the job market than we would if selection and training did not disfavor an entire kind of scholarly personality to begin with.

When people acculturate themselves to academic life by enhancing their tolerance for solitary work and diminishing their intellectual sociability, they reduce their ability to address problems that require collaborative solutions, or even that require close attention to the perspectives offered by approaches or disciplines other than one's own. The structuring of graduate education quietly but pervasively discourages such close attention, fostering instead a culture in which people work alone or within the perspectives and expectations of a small group of like-minded peers.

We can begin to explore this problem by recalling Horowitz' valuable distinction among undergraduate cultures. In the current context, what is needed is a much clearer focus on the difference between undergraduate and graduate cultures. During the century we have lost much of our sense of the cultural differences attendant upon differing levels of study. In Lyman Bagg's day at Yale in the mid-nineteenth century, the freshman societies provided the focal point for first-year students' lives, as did the middle-year societies and the senior societies in turn, just as academically there were largely distinct curricula for each year of study. Colleges today generally suppose that students take introductory courses and then advanced courses, but even these differences have become increasingly fluid over time, and students often take advanced seminars while still taking introductory surveys. We give our freshmen a few days of orientation, but long gone are the close-knit social organizations in which students were often sorted by their year of study throughout their college years.

In the past twenty-five years, the distinctions between undergraduate and graduate life have similarly blurred, both socially and intellectually. Colleges have ceased to stand in loco parentis for their undergraduates and are effectively treating them like graduate students; at the same time, the increased use of graduate-style specialized courses in undergraduate curricula has reduced the difference in the work performed by advanced undergraduates and by beginning graduate students. This change has had both advantages and disadvantages for undergraduates, and the disadvantages have been widely debated; only rarely, though, is it realized that these changes have been a rather mixed blessing for graduate students as well.

Too often, graduate students are caught in a double bind of two opposed but unexamined ways of treating graduate study. On the one hand, in many ways graduate students seem to be thought of as more advanced undergraduates, people who spend two years taking classes, writing term papers, and receiving grades, just like college juniors and seniors (who may even be in class with them). The major difference is that the graduate students will be using more footnotes, adding in some substantial research in the secondary literature. Along with this continuity model, however, there exists a contrary model of discontinuity, whereby graduate study is a process of undercutting the naive preconceptions of the former undergraduates and weaning them from their adolescent modes of thought and of study. Students must become less emotive, more analytic, and their work must move beyond a personal reaction to a text or an issue and situate itself explicitly within the scholarly debate.

I suspect that some such characterization of the shift to graduate study would be assumed by most professors, and that most graduate students themselves would accept these elements of change. Yet much more takes place, and it happens largely unconsciously, not directly reflected on by those involved. We give a great deal of thought to what we need to teach our graduate students, but very little thought to how they learn. And why should we? By the students' own self-selection and by our graduate admissions screening, aren't we getting students who have already proven to thrive in our kind of work? They can simply go on amassing knowledge in courses, then begin to organize fields of knowledge for themselves while preparing for doctoral examinations, until they arrive at the culminating "original contribution to knowledge" of the dissertation, written under the guidance of a professorial mentor.

The problem with this organicist model of developmental growth is that it masks the sharp difference in the *work cultures* of undergraduate and advanced graduate student life. Some make the transition smoothly enough, discovering a taste for an isolated mode of activity—the equivalent of the British public school boy who becomes a budding sergeant major. Those who make it through to the completion of the dissertation might very well be able to form a contented cricket eleven—particularly as so many will have dropped out by then that there may only be eleven Ph.D.s *left* out of an initial class of twenty or more. Given the emphasis on increasing isolation, however, they probably will not be playing a team sport at all; more likely will be those faculty favorites, squash and tennis, excellent sports for communities of one that want to become two, one of whom will defeat the other in a lively hour of play before each returns to the library.

The superficial similarity of graduate and undergraduate academic life is reinforced by the unusual fact that the scene of instruction is the same in both cases. Professional schools at least have separate buildings, often located at the fringe of the main campus or even in another neighborhood altogether. The faculty in a professional school may do little or no teaching of undergraduates, so that the prospective law or medical student is clearly moving to a new situation in such basic respects as locale and faculty. By contrast, graduate programs are normally housed in the same area of campus as the undergraduate major, often in the same building, and the same faculty tend to teach both populations. Everything looks the same, and students have as role models those happy few who have stayed on to be hired as faculty members upon completion of their degree. In no other kind of profession can one remain in the same sort of setting, and sometimes in the very same building, as an undergraduate, a graduate student, and a lifelong practitioner in the field.

This surface continuity puts an unusual and potentially unsettling emphasis on the less visible differences among these levels of study and work, differences that are rarely openly observed, still less taken into account when planning programs. This *disjunctive continuity* must be a significant factor in the high dropout rates observed in graduate programs. Conversations with my wife and her fellow law professors suggest that law students, for example, are no happier as a group than graduate students, but the unhappy law student has a professional goal off campus: to go out and practice. Only a minority think of becoming law professors themselves, and if the law faculty is pressuring students into forms of acculturation that some (or even most) dislike, the students can put up with the law school's culture for a few years without having to *internalize* it. They do not face the prospect, upon graduation, of lifetime servitude within the same sort of organization.

If graduate programs were genuinely continuous with undergraduate programs, these factors would not lead to such high dropout rates. But in reality great disparities persist between undergraduate and graduate student culture. This is a large topic; the issues discussed here can suggest the sorts of results that might be gained from looking at graduate student culture for other purposes as well. The change that concerns me here is the shift from working together to working in isolation, and the problem is that this assumption is both pervasive and yet largely unspoken. Our admissions practices make no direct attempt to identify people who are temperamentally suited for isolated work, and hence we inadvertently take in numbers of people who will find the isolation of graduate study uncongenial; rather than varying our program requirements to suit different emerging scholarly personalities, we present a single norm, forcing the students either to adapt or to fall away.

We could lessen the disruptive effect of the graduate culture's ever-increasing stress on isolated work by formulating the difference explicitly and warning intellectually sociable undergraduates away from graduate study, as Pelikan does when counseling students to focus on how much isolation is presumably necessary for scholars. We might even require more isolated work by our undergraduates so as to have a way to test for this inclination when making our selection of graduate students. Perhaps this could be done, but it is hard to feel confident that it could be done well, and it would be counterproductive to do so if, as I am arguing, we actually could use more collaborative scholarship than we now see.

The fact is that undergraduates like to work together. This too is no simple fact of nature but a socially constructed desire: they have been *trained* to work together during their elementary and secondary education. If anything, their training in the lower years is exaggerated in the direction of sharing and helping one another, to the point that individual needs are often subordinated to group norms. All of us who were good at reading as children know how many hours we spent marking time with textbooks suited to the weaker readers in the class. This pattern recurs even in primary schools based on Montessori-style methods that are supposed to emphasize each child's individual development. My children are in such an elementary school, but "individual development" usually means *small-group* development through cooperative interaction. Even with the activity of reading, that archetypically solitary library skill in graduate mythology, the children spend most of their time in four-person reading groups. Some teachers even make a point of putting together children of different levels of reading ability, on the theory that a disparity in reading skills will require the children to work all the more closely together.

Whereas elementary and secondary education put a heavy emphasis on group learning, undergraduate programs do their best to achieve a balance between individual and group activity—only to have their graduate programs tilt the scale just as strongly in the *other* direction. This reverse tilt comes as an unpleasant surprise to many students, who have spent some sixteen years learning how to work well with others. These ideals have become deeply ingrained by the college years, and they should not simply be ignored. A recent national survey of college freshmen by the Higher Education Research Institute at UCLA shows how strongly social the students are in their habits. This sociability is personal and local rather than abstract; only 7 percent had worked on a city, state, or national political campaign, whereas 78 percent had voted in a student election; only a minority of respondents hoped to effect political change or influence social values, but an impressive 66 percent had performed volunteer work (*Chronicle of Higher Education*, Jan. 13, 1993, A29–32). Twenty-five categories of activity were surveyed, and the highest response of all was to the category "studied with other students" (85 percent), surpassing the percentage who had gone to church (84 percent), stayed up all night (79 percent), consumed alcohol (54 percent), or come late to class (also—the same?—54 percent).

Even if we allow for a certain amount of underreporting on these last two categories, the students' fondness for studying together is very clear. In part, this inclination is the mirror image of the shy freshman's reluctance to trouble the professor with elementary questions; only 19 percent of those surveyed had asked a teacher advice after class. But why should these alternatives be thought of as mutually exclusive? To a very real extent, indeed, the prevalence of the seminar as the preferred mode of teaching advanced undergraduates and beginning graduate students reflects a notion that education should involve learning both from a professor and from other students, and yet we largely abandon this notion after the second year of graduate study. There are good reasons for some shift in emphasis thereafter, yet this shift does not need to be as dramatic as we make it for graduate students. Graduate training will always remain a process of acculturation as much as one of imparting information, and we should think more clearly and more directly about this process. One way to do this is to attend to the sociological literature that examines the influence of culture on education, and in this context the prior student culture is as important as ethnic or regional culture can be.

A good example of such reflection can be found in an intriguing essay by John Van Maanen, a professor at MIT's Sloan School of Management. In this essay, "Doing New Things in Old Ways: The Chains of Socialization," Van Maanen explores the ways in which people learn new skills and adjust to new situations. He emphasizes that people usually assimilate what is new by adapting it to their existing patterns of learning and behavior. Some organizations seek to take full advantage of the varied backgrounds of their new recruits, while others begin by dismantling the preconceptions and behavioral patterns with which people enter. Examples of this disruptive form of organizational socialization, Van Maanen mentions—in an association we have seen before—"include prisons, mental hospitals, military agencies, some homes for the infirm and aged, and many educational institutions" (212).

Van Maanen illustrates his theme with an analogy to windsurfing, an area in which he claims to have been doing extensive fieldwork. He says that, contrary to appearances, windsurfing is not just a skill that people learn and then practice: rather than simply absorb information, people adapt it to their own orientation. They both acquire and use the knowledge in different ways. When Van Maanen was making his observations in the early 1980s, windsurfing was a relatively new sport in this country, and almost everyone who took it up had previously mastered one of three skills: surfing proper, skiing, or sailing. Van Maanen found that each group learned windsurfing differently: skiers liked to take lessons, sailors would read books on the subject, while surfers preferred to teach themselves by trial and error. Having mastered the skill, each group would practice it differently as well: surfers typically windsurf alone, skiers form social groups, and sailors compete in races: "Whereas the individualistic surfer might be spotted in some isolated bay on a windless day in zen-like repose aboard a craft barely moving, and the skier might be found among a cluster of sails heading in the same direction at the same speed, with the same style, the sailor might be recognized only by what appears to the observer as a grim concern for outdistancing rivals along a carefully charted course marked by the ever-present buoys" (238).

Van Maanen argues that organizations can benefit from a similar openness to different modes of learning and performance. Further, he says that many organizations do in fact allow for a variety of work cultures within their ranks, and we should not take as normative those organizations that assume and enforce a singular culture of work, such as "prisons, law schools, Ph.D. programs, concentration camps, police academies, self-help groups, medical schools, lengthy apprenticeship programs, boot camps, sales force training programs, cult indoctrinations," and other organizations that seek to dissociate recruits from their past habits (238). Van Maanen applies his point of view to a comparison of two neighboring business schools, the Harvard Business School and MIT's Sloan School of Management. He details the ways in which the Harvard program emphasizes group work and consensus-building, not only formally in class exercises but also informally, in student study groups, in which students divide up responsibility for an unmanageable amount of assigned work and share their results. According to Van Maanen, "the organization of the B-school produces (and reproduces, year after year) a fairly dense, encompassing, collegial culture wherein the student collective exercises considerable influence over its members and, some would say, over the faculty as well" (224).

The MIT program offers similar courses, but with very different results, for its entire culture emphasizes individual achievement. The Sloan School does not have its own building or eating facilities, and it does less than Harvard to foster a sense of group identity through its classes: Sloan students spend one-third less time in class than Harvard students, and a quarter of the enrollments are non-Sloan students. Friendships form accidentally and are based on nonacademic interests rather than on solving problems for class. As a result, "The Sloan faculty, it seems, has been able, successfully, however unintentionally, to divide and more or less conquer the student body . . . The overall adjustment of students is one that heightens the individualistic and differentiated responses of the student body. Collective solutions to common problems are few and far between, and the students who learn best are apparently those who do so on their own" (225–227).

This difference in the learning environment carries over to a pronounced difference in the corporate cultures to which the students are drawn. Harvard graduates more often go on to work for teamwork-oriented Fortune 500 corporations; such firms hire 67 percent of Harvard graduates but only 48 percent of Sloan School graduates, while 40 percent of Sloan graduates go to work for small entrepreneurial firms and consultant organizations, as against only 11 percent of Harvard graduates. Van Maanen argues that the differences in these programs are all to the good, for different sorts of jobs await differently acculturated students. He does not address the question of how students fare if they choose the wrong school; to the extent that brochures and course catalogues stress matters like course content rather than the broader culture of the school, students must often make poor choices if they lack access to inside information. Presumably this problem could be alleviated if each school were to talk openly about its culture and its processes of socialization; alternatively, each school could try to open more room for the other approach within its own walls.

The analogy to business schools can be useful to us, although it must be used with care. To the extent that the analogy applies, our present-day Ph.D. programs clearly resemble the MIT program rather than the more collaborative mode used at Harvard, which is not to say that we should rush to adopt Harvard Business School methods in our Ph.D. programs. Neither business school shows a fully functioning cooperative community: while the MIT students are pitted against one another, the Harvard students are united *against the faculty*. Van Maanen's description may, of course, be satirically stylized, but to the extent that it is accurate, the Harvard business school looks less like a contemporary graduate program than like a nineteenth-century college, with Horowitz' clubby collegians resisting a haughtily detached faculty. This older model can persist in the business school because the business students do not need to internalize professorial culture. By contrast, many Ph.D. programs train people primarily not to go out into the wider society but instead to remain within the educational system, and so they only show a limited resemblance to professional schools: the ultimate employer will be yet another school, rather than either a Fortune 500 company or a small consulting firm.

The analogy to business schools has limitations, and yet we should not rest content with Van Maanen's semisatirical lumping together of Ph.D. programs with prisons, boot camps, and religious cults. A hundred-year-old university with a thousand instructors, twenty thousand students, and a billion-dollar budget does indeed have some features in common with a large corporation, even as its individual faculty members will have some traits in common with entrepreneurs who run their own businesses.

If we were to pursue the corporate analogy further, it might be best to focus on the changing ways in which people work together within each kind of organization. Like universities, corporations have distinct divisions and departments, and these corporate units have often operated relatively independently. Most collaborative work has gone on within rather than between different departments. More recently, though, an increasing number of corporations have begun to integrate the work of their different units more closely. Traditionally, for example, an automobile would be produced in several quite distinct stages: the designers would do their work and then pass it along to the engineers, who would in turn present their product to the marketers. The Ford Motor Company first began to change this division of labor in the mid-1960s, by incorporating marketing surveys at the design stage, thereby producing the highly popular Mustang. Ford took this process a large step further in the early 1980s by assembling a special working group, "Team Taurus," which brought together people from every stage of the process from the very beginning. The result was the best-selling car in the country.

I do not intend that this inspirational vignette should lead us to create a Team Foucault to boost that thinker's share of the American intellectual market. The point is rather that even within large corporations, collaborative work is now often being undertaken across the lines of specialization as well as within specialized areas like marketing or engineering, and a similar opening of boundaries may be desirable in academic work as well.

Restructuring Graduate Work

How is this opening of boundaries to be achieved? As in the preceding chapter, I would not consider it appropriate to try to invent a template that should be applicable to the dramatically varying situations of different institutions and different disciplines. Real changes can only come about if people on particular campuses get together to discuss such issues, and a whole range of options for improving graduate student culture would need to be explored. Much of the needed change can take place only in the general terms of a gradual changing of perspective: whom we encourage to go on to graduate school, whom we look for in making our decisions on admission, how in our teaching and advising we foster a greater attentiveness to the perspectives offered by other fields and other disciplines.

These changes in perspective are crucial, but they must find expression in concrete form. It is essential that we encourage—and train—our students to work more and better together in their classes; many of the sorts of collaborative learning described in the preceding chapter would apply here as well. Equally, we should attend to the influence exercised by our overall requirements and guidelines. This is a crucial area, although it has received less attention than questions of classroom practice. The importance of requirements may not be evident if we think of them merely as a sort of safety net. On this theory, requirements help to keep students from going astray, and while they may be necessary for our weaker or less focused students, they may seem to be almost irrelevant for our stronger students, who will do good work under almost any circumstances, provided they are given a modicum of funding and individual attention.

This understanding of the uses of requirements has the virtue of modesty but the disadvantage of reinforcing the narcolepsy that comes over us whenever we receive a really meaty memo from the dean's office on almost any topic whatever. Those of us who pride ourselves on our scholarly integrity may even make a point of ignoring memos on matters of direct financial concern to us—we treat major changes to our pensions and health care plans with the same sublime indifference with which we toss out this week's change to the policy on collision loss waivers for automobile rentals while on university business. Are we any more likely to pay close attention to matters as minor as course guidelines, language requirements, and thesis regulations?

Yet these matters are not, after all, so minor. Requirements are as much a glass ceiling as a safety net: they establish the *range* within which good and bad work alike will be done, and this range is more restricted than it may appear to people who overstress the second word in the term "organized anarchy." This is why exhortations for broad cultural change must be rooted in very specific program changes: they cannot take hold in a vacuum. Conversely, merely tinkering with requirements in the absence of a larger vision and a sustained commitment to change will have little effect. The general tenor of an organizational culture exists in an intimate synergy with the seemingly neutral particulars of the ways in which business is transacted. If we really press the question of what would be entailed in fostering collaborative learning at the graduate level, we are likely to be led to alter every aspect of our programs: course requirements, distribution requirements, language requirements, and guidelines for the structuring of doctoral examinations and of the dissertation. No one of these changes could be decisive in itself, and even a systemic change is no be-all and end-all. A thoroughgoing reform, however, can lay the groundwork for a real shift in the "culture of orientation" of graduate students: in their uses of scholarship, and in their interactions with one another and with the faculty. This shift in turn can reflect back on the specifics of program requirements and content, giving real weight to changes that initially can take hold only in a partial and tentative way. The outlook and interactions of faculty themselves can ultimately be affected as well.

If we really wish to carry through the implications of even a single important change in requirements, it is necessary to contemplate corollary changes in every aspect of the program as a whole. And more: these changes must be carried out in light of general considerations of the changing shape of fields at large, and of the relations between disciplines and among different kinds of academic work. In the end, global changes can be initiated only by local means, in our decentralized academic system; at the same time, however, local changes, if they can be carried through gradually and cumulatively, can have profound consequences across the entire system.

If we consider changing the nature and shape of the doctoral dissertation, for example, we must take up a complex of related issues, ranging from the most specific features of graduate requirements to very general questions of the formulation and circulation of scholarly ideas. I offer this example in part as typical of the kind of issue that needs to be addressed, although I recognize and even insist that different departments will not only address such issues in different ways but will even have very different views as to what issues really need their attention. The crucial thing is that departments should develop *some* coherent view of what they are doing and why, and of how they might be doing things better.

Further, I offer this case in point because it seems particularly important. The most extended piece of work our students will do, certainly as students and often during their entire career, the dissertation is the crucial rite of passage of the graduate program and the most important component of students' portfolios as they enter the job market. It is also the hurdle that over a quarter of all students fail to surmount, even after they have finished their course work and their doctoral examinations. This much we know from Bowen and Rudenstine's data, and this is only the most observable sort of failure. An equally real problem, though hard to quantify, is that of the student who struggles along and manages to finish an *unsuccessful* dissertation, after years of suffering the burden of an unworkable or unsalable topic—a minor particle in an obscure language?—or an unapproachable thesis director.

The current mode of work can enable people to produce good dissertations, but it is hardly satisfactory for those who do not, whether because they drop out or because they turn in a mediocre product that is approved reluctantly, defended awkwardly, and de-

posited gratefully into the round file of the library's archives. Sometimes, inevitably, these cases reflect the problems of students who
never should have gone into graduate school to begin with, and yet
the failure rate is so high that I fear that we are often blaming the
victims rather than ourselves and the system we operate. In a series
of interviews with people who had dropped out of Ph.D. programs,
Penelope Jacks and three colleagues found that 44 percent of respondents cited a "poor working relationship with advisor and/or committee" as a primary cause of their departure. This category was tied
for first place with the category "financial difficulties"; close behind
these two factors came the third and fourth reasons, "substantive
problems with the dissertation research" and "personal or emotional
problems" ("The ABCs of ABDs," 75).

If 27 percent of M.Phil. recipients even in the best programs fail
to complete the dissertation at all, and if a certain additional number
struggle through to an unsatisfactory conclusion, then the real failure
rate must be 30 or 40 percent, assuming that the goal is the writing
of a genuinely successful dissertation. The average at all schools is
probably much worse; Ziolkowski estimates that "as many as 70 percent of students who pass their general examinations fail, for one
reason or another, to complete the degree" ("The Ph.D. Squid," 185),
and Ziolkowski's figure too would need to be increased if we add in
a number for marginal productions that barely squeak through.

To an extent, we professors ought to blame ourselves individually,
since we could always give our sponsorees more time and attention
than we now do; but this is not the only problem. Equally, the system
is at fault—an observation that hardly lets us off the hook, as we
are the ones who operate this system, and it is our responsibility to
improve it if it is not working as it should.

The problem of isolation has been compounded in recent years by
the widespread reshaping of the parameters of knowledge. To adapt
David Bromwich's terms, the dissertation has classically been conceived as *a community of two that wants to become one:* student and
sponsor contract to work together for a specific period in their common field of specialization, with the express goal that the student
will finish up in a reasonably timely manner and then *go away,* on
to the job market and into a career that will grow out of and build
on the sponsor's own career. Collaboration as inheritance, as repro-

duction, is symbolized by the traditional German term for the dissertation sponsor: the Doktorvater.

This is a noble model, if genetically a little one-sided, since the candidate is apparently supposed to emerge parthenogenetically from the tutelage of a single paternal authority. (On this analogy, the dissertation would be the fruit produced *parthenocarpically*—like bananas and pineapples—from the unfertilized scion of the single-parental stalk.) I would not wish to suggest that this model can no longer work. Increasingly, however, I find students for whom it works only awkwardly, often not because of personality problems as such, but because students' interests are less fully congruent with those of their sponsors than they used to be. In most fields of study, we find an increasing variety of approaches, perspectives, and materials now in play—"Sociology Branches Out but Is Left in Splinters," to recall the arboreal headline of an article on the state of one discipline (*New York Times,* Aug. 26, 1988). We may condemn or celebrate this change, but first and foremost it is a fact of contemporary intellectual life.

Bowen and Rudenstine devote a chapter to this problem (229–259), and they show statistically that students complete their Ph.D. more rapidly if they are in fields with relatively defined paradigms of their discipline—what it is they are doing, how they should go about doing it, what they need to learn in order to do it. The clarity of the paradigm appears to be as important a variable as fellowship support in determining a student's progress through graduate school. But how can this problem be ameliorated in the less defined disciplines—generally speaking, in the humanities and the social sciences? One way is for faculty members to get together, among themselves and with their students, and talk more about the problem. It is less feasible than it used to be for people simply to do their own work, tacitly assuming a common conception of the field. Departments should give more instruction in the history of their discipline and the relations of varying approaches within it, as a number of departments have begun to do in more or less formalized fashions.

Equally, we need to take much better account of the fact that as students do formulate their interests, those interests may not be congruent with the interests and skills of any one particular member of the faculty. When the student's interests do closely mirror those of a sponsor, the sponsor may still be able to play the old role of the Doktorvater—or Doktormutter, as the case may be. Often, though, our current students' needs may be better served by a much more open and flexible form of the dissertation. A student might benefit most by writing three or four separate articles in two or three different areas, with a different adviser for each, perhaps writing one or more chapters in collaboration with other students. Why should one faculty member be assumed to be the sponsor, with only a secondary involvement, if any, from one or two other people? Why should the dissertation be presumed to be a protobook rather than a series of articles, each produced independently, sharing a common general theme or approach rather than developing a single argument? I suspect that a significant proportion of those 27 percent—or 70 percent—of M.Phil. recipients who never achieve the Ph.D. might do better under this sort of regime. They have already written numbers of 20- or 25-page seminar papers, and often a master's thesis of 50 or 80 pages, and many students who never seem to get going on a dissertation still produce articles and conference papers along the way. Perhaps four or five 50-page projects would be manageable in a way that a single 250-page thesis may not.

Such a new understanding of the dissertation would not only be likely to improve the disturbing rates of completion; it would also reflect more accurately the current state of knowledge in many fields, in which it may be premature to expect a synoptic grasp by someone at this stage of work. A student might gain more from working closely with four different people than from making do with the perfunctory guidance of only one sponsor whose interest is not truly engaged by the topic. As I have been arguing, collaborative work involves a whole range of activities, not only joint authorship or team teaching. These may be the most visible kinds of collaboration, but they may not be the only or even the most common form of work, even for intellectually sociable scholars. Graduate education is a crucial period for fostering the basic collaborative skill of attending closely to other people's ideas, approaches, and perspectives.

Both in its form and in the process by which that form is achieved, the dissertation is one of the root causes of our recurrent failure to engage with more than a single perspective on the issues we take up. When a student has a good working relationship with a sponsor, the result can be a genuine collaboration in my sense of the word. Yet the model of the sponsor as Doktorvater is a model of a rather circumscribed kind of collaboration, essentially carried on within a temporary community of two. Often even the second reader of the dissertation is much less actively involved, while other readers come in only to review the finished product. In the meanwhile, the student may show a chapter to some other reader, but this process is carried on entirely informally and often inconclusively; students rarely feel encouraged to develop a sustained dialogue with someone who is not a primary reader of the dissertation.

My proposal to allow for dissertations conceived as several articles written with a number of different sponsors is meant to give more visibility and weight to this sort of multiple collaboration. By such a process, a student could go so far as to write one or more sections jointly with someone else, doing other sections independently so as to be able to demonstrate individual strengths to potential employers. Yet the process would also be significantly changed for the writing of individual articles or chapters. Not only would a more open structure lessen the problem of perfunctory professorial response in areas in which the student's topic(s) and interests do not truly overlap with one sponsor's; equally, the quality of the *student*'s attention would be expanded. Writing different chapters under the supervision of different sponsors, the student would still be engaging in the unusually close attention and response to a mentor's work and perspective that dissertations now suppose; but now there would be a number of mentors, a number of perspectives, rather than that of the single parental figure. The result would be to increase the student's active engagement with differing perspectives and points of view.

Why Innovations Fail

Books on academia are littered with proposals like this. Why should this one succeed where so many others have failed? Arthur Levine has a sobering book on educational reform entitled *Why Innovation Fails,* but it should have a companion volume: Why Do Innovations Fail to Be Adopted? Too often, critics of academia devote the great bulk of their analysis to detailing what is wrong, and then only sketch out their ideas for reform in a few eloquent concluding paragraphs.

Little space is given to answering the objections that are likely to be raised to their proposals, usually because the arguments have been made, and the objections are tacitly dismissed, on moral grounds. If the professors are preaching tenured radicalism, or killing the spirit, or simply neglecting their students, what more can be done than exhort them to become open to other views, or start to value teaching above research, or just *care* more about their students? Any appeal that is grounded in a reformation of human nature, however fully it is argued, can still work only if human nature is prepared to change. It is interesting to observe how often critics of academia spend much of their time detailing professorial venality, sloth, and indifference, only to turn around in conclusion and call for changes that would require the professors suddenly to become exceptionally altruistic, energetic, and caring.

If a vision of collaborative work were to require scholars to be "nice people," in Rosovsky's phrase, it could hope to take root only among that minority of professors who fit this characterization. Such collaboration requires a small community of congenial colleagues— Julius Getman's dream of what academia would be like before he joined an actual faculty; a utopian-communal bonding that may sometimes occur, as in some contemporary feminist or Marxist scholarly collectives. Such groupings, though, require an unusual harmony of personality and of interests and viewpoint, a wonderful combination when it can be achieved, but not one that can regularly be counted on.

Any proposal for reform must locate itself between two poles: a change should be as substantial as possible while remaining realizable in a significant number of situations. At one extreme, we could make provision for closely bonded several-person working groups, and there are reasons to think that such groups could provide a dramatic improvement over current practice for work on various sorts of projects. The limitation here is that we would need to acknowledge that such groups will only occasionally be formed; once formed, only some of those groups will work as well as we would wish, and they may be difficult to sustain over time.

At the other extreme, a change like putting a page limit on the length of dissertations would be relatively easy to achieve, since anyone who wished to do so could simply place such a limit (say, of 250 pages) on the work of their sponsorees. Here the problem is that a change so easily made may seem too modest to count as much of an improvement. Probably most students who fail to complete the thesis never reach a total of 250 cogent pages to begin with, and those who struggle unsuccessfully onward far beyond that length usually have underlying problems with the topic, with themselves, with the sponsor—or with the mode of work in general. An arbitrary page limit might well help some students to finish somewhat sooner, if they are going to finish at all, but it might not improve the rate of completion, and it would have little or no effect on the quality of work done.

To have some hope of success, then, proposals need to meet two initial tests: they must work within the parameters of human nature as it now exists, and they should ideally be pitched at a middle range, neither too global to accomplish nor too modest to make a difference. These two principles are almost self-evident; I mention them only because so many current discussions seem to ignore them. Beyond these two principles, there is a third I wish to stress, and this has been the most often slighted of all: the proposed reform ought to be beneficial to those who are in a position to put it in place.

People will sometimes carry out ideas that do not bring them any real benefit, or even that harm them personally, if their altruism can be sufficiently engaged or if social or financial pressure becomes sharp enough. Yet altruism alone is hard to sustain over time or across the system, while external pressure produces bad decisions as often as good ones, unless it simply causes people to hunker down and do nothing at all. Both the power of the purse and more general kinds of suasion can be effectively employed by a sufficiently forceful interest group, especially if there is a broad base of institutional support for change. College alumni can be one such vocal group, and even within universities the position of undergraduate education is central enough that deans, presidents, and boards of trustees may become involved. These latter groups can insist on changes they perceive to be in their interest as the people finally responsible for the financial and public-relations health of the institution, and when they want to, they can sometimes force their faculty to adopt disagreeable changes—although here we should recall Clark Kerr's frustrations as an activist university chancellor who could neither wear down nor outlast strong faculty opposition.

In questions of graduate education, the tenured faculty hold almost all the real power, and they are the only interest group with a strong voice within the university in these matters. In this context I would offer the cautionary tale of the fate of the most important call to reform to emerge from the educational ferment of the 1960s, Christopher Jencks and David Riesman's *The Academic Revolution* (1968). Widely praised when it appeared and still often cited today, this remarkably lucid, witty, and informed discussion encountered deep resistance to most of its major proposals for reform. This example can provide a background against which to gauge the prospects of my own ideas for changing the structure of graduate education and the culture it upholds.

Despite its title, *The Academic Revolution* was not concerned with the student revolts that had broken out while the book was in press. Rather, its theme was the emancipation of academics from outside control. Jencks and Riesman analyzed this quiet revolution both historically and sociologically, looking not only at the Ivy League–style schools but also at Catholic and historically black institutions. They wished to explore the implications of the unprecedented degree of control professors had gained during the previous century over the nature and conditions of their work. Not only descriptive, their book was concerned to correct the imbalances and excesses the shift had entailed. In the process, the authors devoted a good deal of attention to graduate and professional education and to the relations between graduate and undergraduate instruction.

Jencks and Riesman advanced two very broad themes, together with a variety of specific recommendations. Of their overall arguments, one was in keeping with the tenor of the times and can be said to have been accepted: they criticized the fact that students were expected to see their work as divorced from their own lives, and called for reforms designed "to put the student closer in touch with himself" (518). In this emphasis Jencks and Riesman were certainly children of their times, and the subsequent rise of subjectivist scholarship and academic identity politics can be said to reflect their perspective. Concerning programs, they called for fewer restrictions on student initiative, more flexibility in requirements, and more opportunity for interdisciplinary work. It is, of course, difficult to say how far Jencks and Riesman's particular discussion influenced developments in these directions, with so many calls for "relevance" being issued around the same time; still, to the extent that they provided both a broad rationale and a variety of concrete suggestions, they probably helped give direction to changes that were beginning to occur.

Their other theme ran counter to the direct interests of research-oriented faculty, and it went nowhere at all. This was a running critique of the hegemony of graduate over undergraduate education. Well before the current academic fascination with imperialism, they used this analogy in trenchant characterizations of the imbalances of power within the modern system:

> we are troubled by the fact that the graduate schools have an essentially imperial relationship with many of the institutions and subcultures on their borders, particularly the undergraduate colleges. Their apparent successes depend in many cases on exploiting these underdeveloped territories. First, the graduate schools import the colleges' most valuable "raw material," i.e. gifted B.A.s. They train these men as scholars. The best of them they keep for themselves; the rest they export to the colleges whence they came, to become teachers . . . we see little prospect that the graduate imperium will yield to outbreaks of unrest among the natives in the undergraduate colleges. If decolonization comes in our time—and we doubt that it will—it will come as a result of strong initiatives from dissidents within the graduate schools themselves.   (515–516)

Fully aware of the power dynamics they were describing, Jencks and Riesman noted that reform could come only from within the ranks of graduate faculties, but they offered no programmatic means by which this result might be achieved. The passage just quoted shows their own expectation that analysis and exhortation alone would be unlikely to effect the changes they desired, such as renewed attention to the specific needs of undergraduates, who were increasingly being treated as future graduate students, swamped by a flood of specialized courses that reflected the research interests of the faculty.

Pessimistic as they were concerning the likelihood of change, even Jencks and Riesman must have been a little taken aback to find their principal arguments dismissed by Martin Trow only a few years later in a foreword to the third edition of *their own book*. Writing in May 1976, Trow refers disparagingly to the relaxation of requirements and the rise of "trendy and superficial 'interdisciplinary' studies," and he declares outright that "the triumph of the specialized undergraduate course, rooted in the research disciplines and in graduate studies, over liberal education does not seem to be the problem it was a decade ago" (xi).

It is an unusual foreword that urges a book's readers to ignore the authors' major themes, but this is what Trow has done. He suggests that the real problems that had emerged in the (eight-year) "decade" since the book was first published were the pressure to shrink budgets and the general flight of students from the arts and sciences into vocational and preprofessional courses. Genuine though these problems were, it is hard to see why they should need to be opposed to the problems stressed by Jencks and Riesman; in fact, they might even be related. Perhaps students had begun to feel that if all they were being offered was specialized courses, they might as well take courses that would prepare them for the specialties they were thinking of going into, rather than for the single profession of university professor.

Trow's other concern, the squeezing of budgets, is in fact now beginning to bring about the renewed emphasis on undergraduate life for which Jencks and Riesman hoped. As sources of outside funding decline in university budgets, there are fewer funds to support phalanxes of graduate students, and graduate course offerings are being trimmed accordingly. Faculty are having to fill their schedules with more undergraduate courses, and at the same time universities are expanding their undergraduate enrollments when possible. Colleges and universities alike are competing ever more strenuously for students who can pay their way, as administrators rediscover that undergraduates are a singularly reliable source of funds, both as students and as alumni—particularly when the alumni see their colleges being given renewed attention.

This may seem to be a highly materialist interpretation of the new shift toward undergraduate education, but it is not necessary to suppose that material factors must be considered at the expense of more intellectual or emotional issues. Take another major factor in the renewed attention to undergraduate programs in universities: the fact that the job market for Ph.D.s in many fields was terrible during the 1970s and remained stagnant even during the boom years of the 1980s. Programs that were established or expanded in the 1960s have endured twenty years in which far too many of their graduates have been getting inadequate jobs or no jobs at all. Scholars usually like to have a reasonable number of devoted students, but the students' devotion starts to wear thin under these circumstances, and their teachers can begin to feel genuinely uneasy about training people for nonexistent jobs. A degree of internal conflict emerges: one still appreciates having enough students to justify a good deal of graduate teaching and to have the stimulation of working through a range of dissertation topics, but much of the psychic reward for all this work comes from seeing one's charges safely off into the profession. It is against our own interests, speaking here intellectually and emotionally rather than financially, to train an oversupply of students, and we may come to feel a renewed fondness for undergraduates whose pleasure in the material is not dimmed by anxiety about our ability to help them get a good job teaching it.

At the time Jencks and Riesman were writing, near the end of the academic hiring boom of the 1960s, this conflict of interests had not begun to emerge; Trow could observe it in 1976, but it would take several years of repeated disappointment in seeing favorite students fail to get good jobs before most faculty would begin to *feel* this conflict. Jencks and Riesman, then, made their arguments twenty years too soon—one reason why their book makes timely reading now. When considering the needs of graduate students, they sought ways to reduce the rigidity and the isolation of graduate student work. (We may note that Riesman began working on higher education only a few years after he cowrote *The Lonely Crowd*.) Jencks and Riesman argued that departments were structuring their programs "on the pork barrel principle. The result is that Ph.D. candidates must know something about the specialty of almost everyone in their department" (524). They suggested that a prospective scholar of American history might do better to study sociology and literature rather than medieval history and German. As they said, "The issue here is not specialization versus generalization. The issue is whether one way of aggregating specialized skills is better than another" (524).

Little has been done to address this issue, which is an important aspect of the isolation of scholarly life. If students receive no sustained training in related fields, they are likely to remain within the perspectives and characteristic methods of a single discipline or to use neighboring disciplines in an amateurish way. Yet Martin Trow was certainly not alone in seeing most interdisciplinary work as superficial and dilettantish; relaxing a department's own requirements would not in itself guarantee that a student would have adequate guidance in working in any sustained way across different fields.

Jencks and Riesman made an ambitious proposal to deal with this problem. They suggested that the power to control programs be given to subdisciplines rather than to departments. They noted that many departments are marriages of convenience among relatively unrelated subdisciplines (cultural and physical anthropology, for example), while many subdisciplines have natural allies across departmental lines. On most campuses, informal interdepartmental contacts already exist, but these contacts are sustained chiefly at the level of the faculty, through a gradual building up of acquaintance over a period of years. Graduate students are largely left out of this network, hemmed in by departmental requirements and lacking any direct access to faculty in other disciplines, aside from taking an occasional course outside their own department.

In view of this situation, Jencks and Riesman proposed that degree programs be directly organized by subdisciplines rather than under the aegis of a department. Any student who wished, or perhaps all students as a matter of course, should be able to ask for the creation of an ad hoc faculty committee to "set requirements for a particular graduate student's graduate work that are adapted to his special interests . . . Each student in effect writes his own ticket, so long as he can find a few faculty willing to approve his plans" (527). In case the students missed some good ideas for emerging subdisciplines, any group of five faculty could establish their own degree program: "Sociologists interested in professionalization and occupational subcultures might, for instance, join with economists interested in manpower problems and psychologists interested in vocational choice to establish a new program. Or anthropologists, political scientists, and economists concerned with economic development might unite to devise a new set of requirements for those who shared their interests" (527).

This bracing vision of anarchic ferment got no further than the establishment of a few area studies programs and some period-based programs like medieval studies. Even these are still controlled by faculty, and usually senior faculty at that; individual student initiative on Jencks and Riesman's model was never seriously encouraged. It is instructive to consider why to this day the great majority of students in the humanities and social sciences are squarely located within the confines of individual departments, following requirements set at the department level and doing almost all of their work with professors housed in their own department.

Jencks and Riesman were mistaken if they seriously supposed that anarchy and individual student initiative would have any appeal to the faculty. Not that professors are opposed to anarchy on principle: as we have seen in Chapter 2, they can live quite comfortably with "organized anarchy" so long as they get to be the anarchists. Free student choice is another matter, for several quite good reasons. How many first- or second-year students are really in a position to formulate a new field of study? How readily would a new and untried field be sold on the job market? And how would an ad hoc faculty committee actually work? A committee put together by a student would have little likelihood of working well, unless its members already had close working relationships. Given the entrenched disciplinary nationalism of most departments, this situation is the exception rather than the rule.

Even if one could gather that rare combination of friends in different disciplines whose interests would severally overlap with the student's own budding concerns, the committee members would need to put in a substantial amount of time in discussion with one another and with the student. Considering the competing demands of one's own department locally and one's discipline nationally, this commitment of time would be unlikely in the extreme, particularly on behalf of only a single student.

These factors do not prevent interested faculty from getting together to create interdepartmental programs, but they also inhibit people from doing so very often. The problems are well known to anyone who has been involved in an interdepartmental doctoral subcommittee, as my own field of comparative literature is organized at my university. Problems come both from those who are on the

committee and from their colleagues "back home" in the departments. Students' funding and teaching opportunities are still largely
controlled by their home departments; we find persistent problems
with noncomparatist faculty, and even with entire departments, who
give preference to "their own" students over the comparatists, even
though the comparatists are supposed to be considered equal members of their department.

Even those on the committee spend almost all their time working
within their individual departments, and have neither the time nor
the inclination to develop a common perspective or common standards for the comparative literature students. As a result, committee
meetings have a tendency to veer in one of two opposite but equally
unfortunate directions. When the committee is taking up an orals
proposal or a dissertation prospectus, often it will just rubber-stamp
it, offering little substantive guidance to a student who is trying to
work across several cultures. Alternatively, the committee may tear
the proposal apart, with several committee members approaching it
from very different and mutually inconsistent points of view. These
problems of warring perspectives occur on our committee, all of
whose members at least come from departments of literature; the
difficulty must be greater when the committee's members are based
in different disciplines altogether.

Jencks and Riesman were right to identify problems of common
purpose within departments made up of disjointed subdisciplines,
but all too often an interdepartmental committee proves to share the
very same problems, and perhaps even to magnify them. Given these
problems, departments always have good reason to send quiet messages to their students that they will receive better guidance—and
have better chances on the job market—if they stay close to home.
Students can and do thrive in good interdepartmental programs, but
the difficulty in finding usable guidance from the committee means
that students must have unusual self-direction or unusually close
and careful advising, and preferably both. By definition, a program
that places unusual demands on both student and adviser will work
well for only a minority of students and faculty.

More generally, an interdepartmental program can thrive only if
the faculty involved in it are passionately committed to it, to the
extent that they will give it the kind of attention and time that they

give to their home department and to their disciplinary work off campus. The explosive growth in women's studies programs in the past fifteen years is the product of such a commitment, and many of these programs display an excitement and common purpose that most departments should envy. Yet the very scale of work involved in creating a broad-based program is hardly less than what is required to start a new department altogether—not an impossibility, but something that happens infrequently in any given institution.

Most faculty lack the motivation to pour such effort into even a single new program; who in their right mind would take on several? Jencks and Riesman's "anarchic" proposal to let a hundred doctoral subcommittees bloom thus foundered on the fact that only(!) the students would stand to benefit. Given the real problems of the indifference or outright hostility of uninvolved faculty and the work load imposed on involved faculty, the majority of faculty could safely conclude that even the students would not, on balance, benefit from such arrangements, since they would too often fall into the cracks—or chasms—between departments, when they were not drawn and quartered outright by the competing interests of their own advisers.

The impetus to reconceive fields usually comes from younger and more restless people, chiefly graduate students and untenured faculty, which is why Jencks and Riesman were right on principle to begin from the idea of individual student initiative in the creation of programs of study. Yet their proposal ran counter to the entrenched interests of the senior faculty and the departments in which they were (and are) generally content to reside. Reforms in academic work will take hold in only one of two ways: either when any single faculty member can institute a change individually, or else when an entire department can be brought to agree to it. Yet decisions at the departmental level are usually heavily weighted toward the interests of the senior faculty, who tend to be accustomed to the status quo, while purely individual decisions lack the reach across departments that Jencks and Riesman required.

This is why real change is so difficult to achieve: although reforms ought to be pitched at a middle range, neither impossibly global nor excessively local, we soon come up against the fact that the nature of departmental culture militates strongly against just such middle-range action. In order to succeed, a change must be shown to be of real benefit not only to the students but also to the majority of the faculty, so that it can be approved by a department as a whole; at the same time, the proposed change must actually operate largely on the individual level, since rarely will a change be instituted—still less survive—if it requires the establishment of yet one more committee. As Levine puts it in *Why Innovation Fails,* reforms too often neglect the decisive criteria of *profitability* (intellectual or otherwise) and of adequate *compatibility* with the system as a whole.

Opening up the dissertation, conceiving it as a group of quasi-independent essays, meets these tests. A change of this sort would be administratively feasible, and it would actually benefit not only the students but also the faculty who must approve it, for it would make the process of advising more pleasurable and more substantive for faculty and students alike. I am thinking particularly of those faculty members who strongly care about their graduate students and who set a high standard for the dissertation. These are the very faculty who would formerly have insisted on the form of the monograph, guided by the firm hand of a senior professor, as the key to good advanced work. The changing shape of many fields has rendered this ideal less plausible than it was even fifteen years ago. The real interest in directing dissertation work has to do with helping the student to gain a clear and effective voice in a sustained scholarly conversation. One can do this, though, only when one is current in the discussion in question. When the student is working in an area we know well, we can give this sort of guidance, and we will regularly find our own perspective refreshed and renewed, in part by learning from our student's argument, and equally by ideas and reflections that come to mind in the very process of working back through the material.

Little of this can happen when the student goes into an area we have not worked in ourselves. We can still give general guidance concerning the overall structuring and presentation of the argument, but so could anyone else; we—and our student—are likely to miss most of the excitement of giving and receiving close attention and sustained guidance, since the adviser will not know the material, and the scholarship on it, well enough to sense what the student may be leaving out or distorting or failing to explore fully. We will have the uncomfortable feeling of shortchanging the student, and while we can always learn something from a dissertation on unfamiliar material, it is a rare dissertation that is a pleasure to read in itself; we would do better to be reading the best published work on the issue if our concern really were to learn a new area.

What the classic form of the dissertation is designed to produce is disciples, and indeed the very concept of the *discipline* means, etymologically, the thing that a group of *disciples* practices. In the Middle Ages, "discipline" was a function of "doctrine," the property of the *doctor* or teacher, who would translate his doctrine into disciplinary applications and exercises for his disciples. I do not mean to argue that the idea of discipleship can no longer hold good; the relation of mentor and disciple is an ancient and honorable one, a mutually illuminating and informing relation when it works as it should. It should remain one of the available modes of advanced education, just as the individual disciplines retain their value for many kinds of inquiry. Yet like the disciplines, discipleship should no longer be thought of—or taken for granted—as the *sole* model for the culmination of graduate education.

The alternative need not be mere dilettantism. Rather, students who become aware that their developing interests do not fully coincide with those of a single faculty member should begin from an early date to work in a sustained way with several faculty members. This, after all, is just what we actually require students to do during their course work, and to a lesser extent in preparing for their doctoral examinations. It would be perfectly possible for us to find ways to strengthen the ties between this base of work and the superstructure of the dissertation, so that we are not enforcing an intellectual culture of increasing isolation.

In preparing the ground for a more open dissertation, we could well begin by reconsidering our expectations and requirements for the doctoral examination. The structuring of these examinations may seem a small matter, especially as their form can usually be described very simply and may seem very flexible. Our requirements, however, are symptomatic of very basic assumptions underlying our construction of knowledge and our acculturation of our advanced students. These requirements shape our students' entire work for a year or more, and not just any year but precisely the period of transition from broad-based course work to the culminating stage of the dissertation. As a result, the doctoral examination deserves direct attention.

In my department, for example, we give a two-hour oral examination, consisting of a one-hour major field (with two examiners) and two half-hour minor fields, each with one examiner. The examination is preceded by a written pre-oral, devoted to the material to be discussed in the major field, given and read by the two major examiners but not by the minor-field examiners. We moved to this model a few years ago from a structure of a major field and three twenty-minute minor fields, for we felt that the third minor field was often tacked on arbitrarily, simply to fulfill the requirement. I argued for the change, but now I wonder how it was that "often" turned into "always." Why did we suppose that we had to make the choice and enforce it upon all our students? Why not have them decide, in consultation with their prospective examiners, how many fields to have? Why not allow for options such as two one-hour "major" fields, or else two forty-five-minute fields and one or two ancillary fields?

As it is, the very structure of our orals examination makes two assumptions that now seem unwarranted: first, that students will have one primary field and two (or three) decidedly secondary interests, an assumption reinforced by the fact that only the "major" examiners assign and read the written pre-oral. Second, we assume that whatever we currently decide is best for the majority should be the single standard for all students. Yet the alternatives I have outlined would be easy enough to arrange administratively, and they could make a real difference in allowing for different students' particular configurations of interests. Students and their examiners would have to give some thought to the form as well as to the content of the examination, but as it is, we spend considerable time deciding how to shoehorn a student's interests into the fixed form of the three-field orals. A range of formal options could inspire students and their advisers to think more actively and more creatively about the relations among their interests and the ways they could be put together.

Often, students will find that all their interests can be pursued within their own department; sometimes, though, they need to work extensively with someone in another discipline altogether. At present this happens only by student initiative and as an act of individual generosity by faculty members who are willing to give time to students who are not "their own"—language of possession that we would do well to loosen up. Too often, departments seem to sort students by discipline the way the University of Geneva does by region. Their students are registered in the categories of "Genevois" or of "Etranger"—with students from the other five Swiss cantons included among the foreigners.

But how, really, are students to gain a solid grounding in another discipline? They can be greatly aided in doing so if departments change their treatment both of their "own" students and of students from other departments. Consider Jencks and Riesman's point that a student of American history might do better to study sociology than German. This analogy is more apt than they may have realized: for its practitioners, sociology is very much a kind of language in its own right—a language made up of clusters of terms, concepts, and characteristic questions. Why not give graduate students the option to learn this language instead of German, if they can show that this will be the more useful language for them to know? Our current foreign-language requirements date from the close of the last century, when the older requirements of Latin and Greek were reluctantly being given up, and when most scholarship was being written in German and French. At that time, there was a real logic to supposing that one could hardly be a scholar in most fields without a good working knowledge of at least those modern languages.

This situation has changed dramatically in the past fifty years, since English has increasingly achieved prominence as a major language of scholarship. Much more scholarship is now being written in English to begin with, and English has joined French as a common language in international journals. In addition, more foreign-language scholarship than ever is being translated into English rapidly and accurately. Yet the language requirement persists unchanged, as university requirements regularly do if they are not subjected to direct examination, and any number of graduate students now struggle to obtain a superficial acquaintance with one or two foreign languages that they will never seriously use in their scholarly careers.

In Chapter 1 I noted with regret that foreign-language scholarship is rarely given the same attention as scholarship in one's own language. Yet this parochialism has grown up under our current system. We nominally require competence in two or three foreign languages, but we give our students no credit for learning them, and we then measure their competence so minimally that students rarely attain— still less *retain*—anything approaching a comfortable reading ability.

Our present requirements are not a meaningful response to the linguistic parochialism of modern academia, but only a form of denial of the severity of the problem. My own preference would be for arrangements at once more rigorous and more flexible than our present requirements. Students should be asked to make a case for whatever combination of foreign and disciplinary languages they genuinely need, and then be expected to demonstrate a real grasp of each.

Course requirements are similarly parochial. Departments commonly husband scarce resources, and coincidentally police their borders, by restricting introductory courses to members of their own department, or by a general tacit policy to exclude other departments' students from their advanced courses anytime the course begins to be crowded with students from their own department—even though some of "their" students may be taking the course only out of the most casual interest or in order to fulfill some distribution requirement, a requirement that may well reflect a forty-year-old understanding of the distribution of knowledge needed to practice the discipline. Often the need to exclude "outside" students is avoided by the simple recourse of filling seminars by preregistration, with the preregistration information circulated only within the department.

Work in other fields, departments, and disciplines can be fostered by many means, not by a simple relaxation of requirements but by an effort to define what might be needed for a student to gain a working fluency in the language of a different period, approach, or discipline. The fact of the matter is that such cross-disciplinary work is now being carried on by our graduate students, usually largely on their own and rather haphazardly. Far too much interdisciplinary work involves a routinized circulation of a few received ideas and articles from a given discipline, almost always taken out of the historical context—usually twenty or thirty years old—in which they were formulated, not to mention out of the longer disciplinary debate against which they were developed. We can hardly keep our students from reaching across departmental lines; all we have been doing to date is keeping them from doing so *well*.

The Circulation of Scholarly Ideas

I have tried to suggest some of the ways in which the earlier years of graduate study can be reconceived if they are thought of as leading toward a more open form of the dissertation. Given more extended and sustained work in their different areas of interest in the earlier years, students would be in a position to make the best use of the flexible dissertation I am recommending. I have already argued that such flexibility would benefit faculty as well, freeing them to work closely with students whose interests genuinely overlap with their own: sometimes on an entire dissertation, often on only one or two component essays.

It is still necessary to ask what disadvantages may attend, or may seem to attend, a dissertation made up of quasi-independent articles rather than structured as a single argument. Like so many entrenched aspects of university education, the idea of the dissertation-as-monograph is so widely assumed that it is rarely discussed. In "The Ph.D. Squid," for example, Theodore Ziolkowski recommends, among other things, that "the humanities might also emulate the sciences (and such social sciences as economics) in their tendency to accommodate the thesis to the current practices of the field." But he adds a parenthetical caveat: "(This is not to suggest approval of the practice in some fields of accepting as dissertations works that amount to published articles bound or stapled together)" (192). Yet Ziolkowski gives us no argument to support his demurral; apparently the reasons should be self-evident.

Looking at Ziolkowski's own definitions of what the dissertation should be, I find it hard to see why a group of articles could not fit the bill just as well as a book-length monograph. Ziolkowski himself remarks that "the 'dissertation' is increasingly no longer a monograph in the traditional sense of the word but a presentation according to the publication practices of the field: it often includes material presented at conferences and published by the candidate and his or her research group" (191). Perhaps someone might insist that in the present advanced state of most fields, one needs two or three hundred pages to develop an original piece of research—and yet Ziolkowski himself does not accept this by now rather romantic idea of the dissertation; he notes that many dissertations are not best described as original pieces of research at all, "but rather—and perhaps more important—a 'contribution' to knowledge certifying the ability to carry out research according to the current standards of the discipline" (191). The real contribution, he refreshingly notes, is not to the field but "to the candidate's own knowledge: it should have taught him or her to identify and analyze a reasonable problem in the field, to treat it according to accepted procedures, and to present it in an accessible manner. At the very least, the dissertation as an exercise should prepare the new Ph.D. to organize his or her first college course and to appreciate what it takes to write a good book" (193).

I see no goal here that could not be achieved just as well by a well-planned series of articles, though I would doubt that dissertations on either model can often provide the basis for one's "first college course." Leaving aside the fact that most graduate students have begun teaching well before completing their degrees, the very idea that new professors should base their first college courses on their dissertations only shows how heavily undergraduate education is still overshadowed by graduate-level research, at least in theory. In fact, most dissertations today give little help with course planning, since introductory college courses much more closely resemble orals fields than the intensive study of advanced topics typical of dissertations.

The heart of Ziolkowski's objection to a group of articles must be the idea that they would not prepare the candidate to write a good book. I would not wish to counter this argument simply by suggesting that far too many dissertations now end up as rather *dull* books—when they are not simply mined for one or two articles after all; much more to the point are several considerations that challenge the book-length study as the sole model for mature scholarship. Not only in the sciences, but in other fields like law, articles rather than books have long played the central role. In the humanities and social sciences, however, books have increasingly become the norm by which scholars cement their reputation and by which untenured faculty are evaluated for tenure. The differing emphases given to articles as against books suggest that there is not necessarily any intrinsic difference in the scholarly value of one book as against several articles; rather, looking across different disciplines, and looking across time within single disciplines, we can see that the relative value of the two forms is bound up with changes in general practices of publication and reception. A detailed picture of these changes would require a volume in itself; here it may be sufficient to make several observations.

It is fair to say that into the early 1960s, books and articles stood at relative parity in many fields. The reason for this is that they shared much the same readership: within a given field, there would be a handful of leading journals, and a rather small number of books would appear annually from major presses. People active in the field would subscribe to the most important journals, and the visibility of articles was such that a scholar could readily rise to prominence in a field by means of several important and well-placed articles.

This situation began to change during the 1960s. Journals proliferated to such an extent that by the late 1970s a field might have thirty journals instead of four, and no one would subscribe to all of them or even keep up with them via the library. This multiplication of journals vastly outpaced the growth in university presses. Each of the major research universities had previously had a press and a handful of journals, but by the end of this period they still had one press and *many* journals. As more and more universities began to emulate the major research universities—only two dozen or so in 1950—they too each established one press and an increasing number of journals.

Journals were particularly adapted to multiply within the scholarly ecosystem because they could thrive in many different niches: a single department could produce one or even several, either linked to their university press distribution network or circulated quite independently through professional organizations and other private channels. One senior professor could take charge, with a modest subsidy granted directly by the administration (often as part of a deal to keep the popular person from accepting an offer elsewhere), and while university presses would have substantial fixed costs in salaries for permanent staff such as acquiring editors, in the case of journals many of these jobs could be farmed out within departments as unpaid labor by untenured faculty and by graduate students. Furthermore, contributors would not expect the royalties that a press would have to pay on a book.

The proliferation of journals had the unintended effect of lowering the value of articles relative to books. The fact that just about anyone could get just about any article published somewhere reduced their collective prestige, and moreover the impact of an article became less than that of a comparable article published twenty years before, since a much smaller proportion of the scholars in the field would see any given journal. Meanwhile, books from major presses retained more of their value, partly because the increase in numbers was proportionately smaller, and partly because the greater expense of publication and distribution continued to give an edge during this period to the older and larger university presses, even as their direct connection to the prestige of their home institutions continued to command closer attention to their advertisements and catalogues.

For many reasons, this picture has begun to change in the past decade. The very superabundance of journals has in and of itself led to an interesting *lessening of competition* between journals and books. As recently as fifteen years ago, it was common wisdom that a press would be reluctant to publish a manuscript if more than one or at most two of its chapters had already appeared in print, the logic being that too many of the potential audience would have seen the material and would not buy the book. Currently, the situation is almost the opposite: except in some small fields, the market is so fragmented that presses actually benefit if most of a book first appears in various journals. The average reader will still see only one or two of these articles, which will ideally serve as advance publicity for the book.

In scholarship as in advertising, the sheer volume of publication has become a form of background noise against which a new idea must make itself heard. Just because the market is now so crowded, a scholar's impact will be greater if the work appears in pieces in several venues. We now find the phenomenon, unheard of until recently, that a given *chapter* may have appeared in two or three journals and collections, slightly revised or reprinted outright, before the publication of the book. Scholars now regularly gain prominence by a reversal of the traditional process. Formerly, someone would write a few articles and then the "big book" synthesizing ten or twenty years' work, bringing the author to prominence in the field. Increasingly we find that someone writes a solid first book (usually dissertation based), well enough received but not decisive in itself, which serves chiefly to get the young scholar onto the lecture circuit and leads to invitations to contribute to some of the hot—that is, new— journals in the field. After a few years our young scholar collects several of these articles and conference papers into a volume with some general theme, and it is this collection that really establishes the author as a figure to reckon with. The articles have to be published in book form to achieve this effect, but the fact remains that this is a collection of articles, something scholars of the previous generation would usually not have thought of assembling until quite late in their careers.

Academic habits often lag some time behind such changing circumstances. The heyday of the book as *tenure fetish* began in the 1970s, a decade after the market had changed in such a way as to devalue articles; the book is still fetishized in tenure decisions today, even though the market no longer holds the two forms in opposition. This new shift in the market is bound to intrude gradually on our collective consciousness, however, particularly as the university presses have come under fierce financial pressure. Even major presses find only half as many libraries as before—only five hundred or so across the country—buying their list as a matter of course. A single hardcover book can cost more than a year's subscription to a journal, and even paperbacks have become expensive for individuals to buy. The output of university presses is consequently going to remain stagnant or even decline, and their print runs are shrinking already, thereby reducing the relative advantage in impact that books had been having in the past twenty years. Further, editors are now putting a new premium on *short* (less expensive) books, thereby reducing the difference in scale between books and articles. Many a book is now only the length of four or five articles, even if it did not literally begin life in that form. Journals are also under financial pressure, but their fixed costs remain lower, and many are tied to dues paid for membership in professional organizations and to the funds raised for conferences. Further, the rapid spread of electronic mail and of electronic publishing in its various forms will give journals a further edge over books, since book-length manuscripts are cumbersome to transmit and read via faxes and computer screens, while articles can be quite easily adapted to the new formats.

For all these reasons, a book that is composed of several thematically related articles may reach a wider audience than one that develops a single argument over several hundred closely connected pages. Insofar as a dissertation is supposed, as Ziolkowski says, to reflect "the publication practices in the field" and to teach the candidate "what it takes to write a good book," it is now fair to say that writing a series of articles should be at least as valuable training as writing a monograph.

An advantage of putting the case in these terms is that we are not driven into a sterile opposition between the two forms, as though we had to agree with some enthusiasts of "hypertext" that the traditional book is a dead form. The conservatism of the university will ensure that the monograph will no more disappear after the invention of the computer than the classroom lecture disappeared after the invention of printing. At the same time, the progressivism of the university will allow our practices to adopt the new along with the old: just as the invention of printing paved the way for the seminar—a form possible only once a teacher could expect the students to have read the material before class—so too the electronically published article, saved on disk or bound in hard copy, will flourish along with the more capacious but expensive monograph.

Since we need not choose between these forms, we have the further advantage that we do not have to impose on sponsors the new form of the dissertation as a series of articles, or deny the form of the monograph to students who genuinely have a project best suited to that scale. Students could still do all their work with one or two sponsors, on one topic or on several, or they could do several different pieces with different advisers—even writing some pieces collaboratively with other people.

These latter options would do much to combat the isolation of advanced graduate study; they would also be beneficial when a student would otherwise be driven to a premature synthesis of a single complex field or of several interests. Increasingly, I find that students in my department have begun to work actively in two or three rather distant fields, as these fields have traditionally been conceived—medieval literature and modernism, for example, or law and literature. Sometimes such a student finds a way to bring these interests together within a single dissertation topic, but often it proves simpler to put one area aside indefinitely, or else to manufacture a somewhat specious quick connection so as to be able to formulate a single thesis. In these latter instances, students' scholarly development would be better served if they could write more or less independent essays, deepening their understanding of each area. In subsequent years they could work to synthesize their interests, or simply work actively in two fields. Some careers evolve in this way even now, but they have been hindered rather than helped by the dominance of the ideal of the dissertation as monograph.

These broad perspectives should be kept in view as we undertake specific reforms, which require detailed work on policies and requirements. The reforms I am proposing can be adopted by individual sponsors and students but do not require a wholesale alteration of departmental culture. Over time, substantial cultural changes can follow from such changes in the form of the dissertation, and from collateral changes in language requirements, course requirements, doctoral examinations, and student contacts across departmental lines. A culture of cooperation can grow up alongside the culture of isolation, not replacing it but providing a livelier cultural landscape than now exists, yielding a more varied intellectual diet than the parthenocarpic fruits we now cultivate in our enclosed academic fields. Gradually and cumulatively, this greater variety can have profound effects on the way established scholars carry on their work, helping us to address problems in our current scholarly practices and to take advantage of the opportunities ahead of us. These problems and these opportunities are the subject of the concluding chapter.

6

The Next Intellectuals

Throughout this book, I have been arguing that scholars should be able to do better at working together and at listening to one another. Having suggested some of the ways in which we can begin to train future scholars so as to enhance, rather than repress, their intellectual sociability, I must now show more fully the benefits that can grow out of such a reorientation. Though intellectual in nature, these benefits cannot be described purely in terms of abstract ideas, for they are directly tied to the ways particular people work within specific institutional contexts. This social and personal grounding means that my argument will continue to be sociological in emphasis and ethical in intent. A real shift in academic culture can enhance the quality of ideas, strengthen the links among all aspects of scholarly activity, and lessen the often-regretted but too rarely bridged rift between scholarly and public life.

Academic and public institutions today are under similar kinds of stress, as a result of the explosion of information and the increasingly complex political and financial integration (or integration/disintegration) of societies around the globe. The best analogy I have encountered for the situation on our campuses came in a talk not long ago by Sir Brian Urquhart, former under secretary-general of the United Nations. Speaking to a group of international lawyers, Urquhart emphasized the need for the UN's agencies to recognize that "it is impossible any longer comfortably to compartmentalize most big problems, which now seem to be inextricably connected with each other" ("Address," 45). Each UN agency, however, was established to deal with a separate problem—health, education, labor, poverty, and so on—and each developed its own bureaucracy and methods. Their separation was compounded by "a long tradition of lack of genuine coordination" (Urquhart and Childers, *Towards a More Effective United Nations*, 33). Urquhart puts the problem in less measured terms in his memoir, *A Life in Peace and War,* describing his own early involvement in trying to foster a modicum of cooperation among these agencies. He describes this work during the late 1940s as

> a singularly futile and bleak period in my career . . . Our work epitomized, in its futility, the built-in diffuseness of the United Nations system. There was, and is, as little chance of the Secretary-General coordinating the autonomous specialized agencies of the UN system as King John of England had of bringing to heel the feudal barons. Indeed, the situations are in some respects similar. The agencies each have their own constitutions, budgets, and national constituencies, and have no intention of being coordinated by the UN, although they must pretend to be in favor of it.   (119–120)

The analogy to the modern university is clear. Indeed, Urquhart's own sense of the similarity of the institutions can be seen from the fact that in remarks prefacing his international law address, he commended F. M. Cornford's trenchant satire of academic politics, *Microcosmographia Academica,* as the best book ever written on political behavior.

The protectionistic nationalism of our departments certainly needs to be countered as strongly as possible, although it may be too much to expect that we will live to see the abolition of the existing departmental structures. In the current rudimentary state of collaborative work, indeed, it would be hard to impose a new structure with any confidence that it would work better than what we have now. What I propose are steps that can begin to take hold within our present system; ideally, over time, substantial structural change will follow, but it would already be a great improvement if people could work more creatively from within the departments and disciplines we now have. We need not only to develop the inner imperatives of our disciplines as we usually do, but also to go against their grain, trying to work together to see better those questions to which our institutions normally blind us.

The myth of the scholar as isolated individual has harmful consequences in two opposite ways: first, it inhibits people from working directly together; equally, it conceals the extent to which individuals do bear the marks of the disciplines and departments in which we live. A herd of independent thinkers is still a herd. I think I do not need to detail examples of the faddishness and bandwagonism that are endemic—and even seem to be increasing—in academia, and it may seem paradoxical that my solution to this problem is to urge *more* group activity. Yet I believe that contemporary academic group-think is closely bound up with the isolation of much scholarship; it is often nothing other than a magnification of the individual-think discussed at the end of Chapter 3. When people do work together, the result is likely to be a *pseudo*-collaboration rather than genuine collaboration. Individual and pseudo-collaborative work alike then reinforce the circulation of tendentious truisms that too often set the tone and the terms for the work being done.

"Institutions create shadowed places," as Mary Douglas says, "in which nothing can be seen and no questions asked. They make other areas show finely discriminated detail, which is closely scrutinized and ordered" (*How Institutions Think,* 69). Pseudo-collaboration only masks this process, thereby allowing it free rein, as people go over and over the established issues, perhaps using the revisionary optic of some hot trend, but often doing little more than "filling in the third and fourth decimal places" (as a friend of mine describes the current state of the field of cellular immunology). Having sporadic contacts with someone from another department or reading a couple of articles by the thinker of the month from the discipline of the year will rarely cast any sustained light on the areas put in shadow by one's home discipline. All too often, the result is merely to provide a new metaphor or a temporarily interesting issue to apply to much the usual material in much the usual way, and the new ideas quickly become banal as they make the rounds of different disciplines. Individuals in themselves can have only partial success in standing outside the norms of the disciplines and departments within which they live and work: this is why genuine collaboration across fields and disciplines can be so valuable.

Scholarly collaboration involves sustained and careful attention to the ideas and approaches of people working on related issues from differing perspectives, and this quality of attention should also carry over into work one does on one's own. Joint authorship of written productions is the most visible mode of collaboration; other, equally important, forms include conferences, colloquia, and coordinated journal issues and collections of essays. These kinds of genuine collaboration can certainly be found today, and they show that the ideals advanced here are not simply unrealizable utopian projections.

My call for genuine collaboration runs against two opposed assumptions: first, that it is impossible; second, that it is already being done all the time anyway. On the one hand, joint authorship is widely thought to be somehow impossible under most conditions in the humanities, while on the other hand it is already constantly practiced in the natural and social sciences. Similarly, conferences have proliferated for decades, so that scholarly interchange of this sort is already perfectly well established—unless like many recent writers (Martin Anderson, Julius Getman, David Lodge) one takes the opposite view that conferences are merely social events masquerading as intellectual occasions, exercises in tedium enlivened only by the chance to snub one's inferiors, suck up to one's superiors, and sample the restaurants of New Orleans. All these views have a measure of truth, yet none of them is satisfactory in the long run.

Collaborative Writing and the Mentalist Myth

A given social institution establishes certain relations of authority and influence; it characteristically maintains and justifies these relations not by brute force alone but by grounding these power relations in a mythic analogy, whether seen cosmically as the will of the gods or in earthly terms as the physical determinants of life. As Mary Douglas argues in *How Institutions Think* (31–53), the members of a society often assume these mythic analogies unconsciously, expressing them directly only if the reigning system of relations is challenged.

The ideal of the scholar as isolated individual is openly held, al-

though it is close enough to the realm of myth that it is rarely debated. Full-scale myths, even more rarely enunciated, underlie this
ideal. In our naturalistic age, the supporting myths take a physical
rather than a directly theological form; if we advocate a contrary ideal
of collaborative scholarship, these myths are forced to the surface.
Either the mind or the body itself, we will be told, is constitution-
ally—by natural law, so to say—incapable of meaningful collaborative writing. Any ideas that can be generated in conversation are
somehow trivial or inauthentic. "Virtually all original, important
ideas," Martin Anderson tells us, "spring from one brain" (*Impostors
in the Temple,* 110). Similarly, David Bromwich insists that whereas
conceits and dogmas take refuge in groups, "thoughts, in turn, come
into the mind alone, which could never pass through the sorting
medium of the group . . . Group thinking is not thinking" (*Politics
by Other Means,* ix). Or, as I've been told in the somatic equivalent
of these mentalist claims, "a committee can't hold a pen."

I counter such remarks with the observation that our own experience shows that original thoughts can in fact arise through the process of conversation, and extended discussion can add depth and
perspective that a single person may lack. The results can even be
written up by more than one person. I then sometimes find my inter-
locutor falling back on history to dispute the efficacy of this process:
"But can you really give any examples of good books written by a
committee?" Although they may acknowledge that documents by
multiple authors exist in the social sciences, humanists in particular
will take their stand on an ideal of quality that ultimately relies on
an individualist mentalism: "Of course a committee can assemble statistics, but in *our* field the really important work is always the result
of the play of a mind, expressed in a unique and compelling style;
how could a committee do anything like that?" The mythic quality
of all these responses can be seen in the fact that my respondents
forget important books I know they have read. Further, they pose
an unnecessarily stark alternative, as though the choice were that
we must give them personal liberty or give them the living death of
committee prose. Yet coauthorship is usually a much smaller-scale
and more personal activity than the writing of committee reports.

In every field known to me, there are seminal works of joint authorship—certainly a small minority of work in most fields, but fully

sufficient to show that the thing can be done. The prefaces to these works regularly testify to their authors' pleasure in formulating their ideas together and in drafting and redrafting chapters in light of each other's comments. The resulting work may either retain their differing voices or else blend them. René Wellek and Austin Warren, for example, wrote in the preface to the first edition of their *Theory of Literature* that their book was "a real instance of a collaboration in which the author is the shared agreement between two writers" (8).

So strong is the myth of individual authorship, however, that even people who themselves have worked closely with coauthors seem to forget their own experience when formulating their ideas on academic life. We have already encountered the case of Julius Getman, holding to an entirely individualistic conception of scholarship despite his own happy experiences with joint authorship. Equally noteworthy is Bowen and Rudenstine's collaboratively written *In Pursuit of the Ph.D.*, the best book on graduate education in at least twenty years—and not at all badly written, so far as style is concerned. For all their extended discussions of problems and possible reforms in graduate education, it is notable that Bowen and Rudenstine devote only a single page to a section on "Combating the Problem of Isolation." There they note that humanists are not encouraged to work collaboratively as scientists regularly do. To lessen the isolation of humanists' advanced training, Bowen and Rudenstine offer a single idea, an increased use of dissertation seminars in which students can read dissertation chapters to one another (263).

It is a measure of the extreme isolation of much advanced graduate work that this minimum of collegiality should be seen as exceptional—and that so modest a response to the problem should be all that Bowen and Rudenstine propose. Although they begin by noting the prevalence of collaboration in science, they say nothing to suggest that humanists might actually think of working together. This silence is rather surprising, especially if we consider the terms in which they describe the genesis of their own book: "We now wish to thank the extraordinary group of colleagues and friends who have participated in this research project. Without attempting to mention everyone who has helped, we find that we still have an exceptionally long list of debts to acknowledge—which is itself a commentary on

the collaborative nature of the process that has resulted in this book"
(xvii). Several pages follow in which they detail the contributions of
their "four principal collaborators"; numbers of Mellon Foundation
staff members; dozens of administrators and colleagues at the universities they studied; "Robert Goheen, who has been a teacher, colleague, and friend of both authors for over 20 years"; and various
assistants, editors, and foundation trustees. They conclude, in a mini-
manifesto for extended collaborative work:

> No one person, or small group of people, could be expected
> to have the substantive knowledge of particular fields of study,
> computer skills, familiarity with at least basic statistical tech-
> niques, and the historical-institutional perspective that have
> seemed to us to be necessary. A blending of skills, tastes, and
> experiences has without question enriched the research process
> for us, and has, we hope, improved the product.
>
> Of one thing we are certain. Our personal partnership, which
> has lasted for some 23 years, has survived yet another test! And
> that is the most extreme understatement. We have benefited
> once again by counting on each other to do those things that
> one of us could not do at all, or hardly at all. Writing this book
> has been a new and most rewarding experience for two very
> good friends who will always be grateful for the extraordinary
> opportunities that they have been given to work together.   (xx)

The very warmth of these acknowledgments makes it all the more
notable that the collaborative pleasure of the project's own execution
has not carried over into any discussion of ways in which graduate
training might foster work of a similar sort.

More and more problems today are of the sort described by Brian
Urquhart and by Bowen and Rudenstine: complex questions whose
answers can most effectively be undertaken by collaborative work
among two or more people who possess the needed range of interests
and expertise. So entrenched is the individualist ethos, however, that
academic culture casts most truly interdisciplinary questions into
deep shadow. At best we see some two-dimensional, flattened-out
version of the problem, all too readily subsumable under the heading

of a catch phrase from whatever theory is currently in fashion, all too susceptible of some dramatic global solution.

The collaborative work that is being done today shows that we can do better than we have been doing, if we can foster an academic culture in which it can thrive. I am not saying that we must forswear the pleasures of watching a single mind develop an idea in a compelling and idiosyncratic style; I am simply arguing that we should realize that this is only one model for scholarly excellence, suited more to some sorts of questions and approaches than to others. Current collaborative work can point the way toward the future, although this future may be something other than more of the same sorts of collaboration we now see. Just because collaboration is now an exotic growth in a hostile environment, it is forced in certain directions rather than in others, and it takes more limited forms than we may expect to find in the future. To gain a sense of the real potential for collaborative work, we must begin from an understanding of the limitations as well as the strengths of the collaborative work that is now being done.

Too often, present-day collaboration has one of only two bases: authoritarianism or close personal friendship. The authoritarian mode of collaboration is perhaps most clearly seen in some European systems, such as those of Holland and Sweden, in which the director of a department often sets the research agenda for the entire department; the others must tailor their work to feed into the overall project, or to seem to feed into it, or at least not to compete with it. The directors of laboratories in this country often set the agenda in similar ways. We may not wish to endorse the view of a paleontologist friend of mine, that "most labs are run like fascist states," but at least it would seem that a good deal of scientific collaboration is strongly hierarchical in nature. Both in the natural sciences and in the social sciences, papers by multiple authors often (though by no means always) reflect a relatively limited degree of genuine collaboration in the formulation of ideas, fleshed out by a good deal of routine work—running experiments, conducting interviews, crunching numbers—by the junior members of the team.

Collaborations that are not authoritarian in basis are usually grounded in personal friendship. Genuine though such collaborations are, however, personal friendship is a very selective basis for work: the requirement that the collaborators be friends eliminates most of the potential combinations that can be found on a typical campus. The objection to this prerequisite is the same that must be raised to any vision of collegiality that would require one's colleagues to be "nice people," to recall Rosovsky's phrase: academics simply aren't nice enough, to enough of their colleagues, enough of the time, for this to be a general basis for academic life.

Further, personal friendship usually seems to result in collaborations between only two persons. Such collaborations most often flourish in cases in which the participants have already enjoyed a long relationship—think of Bowen and Rudenstine's twenty-three years together. To extend the reach of a project beyond two people seems, under existing circumstances, to require exceptional conditions to prevent either the project or the relationships from falling apart.

Bowen and Rudenstine clearly enjoyed ideal working conditions and extensive resources: they had earlier worked together as president and provost of Princeton, then moved in tandem to serve as president and executive vice president of the Mellon Foundation. From these positions they could extend both their own friendship and their patronage to involve colleagues and hire numerous assistants, all backed by the "encouragement and support" of their "endlessly patient Trustees" (xx). When conditions are less favorable, even a three-person working group is likely to run into difficulties of personality or simply lack of enough commitment to coordinate and complete a project.

In 1990 Harvard University Press published a major critical edition of the aesthetic treatises of two classical Sanskrit theologians and poeticians, Anandavardhana and Abhinavagupta, translated and edited by a three-person team: Daniel H. H. Ingalls, Jeffrey Moussaieff Masson, and M. V. Patwardhan. This eight-hundred-page volume had evolved in several stages. Originally Masson had translated part of these works as his dissertation, which he completed under Ingalls' sponsorship in 1970. After studying in India with Professor Patwardhan, he completed his translation and a commentary on the treatises and submitted the whole to Ingalls in the mid-1970s, for publication in the Harvard Oriental Series, of which Ingalls has long been the general editor. Ingalls decided that the translations needed polishing and that the commentary could use expansion. He and Masson agreed to do these revisions and additions together.

Further, in a notable departure from the prevailing tendency of Western academics to work in isolation from Asian scholars, Ingalls and Masson also determined to invite commentary from Professor Patwardhan. The result was a splendid volume, one that presents these important but enigmatic treatises in a form comprehensible even to people outside the field. Their extensive notes carry on in an interesting way the dialogue of Abhinavagupta's own commentary on Anandavardhana. Some notes, written in the first person plural, express a common view; others are written by Ingalls alone, often with rejoinders or demurrals from Masson or Patwardhan. Far from damning their subject with faint prose, as the myth of "committee" authorship would lead us to expect, the three scholars have achieved a lively and multiple-voiced analysis.

This result was not achieved, however, without costs. In his preface Ingalls acknowledges that "I have spent what my colleagues must have thought an unconscionable time" in completing his share of the book (*The Dhvanyaloka*, v). As the project had taken more than a dozen years even after Masson had completed the first full translation, Ingalls may be using ironic understatement, although he may also be expressing a genuine metaphysical uncertainty, Professor Patwardhan having died while the book was in press. Masson, meanwhile, had undergone psychoanalysis, developed a scholarly interest in that discipline, and left the field of Sanskrit studies altogether, some years before his senior colleague finally completed his contribution to their joint production.

To move beyond the scale of two-person work, it appears that considerable care is needed to ensure steady involvement by all parties, lest the contributors' other commitments add years to the duration of the project. Moreover, for projects on any scale there needs to be concrete institutional support for collaborative work—such as favorable notice in tenure reviews—if collaborations are not to depend on long-standing friendships among securely tenured faculty.

For all its personal advantages, friendship is actually a somewhat mixed basis for scholarly work. More often than not, friends who choose to work together already share many assumptions and much the same expertise. Their work together may well produce better results than either could do alone—Wellek and Warren's *Theory of Literature,* for example, for years the best-selling work in literary theory, has had a greater impact than any single work either author has written on his own. But a different order of benefit can come from work by people who do not have common interests and views, as is evident in M. S. Silk and J. P. Stern's excellent *Nietzsche on Tragedy.* A German historian and a classicist at the University of London, they found themselves arguing over Nietzsche and came to realize that their differing perspectives could be brought to bear in an interesting way on the problem of Nietzsche's uses and abuses of the classical tradition. They began by dividing up the project along the lines of their differing expertise, with Silk working up sections on German literature and thought while Stern worked on classicism and Greek tragedy. But over time, "each step of the writing was preceded by so much discussion and followed by so much intensive rewriting on both sides, that the final version cannot be regarded as anything other than the joint effort of the authors, who accept equal responsibility for it. When they first mooted the idea of a collaboration (at the institution to which this book is dedicated), the authors did not, as a matter of fact, share a common view of their subject. The final version is the product of mutual correction and convergence" (iii).

This is collaborative work in the best sense; it is work that could not have been done nearly as well by a historian alone swotting up some classical scholarship, or by a classicist doing the reverse. Their disciplinary differences influenced the project as much as their personal friendship did. While a strengthened friendship may well have followed from this process of work, the really essential thing was *a commitment to the project,* fueled both by the topic itself and by the challenge of arguing out their ideas with—and even against—each other. Their project was also grounded in an institutional space, provided by "the Masters and Fellows of St. John's College, Cambridge," to whom the book is dedicated.

It is notable that Silk and Stern had not thought of working together while pursuing their daily business in their different departments at the University of London; it was while both were visiting at St. John's that they realized their common interest, or more precisely the potential overlap between their very distinct interests. Perhaps Rosovsky should not be so quick to dismiss the clubbishness of Oxbridge life, and we might do well to think of ways to foster similar sorts of interchange in our American environments. At the very least, such examples of collaborative work—more could easily be given—can loosen the hold of the myth that original ideas come into the mind alone and in no other way.

Collaboration and the Exchange of Ideas

Valuable as it is, collaborative writing proper is only part of the story. The collaborative interchange of individually written work is equally important and equally in need of improvement. This involves both the production and the circulation of ideas. The need for a cultural shift in academic life and work is nowhere more apparent than in the sad parodies of collaborative work that conferences and collections of articles now represent. Twenty-five years ago Jacques Barzun referred sarcastically to conferences as "the waxworks of the intellectual world," although the only improvement he could suggest was that the papers "should be read by machine in some empty ballroom, to permit the absent listeners to stay at home and work" (*The American University*, 250). What would it take to find ways in which scholars might manage to do real work together outside their homes?

It would certainly take a major change from the practices that prevail today. Over the years, I have contributed to special issues of journals and to several thematically organized essay collections in book form, and I have spoken at conferences large and small, organized in several formats by people in a number of disciplines. Yet I have never had the good fortune either to contribute to a collection or to participate on a panel that could be described as genuinely collaborative. Only rarely have I even attended a panel, or read a collection, that was the product of sustained discussion beforehand or that yielded a meaningful discussion among the participants.

Again and again in conference panel sessions, the introductions and the speakers' presentations take up almost all of the time, with at most only a few minutes for questions at the end. Usually the papers have not been circulated in advance, even to the other panelists; never in my own experience has there been any organized process of revision in advance of the conference on the basis of comments received. We may suppose that practical problems of reproduction and distribution are involved here, but such problems are surely more of an excuse than a determining force. Similarly, it would be a simple matter to establish a two- or three-stage process of sharing and revising of drafts among contributors to a special issue of a journal or a collection of essays on a topic, and yet I have never found this done in the several such projects to which I have contributed. To the extent that the time and expense of photocopying and mailing have inhibited such processes, the burgeoning use of the Internet is very rapidly reducing the problem to minor proportions.

Even electronic mail can work only if one has prepared a text to transmit. The fact that many participants wait until the last minute to produce their papers is only a reflection of the underlying ideology of individual production, reinforced by the fact that conference organizers and journal editors rarely ask—still less insist—that people do things differently. It is perfectly easy to set a conference or publication schedule with clearly defined dates for the circulation of first drafts, receipt of comments, and submission of final drafts. Would anyone seriously argue that such a process would not improve the finished products? Apparently, the tacit assumption is that the contributors' excellence is so unqualifiable, or their stubbornness is so intractable, that any resulting improvements would be too minor to justify the effort.

I will not counter such assumptions in detail; rather, I hope that the whole force of the preceding chapters will be to show how threadbare such ideas are, how dependent on an unreflective acceptance of century-old myths about the nature of scholarly work. The only substantive objection I would acknowledge is a practical one, that more serious preparation for conferences and collections would take more time than we now need to give them, perhaps more than we *can* give them. Life is short, and trade-offs must sometimes be made; would we really have the time to read our fellow participants' drafts, make suggestions, and revise our own draft in turn?

Anyone who has, as I do, three small children must always take seriously any argument grounded in the limited number of hours there are in the day. And it is true that good work can sometimes be done at the last minute. I would reply, though, that most conferences and special issues fall rather flat, far short of the real excitement, and the full benefit to participants and audience or readers alike, that they would offer if they were genuinely collaborative in nature. How much extra time would be needed to do these things better, if one commented on three fellow panelists' drafts and rewrote one's own draft? (More extensive versions of collaboration could of course be imagined, but even this modest program would represent a sea change from the current state of affairs.) Perhaps someone who now speaks at four conferences a year would have time only for three. Yet it might be better to go to three conferences at which we truly learn something, and at which we strengthen some real working relationships, than to attend four conferences of which we can recall little a week later. Surely most of us have heard far too many half-baked presentations, and had far too little useful feedback on our own productions, however well or poorly baked. Suppose the price of really learning from these experiences was that we would have somewhat fewer of them: would this be such a loss? As gratifying as a lengthening résumé can be, a nagging sense of issues not quite thought through can produce, in the end, a certain *taedium curriculum vitae.*

Such literature as exists on the organization and planning of conferences—consisting largely of titles like *Let's Have a Conference!*— includes little reflection on the broader social and intellectual implications of the ways we arrange these events. One exception is a detailed account by Mary Catherine Bateson of an intensive weeklong conference held in Austria in 1968. One could wish that more conferences would have the effect that Bateson describes, of giving its fourteen participants "both a new understanding and a new concern about the human condition" (*Our Own Metaphor,* ix); for the participants, the conference itself became a metaphor for their theme, the challenge of making conscious thought adequate to the complexity of relations in the social and natural environments.

Not every conference, of course, is sponsored by a foundation that owns a fortress "on a peak above the town of Gloggnitz, guarding the Semmering Pass" (Bateson, 23), but intensive intellectual exchange can be produced under less exalted circumstances as well. Too often, indeed, the participants at a typical conference would be spending more time going out for grog in Gloggnitz and opera in Vienna than absorbing and talking through long papers on cybernetics and the environment.

Problems of locale and scale were shrewdly discussed by Bateson's mother, Margaret Mead, in an essay from 1962. Mead celebrated conferences as opportunities for the participants "to act as whole individuals, using all their senses as they seldom do in the narrower, more specialized contexts" of their other work ("Conference Arrangements," 45). She emphasized the influence that practical arrangements can have in promoting or inhibiting a "conference ethos." Whether they stimulate all the senses or not, conferences provide an important testing-ground for very practical as well as broadly theoretical concerns about academic work, and they also illustrate the close connection among writing and other forms of scholarly activity.

Too often, those who love to present papers at conferences shun the "ward heeling" of practical discussions at the departmental level, to recall the closing pages of Chapter 2, and yet the general desiccation of departmental life has unfortunate consequences for conferencegoers themselves. These consequences are both intellectual and administrative. Intellectually, people who do not participate in departmental life lose a major venue for sustained collegial interaction; they thereby risk unfitting themselves for the business of really listening to people at conferences and learning from them. If you get a good audience for your paper, you will, of course, disseminate your ideas and improve your professional standing; but if there has been no opportunity for feedback as you prepared the paper, and next to no time for discussion after you present it, has the experience really been so very substantive?

You may also happen to hear one or two good papers at other sessions, always assuming that they are scheduled at times when you are not exploring the latest in Cajun cooking, but most of them— perhaps in contrast to your own—may seem a little slipshod and rather tendentious. A really subtle argument, on the other hand, may require some reflection before you can formulate a response. For a real discussion to occur, you may have to think about the issue for a while, then buttonhole the speaker later, always assuming that you run into one another on the tour of Storyville. In the end, the scene of the conference itself is hardly any more of a genuine scene these days than is the departmental office back home in Tammany Hall.

These intellectual problems breed administrative arrangements that powerfully reinforce the problems themselves. Colleges and universities usually assist professors with funds for travel to conferences only if the professor is speaking at the conference. As most conferences are now run, there is a certain logic to this choice, since no dean who has ever been a professor is likely to suppose that it's worth several hundred dollars just to *listen* to the papers being presented. The prestige of the institution will be increased, and the professor's work will be advanced, only if the professor performs, giving a paper or at least chairing a session.

This is a good example of the way in which institutional arrangements can substitute for thinking. Why should it be assumed, a priori, that "participation" really means "performance"? I write these pages having just returned from the annual meeting of the Modern Language Association, where I gave a paper, went to a variety of sessions, and consumed large quantities of several sorts of beverage while talking to old and new friends. My university paid my way on the strength of my presentation, which did involve twenty very pleasant minutes talking about Buster Keaton to an audience of thirty. Yet my own research, and perhaps even my institution's prestige, were at least equally advanced by all the other hours of conversation and by my presence at those other sessions, a few of which actually provided food for thought even if little time for discussion.

A more rational administrative arrangement would grant funds up to a certain annual amount for people to attend conferences in order to speak *or* to listen, so long as they could justify the importance of the conference for their work and professional development. Some schools do this, but I cannot help feeling that most deans secretly suspect that conferences are really vacations in disguise, and so they enforce a bare minimum of obvious work. They could always require their faculty to certify that they had actually attended a set number of sessions—as lawyers do in order to write Caribbean conferences off their taxes—but given the quality of so many sessions, this might look too much like outright punishment. Taking conferences seriously would entail changing these arrangements, and would indeed provide the justification for doing so. I can hardly argue to my dean that I participated actively in those other MLA sessions I attended, as the speakers ran over their time at all of them, leaving even less chance for discussion than the minimum that had been allotted. More fully collaborative conference arrangements—much more the exception than the rule today—would give such an argument more force.

This sort of claim would be even more persuasive if more professors were seen to be serious about work on campus itself. There is, in fact, encouraging evidence that professors around the country are taking a renewed interest in their home institutions: a survey in 1989 showed 40 percent of respondents describing their home institution as "very important" to them, a significant increase from a mere 29 percent five years before—though still well below the 77 percent who described their *discipline* as "very important" to them (Boyer, *Scholarship Reconsidered,* 56). This moderate level of attachment to work on campus can be strengthened if we can move beyond the false dichotomy of department versus discipline. We need to understand the full extent to which the different phases of our academic life can work in synergy together, recognizing conversely that they undercut one another if we try to hold them too strictly apart, especially if we devalue half of what we do.

Strengthening collaboration both on and off campus would help to allay administrators' suspicion that faculty think poorly of working on campus with their colleagues and students and venture off campus to avoid them. I have heard of quite open expressions of this view on some college campuses, but there is only a difference of degree between colleges and universities in this as in many areas. My own university prides itself both on its commitment to research and on its cosmopolitanism, and yet our administrators have an odd way of letting slip from time to time their view—or awareness—that the faculty must be kept in line, lest they either do no work at all or else do so much off campus that no student can ever find them.

The most forthright expression of this view that I have encountered firsthand came, of all times, in the letter I received from the Secretary of the University when I was awarded tenure. This letter, embossed with the University seal in the school color, imparted two pieces of information: first, that the Secretary had the honor to inform me of my appointment; second, that this appointment was to be held, during the pleasure of the Trustees, under the terms noted within. The terms of appointment were expressed in two paragraphs.

The first informed me that "full-time service implies [a tactful term!] a program of teaching and scholarly research." The second paragraph was more emphatic:

> Except in the Faculties of Medicine and Dental and Oral Surgery, where appointments are for twelve months of service, any teaching assignment entails a period of residence of two terms totaling not more than nine months (less stated holidays), and including, if required, one week before and after each term. All absences during a period of residence must either be excused by the President or be taken on leave requested from the appropriate Dean.

Thus the tenured professor, that pinnacle of the university community, is also a kind of truant schoolchild, who must be sternly admonished not to wander off to the playground before recess begins. The administration has reasons for this double view, and not only because of cases such as the time the chair of one of our departments had to miss registration and the first week of classes in order to lecture on a cruise ship in the Mediterranean. Our institutional role is at issue here as much as the proclivities of any particular colleagues. If we can achieve a more integrated and collaborative sense of scholarly life, we can dismantle the false oppositions between on-campus ward heeling and off-campus work (or is it play), between our teaching and our "own" work, thereby reducing the structural schizophrenia of our professional lives.

What's an Administrator to Do?

One of the few truly positive effects of the current financial pressures on our academic institutions is the fact that faculty and administrators are beginning to talk to one another about systemwide issues. This is a welcome change from the norm during the past generation, well described thirty years ago by the sociologists Paul Lazarsfeld and Sam Sieber: "We are confronted nowadays, in our universities, with a very serious problem which may be called an 'academic power vacuum' . . . Academic freedom is more and more interpreted in such a way as to keep the administration out of any truly academic affairs;

the faculty, in turn, has come to consider administration beneath its dignity" (*Organizing Educational Research,* 13). Taken seriously, the sorts of strategic planning now under way on many campuses can go beyond considerations of health plans and the fate of schools of library science, and can become venues to set in motion broader changes in campus culture.

Ideally these changes would influence administrative as well as scholarly culture. Administrators themselves may not be entirely free of the problems entailed by the reigning scholarly ethos, partly because so many are current or former faculty members themselves. This background may lead them to accept scholarly values that should be questioned, even to reproduce them within their own sphere. Ten years ago, in a book on academic management, George Keller celebrated the newly reemerging administrative activism on many campuses, but he also noted that university presidents "often accept needless engagements or take peculiar trips rather than thrash out an issue thoroughly or pry a hard decision affecting the future of their campus out of their colleagues and aides" (*Academic Strategy,* 173). Administrators too may need to rethink the uses and abuses of conferences.

They can also play an active role in combatting the individualism of scholarly work. Too often, faculty research funds are distributed entirely on an individual basis; nothing actually prevents faculty from collaborating, but nothing actively encourages them to do so either. Funds specifically earmarked for collaborative work have, to my knowledge, come more often from foundations and governmental agencies than from campus administrations. For several years, for example, the National Endowment for the Humanities has had a program for collaborative research, although its funding is still a small fraction of the funding distributed to individual scholars. The Mellon Foundation for some time has provided funds for faculty seminars involving people from a variety of institutions in a given region. Yet such sources can reach only a small proportion of faculty in a limited number of our three thousand institutions of higher education. Colleges and universities themselves need to be much more active in promoting, and funding, such work.

The funds involved are not necessarily very large; even a relatively nominal amount, paying for refreshments, photocopying, and some travel costs, can make an enormous difference to the vitality of such a seminar. Equally, administrators should become much more active in sharing information, across disciplines and institutions, concerning creative forms of collaboration that have proved successful elsewhere. We do not necessarily need a new influx of faculty seminars in the mode of a miniconference, in which people gather to hear monthly talks by onetime guest speakers. Administrators and faculty alike should work together to develop more sustained collaborative projects and venues, and large numbers of participants should not be taken as a primary measure of success. Existing scholarship suggests that projects involving two to six people may be more fruitful than projects involving two or three dozen. Much more needs to be done to build contacts among faculty at different area institutions, so as to create the preconditions for such small-scale collaboration. More then needs to be done to support such collaborations, including summer travel funds and flexibility in sabbatical arrangements, to help different people coordinate their research time.

On their own campuses, administrators might also consider ways to help scholars attend to the differences in culture between small departments and fields as against large ones. The postwar growth of large campuses with more than ten thousand students has involved a concomitant increase in the numbers of faculty members working within large departments. Like small fields within disciplines, small departments may have little visibility on campus, yet they exhibit both the best and the worst features of academic culture. At their best, they can form a genuine community, and their faculty often still make a real effort to read scholarship in a variety of disciplines relating to their area of interest. Further, the relatively small output of scholarship in fields like Egyptology and Icelandic studies allows scholars to carry out this intention with some thoroughness. People in larger departments and fields have often simply thrown up their hands before the numbers of people and books they would have to deal with, but the example of the genuine interdisciplinary work often done by medievalists and Mesoamericanists could inspire people in larger fields to make new efforts to do more serious work across fields and disciplines.

Conversely, smaller fields and departments too often accept and even reinforce their own Balkanization, priding themselves on staying out of the "faddism"—that is to say, current discussion—in the larger fields, and jealously guarding their control over their already small number of students. Administrators can do much to combat the isolation and mutual disregard that often grow up between small and large departments, by encouraging joint appointments, finding ways to keep small departments from suffering if their students register for courses in other departments, and encouraging team teaching across departmental lines.

Teaching itself, properly conceived, is a learning experience for faculty as well as for students, and it is one in which administrations have a great deal of say. As Kenneth Boulding has rightly remarked, "there should be a principle of university administration that if you take care of the education of the faculty, the education of the students will take care of itself. Unfortunately, there are very few administrations that give a high priority to this principle, and the education of the faculty is left almost entirely to its own initiative." He proposes that although sabbaticals are all very well for individual faculty projects, administrations should do much more "to promote the education of the faculty by each other" through team teaching ("Graduate Education as Ritual and Substance," 149).

All in all, it is high time for us to get to work to break down the severity of the antinomy between faculty and administration, an antinomy that has too often been a matter of pride and mutual resentment, when it should be a matter of regret and mutual effort to overcome it. At my own institution, the story still circulates of the dramatic confrontation at a faculty meeting in the 1950s, when Dwight D. Eisenhower was president of Columbia. Faced with faculty resistance to an administration proposal, Eisenhower expressed his expectation that "the employees of the university" would adopt the proposal. At this, a senior faculty member rose to declare, "Sir, the faculty *are* the university!" If the choice is between administrative condescension and professorial hubris, we need some better choices. A collaborative perspective will really have begun to take hold when faculty and administrators learn how to learn from one another.

Scholars in Society

Better patterns of interaction are thus needed at all levels of campus work. There is reason to expect that scholarly perspectives could be improved in the process. Over the years, sporadic complaints have been lodged in a variety of fields—economics, psychology, political science, history, and literature among them—that academic writing presupposes an exaggerated individualism in society at large. Feminist literary scholars, for example, have begun to criticize what they see as a male-oriented emphasis on the lone hero, hostile to his culture, who must break free of the maternal home and strike out on his own. They have argued that such an emphasis distorts the analysis of many works, and in particular causes a systematic undervaluation of writing (often by women) that focuses on the protagonists' ties to society, culture, and home. Economists, meanwhile, commonly continue to employ the "rational choice" model of economic behavior, in which society is assumed to operate as the sum of individual decisions, each individual working out what is rationally—self-interestedly—the best choice; versions of this model are widely assumed in political science as well. Local studies may challenge such assumptions, but somehow the paradigm soon resurfaces. Society as a whole is imagined as the individual mind writ large.

Mary Douglas proposes that we reverse this analogy and think of the individual mind as "society writ small" (45). She argues that such a perspective is needed to overcome the common inability of political scientists and economists to deal meaningfully with collective action and group solidarity. She quotes a similar complaint from a pair of psychologists in 1981: "We have lost sight of the collective nature of attitudes because attitudes have been impounded by social psychology . . . Recent developments in attitude research and scaling techniques have led to a complete individualization of the study of attitude" (Jaspers and Frazer, "Attitudes and Social Representations," quoted on 82). Douglas comments: "There must be hundreds of such isolated complaints, insights, and independent discoveries. They have been doomed" (82). She argues that our difficulty in redressing such imbalances stems from our neglect of the role of institutions in society, especially the positive roles they play. In the concluding pages of her book, she argues powerfully that talking about reforms on an individual level is insufficient:

> Preaching against wife battering and child abuse is not more likely to be effective than preaching against alcohol and drug abuse, racism, or sexism. Only changing institutions can help

> . . . Once it were conceded that legitimated institutions make
> the big decisions, much else would be changed. Psychologists
> would not be able to claim that this extension of cognitive func-
> tions is a trivial matter, to be left unstudied in favor of children's
> uncultured perceptual and moral growth. Once it were con-
> ceded that the big decisions always engage ethical principles,
> then philosophers would not focus single-mindedly on individ-
> ual moral dilemmas . . . A theory of justice has to be balanced
> between theories of human agency, on the one hand, and theo-
> ries of community on the other.   (126)

As the son of two generations of preachers, I am hardly averse to
preaching against social ills: what is Douglas' book—or this one—
if not a kind of secular sermon? The point is that such sermons need
to take institutions into account, both as important subject matter
and as a crucial staging ground for reform.

In part, Douglas is pleading for a wider recognition in other fields
of the special expertise of her own discipline, anthropology, in studying cultural institutions. From the perspective of the present argument we can go further, to suggest that there is a rather specific
institutional reason why such insights have so often been neglected:
the academics who somehow cannot keep their minds on the influence of institutions are *by this very fact* showing the clearest influence
of our own institutional environment, with its pervasive, archaic
hyperindividualism. Breathing such an atmosphere, whose very nature is to render itself as invisible as the supposedly rarified air we
breathe, is it any wonder that we project its assumptions onto the
society around us?

I began this book by arguing that we should not see the university
as simply a microcosm of society; it is even stranger to treat society
as some colonial extension of the university. We are caught in a paradoxical and unhealthy double bind: at once imagining ourselves as
alienated exiles from society at large and yet also continually trying
to recreate society in our own image. We would do better to open
our modes of work to incorporate a more contemporary political
economy, while striving for a livelier sense of the real differences
that will persist between our "partially autonomous subsystem" and
the society around us.

These changes can pave the way for a more dynamic and more

fruitful relation between scholarship and other forms of intellectual work. The rift between them has been widely discussed in recent years. Russell Jacoby has gone so far as to claim that broad movements of suburbanization and urban decay have deprived us of the very space in which public discourse can flourish—inexpensive and congenial urban environments like the Greenwich Village of an earlier era, in which a critical mass of intellectuals could gather, debate public issues, and write of them in publicly accessible prose. As these neighborhoods first declined and then gentrified, intellectuals retreated to the enclosed spaces of campuses, and their writing in turn dried out: "a prose desert, certain death for anyone unprepared for an extreme academic environment" (*The Last Intellectuals*, 56).

In one of contemporary history's small ironies, the same year Jacoby's book was published also saw the first of an unbroken series of widely read books by professors on issues of simultaneously academic and public interest, beginning with Allan Bloom's *The Closing of the American Mind* and soon followed by—to name only a few—E. D. Hirsch's *Cultural Literacy*, Harold Bloom's *The Book of J*, Paul Kennedy's *The Rise and Fall of the Great Powers* and *Preparing for the Twenty-first Century*, Deborah Tannen's *You Just Don't Understand*, Stephen Carter's *Reflections of an Affirmative Action Baby* and *The Culture of Disbelief*, and doctoral student Katie Roiphe's *The Morning After*.

In some ways, then, the problem can hardly be as drastic as Jacoby supposed, particularly as campus environments reproduce most of the sociological features he emphasizes in the Village of the 1940s and 1950s: clusters of people interested in ideas and skeptical of social commonplaces, plenty of cheap cafés, flexible schedules that leave time to frequent them, even the group solidarity that comes from a certain stylish raffishness. ("I wanted to be a literature major," the line went at Yale a few years ago, "but I couldn't afford the wardrobe.") All these preconditions, of course, have little force if people do not actually learn from one another, but academics are not alone in this difficulty.

Jacoby himself, great proponent of public intellectual life, holds to a university-style individualism that infuses his book. He sees no contradiction when he defines the public intellectual as "an incorrigibly independent soul answering to no one" who is supposed at the same time to be committed to "a public language, the vernacular"

(235). This perspective reappears throughout Jacoby's book, as when he sees the rise of jointly written sociological articles as prima facie evidence of intellectual decline (158). Even a scholar's simple generosity to others puts him off: "Sennett is a New York intellectual without the caustic intelligence that marked the species; rather he nods to and compliments everyone he encounters. The warm collegiality that flows through his books douses the spark of ideas" (212). No doubt collegiality can overheat, but Jacoby does not pause to show this; collegiality in and of itself seems to have a baleful effect.

I almost hesitate to lower myself in Jacoby's estimation by praising his book, and yet it is admirable in its sociological emphasis—rarely addressed in subsequent discussions of his argument—and in its own warm evocation of at least a disputatious mode of intensive intellectual exchange. For my part, I think there is already enough polemical antagonism at play both on and off our campuses; debaters in the public sphere divide as readily as academics into opposing camps who, like Tannen's men and women, just don't understand what the other side is saying. More positively, the best-sellers I have mentioned show a healthy movement toward a constructive engagement between academics and other intellectuals.

This engagement is made both more possible and more necessary by the fact that the growing complexity of society at large is undercutting the very distinction between "academic" and "intellectual" questions. This distinction looked quite clear to Christopher Jencks and David Riesman twenty-five years ago:

> We have used the term "academic" to describe a professional guild and its activities. An academic question is therefore one raised by some lacuna or ambiguity in the data or interpretations of a world-wide discipline. It is a question asked by one's colleagues or on their behalf and answered primarily as a service to these colleagues. The term "intellectual" refers to an amateur role . . . Intellectual questions grow out of reflection on experience, are asked by all sorts and conditions of men, and are answered, insofar as they can be answered, in ways that make sense to such men. (*The Academic Revolution*, 242–243)

Jencks and Riesman allow that intellectual debate and academic inquiry should ideally exist in "creative symbiosis," but they stress the

essential difference between the two activities. Thus, "only an exceptional scholar would say that his life style—or even his voting behavior—could conceivably be altered by his research findings" (243).
Differences in culture and orientation certainly persist, and yet surely
these cultures overlap much more these days than such clear distinctions would suggest, partly because the social composition of faculties is beginning to resemble that of society as a whole in new ways;
the faculty itself is now likely to contain more "sorts and conditions
of men," notably many more people from a greater range of ethnic
backgrounds and more women, and these newly arrived scholars are
often trying precisely to alter life styles and even voting behavior by
their scholarship.

The differences in motive and audience of which Jencks and Riesman speak have their equivalent in a division that Jacoby makes between genres: "café society gives rise to aphorism and essay; the college campus yields the monograph and lecture—and the grant
application" (31). These generic lines too are blurring. On the one
hand, my friends in SoHo and TriBeCa seem to spend as much time
writing grant applications as my colleagues on campus do; on the
other hand, a wide range of writing is now located somewhere on a
continuum in between the aphoristic essay and the academic monograph. Or better: more and more writing now combines pronounced
elements of both ends of the continuum.

Such a process of overlay creates the conditions for a dynamic
interchange between public and academic concerns, a dynamism that
was present at the turn of the century when academic life was achieving its modern form in dialogue with the society of its time. If we
can create a contemporary academic culture that is as intellectually
open as it is becoming socially varied, the next intellectuals can carry
much further the interfusion of modes of inquiry, whatever their
place of work. Academics and "public" intellectuals are already beginning to engage one another more closely, though still with a
somewhat quizzical regard, well expressed from a nonacademic perspective by Barbara Ehrenreich:

> Sometimes I envy my friends in academia because they get paid
> *even if they don't think of something new,* even if they teach the
> same thing over and over for months at a time. But, like most

free-lancers I know, I am congenitally incapable of specialization . . . The important thing, to me, is being a *political* intellectual: trying to "shift the discourse" through every available medium and, equally important, keeping in touch with all kinds
of streams of protest and dissent so as to know what's important
to say. And I would really emphasize the latter because of the
class insularity of so much intellectual culture.   ("The Professional-Managerial Class Revisited," 177–178)

The next intellectuals already exist in growing numbers; they include
general-interest writers like Ehrenreich who are willing to pay serious attention to those specialists who have a congenital (or acquired)
capacity to stay with an area for a long period of time, and they
include academic specialists who resist the insularity of their disciplinary culture, attending to differing kinds of voices in their own
fields, in neighboring fields, and off campus altogether, always asking
themselves what is really important to say.

Modern debate concerning the proper role of academia has often
focused on the contrast between an economy of production and an
economy of conservation. We need not choose between these alternatives; our colleges and universities obviously transmit our cultural
heritage and produce knowledge at the same time—not only new
information but also new ways of looking at the transmitted culture
itself. Perhaps there is a missing term, though; in our contemporary
"postindustrial" economy, we need a strengthened *economy of circulation*. The explosion of knowledge threatens to become an *implosion*
of knowledge, into ever more densely crowded databases and hard
disks, black holes we enter at the risk of never returning to public
view. If we are not to retreat within the sheltering confines of the
nearest disciplinary or ideological coterie, we need to coordinate and
share knowledge better, and to listen more attentively to people with
whom we do not already agree. New ideas must be circulated with
greater care than they often are now, if they are not to lose their
specificity or get lost in the shuffle altogether. Equally, the press of
new knowledge should not be allowed simply to drive out what is
already known; historical diversity is as valuable as modern cultural
diversity, and our American culture has always been prone to particularly rapid processes of forgetting.

Too often, like Charles Eliot Norton ninety years ago, American scholars still hold fast to a hermeneutics of exile, using their specialized knowledge to dwell in a distant time or an esoteric disciplinary space, returning periodically like Rip Van Winkle from his inaccessible mountain retreat—his spouse now safely deceased—to tell the forgetful villagers what life was like in the distant past, twenty years before. We scholars rightly cherish our independence of mind and our originality of perspective, but we need to balance the hermeneutics of exile with a more creative hermeneutics of community.

The intellectual tension between withdrawal and community must periodically be addressed anew, although it is as old as scholarship itself. The tale of Rip Van Winkle, in fact, has an ancient antecedent in a story about a scholar. The story concerns Honi the Circle-drawer, subject of some striking passages in the Talmud and midrash. What turns him into the first Rip Van Winkle is his inability to understand a metaphor in a psalm of David, appropriately concerning the community's return to Israel after seventy years in exile in Babylon. In the *Midrash on Psalms* (126:1), we are told of Honi's difficulties with this verse; apparently, he refuses to accept the interpretations of it given by any of his rabbinical colleagues—and these were rabbis who prided themselves on their ability to offer seventy interpretations for any passage in scripture. It may be noted that this tale itself has been collaboratively created, its plot furnished by one rabbi and its crucial moral adduced by another. The individualism of the modern cry "Give *me* liberty or give me death" is here countered with a double emphasis on the intellectual and social communities, one that we would do well to ponder today. It seems fitting, then, to give the last word to this early manifesto for scholarly community:

> "When the Lord brought back those that returned to Zion, we were like those who dream." Rabbi Johanan said: All the years of his life, Honi, that man renowned for righteousness, was troubled about this verse. He said: "Is it possible for a man to lie sleeping for seventy years?" One day, while Honi was walking along the road, he saw a man planting a carob-tree. Honi asked: "Tell me now—in how many years will the carob-tree bear fruit?" The man replied: "Seventy years." Said Honi: "Are you sure that you will live for seventy years more?" The man replied:

"Me, I found carob-trees already planted in the earth. And so, like my fathers who planted carob-trees for me, I plant carob-trees for my children."

Then Honi sat down to eat, and sleep came upon him. As he slept, a hedge grew up around Honi and concealed him from human eyes, and so he slept on for seventy years. When Honi awoke, he saw a man gathering fruit from the carob-tree, and he asked: "Are you the man who planted it?" And when the man replied: "I am the son of his son," Honi said to himself: "This seems to prove that it is possible to sleep for seventy years." And when he saw his ass which by this time had borne many mules, Honi said: "Now it is certain that I have been asleep for seventy years."

Honi went to his house, and said: "I am Honi the Circle-drawer," but his household did not believe him. He went to the house of study, and heard the rabbis say: "This tradition is as clear to us as it was in the days of Honi the Circle-drawer,"—for whenever he had come to the house of study, he had solved for the rabbis every moot point they had—and he said: "I am Honi." But they did not believe him and did not give him the honor that was due him. Full of despair, he asked for the Lord's mercy, and his soul went to its rest.

Rabba declared: People rightly say, "Either fellowship or death."

Bibliography
Index

Bibliography

Adams, Hazard. *The Academic Tribes*. 2d ed. Urbana: University of Illinois Press, 1988.

Anderson, Martin. *Impostors in the Temple: American Intellectuals Are Destroying Our Universities and Cheating Our Students of Their Future*. New York: Simon & Schuster, 1992.

Augustine. *On Christian Doctrine*. Translated by D. W. Robertson. New York: Liberal Arts Press, 1958.

Bagg, Lyman. *Four Years at Yale*. New Haven: Chatfield, 1981.

Baldridge, J. Victor. *Power and Conflict in the University: Research in the Sociology of Complex Organizations*. New York: John Wiley & Sons, 1971.

Barzun, Jacques. *The American University: How It Runs, Where It Is Going*. New York: Harper & Row, 1968.

Bateson, Mary Catherine. *Our Own Metaphor: A Personal Account of a Conference on the Effects of Conscious Purpose on Human Adaptation*. New York: Alfred A. Knopf, 1972.

Baum, L. Frank. *The Wonderful Wizard of Oz*. Chicago: G. M. Hill, 1900.

Beerbohm, Max, "Diminuendo." In *The Incomparable Max: A Selection*. Edited by S. C. Roberts. London: Heinemann, 1962, 59–66.

Bell, Daniel. *The Reforming of General Education: The Columbia College Experience in Its National Setting*. New York: Columbia University Press, 1966.

Bellah, Robert N., et al. *Habits of the Heart: Individualism and Commitment in American Life*. Berkeley: University of California Press, 1985.

Bender, Thomas. "The Erosion of Public Culture: Cities, Discourses, and Professional Disciplines." In Thomas Haskell, ed., *The Authority of Experts: Studies in History and Theory*. Bloomington: Indiana University Press, 1984, 84–106. Reprinted in *Intellect and Public Life*.

———*Intellect and Public Life: Essays on the Social History of Academic Intellectuals in the United States*. Baltimore: Johns Hopkins University Press, 1993.

Berelson, Bernard. *Graduate Education in the United States*. New York: McGraw-Hill, 1960.

Bess, James L., ed. *College and University Organization: Insights from the Behavioral Sciences*. New York: New York University Press, 1984.

Blau, Peter M. *The Organization of Academic Work*. New York: John Wiley & Sons, 1973.

Bloom, Allan. *The Closing of the American Mind: How Higher Education Has Failed Democracy and Impoverished the Souls of Today's Students*. Foreword by Saul Bellow. New York: Simon & Schuster, 1987.

———*Giants and Dwarfs: Essays 1960–1990*. New York: Simon & Schuster, 1990.

Bok, Derek. *Higher Learning*. Cambridge, Mass.: Harvard University Press, 1986.

———*Universities and the Future of America*. Durham: Duke University Press, 1990.

Boulding, Kenneth E. "Graduate Education as Ritual and Substance." In William K. Frankena, ed., *The Philosophy and Future of Graduate Education*. Ann Arbor: University of Michigan Press, 1980, 143–154.

Bowen, William G., and Julie Ann Sosa. *Prospects for Faculty in the Arts and Sciences*. Princeton: Princeton University Press, 1989.

Bowen, William G., and Neil L. Rudenstine, in collaboration with Julie Ann Sosa, Graham Lord, Marcia L. Witte, and Sarah E. Turner. *In Pursuit of the Ph.D.* Princeton: Princeton University Press, 1992.

Boyer, Ernest L. *Scholarship Reconsidered: Priorities of the Professoriate*. Special Report of the Carnegie Foundation for the Advancement of Teaching. Princeton: Carnegie Foundation, 1990.

Bromwich, David. *Politics by Other Means: Higher Education and Group Thinking*. New Haven: Yale University Press, 1992.

Bruffee, Kenneth A. *Collaborative Learning: Higher Education, Interdependence, and the Authority of Knowledge*. Baltimore: Johns Hopkins University Press, 1993.

Cain, William E. "English in America Reconsidered: Theory, Marxism, and Social Change." In Gerald Graff and R. Gibbons, eds., *Criticism in the University*. Evanston: Northwestern University Press, 1985, 85–104.

Campbell, Donald. "A Tribal Model of the Social System Vehicle Carrying Scientific Knowledge." *Knowledge: Creation, Diffusion, Utilization* 1 (1979):181–201.

Carnegie Council on Policy Studies in Higher Education. *Three Thousand Futures: The Next Twenty Years for Higher Education*. San Francisco: Jossey-Bass, 1980.

Chiseri-Strater, Elizabeth. *Academic Literacies: The Public and Private Discourse of University Students*. New York: Boynton/Cook, 1990.

Clark, Burton R., ed. *The Academic Profession: National, Disciplinary, and Institutional Settings*. Berkeley: University of California Press, 1987.

Cohen, Michael D., and James G. March. *Leadership and Ambiguity: The American College President*. New York: McGraw-Hill, 1974.

Cohen, Michael D., James G. March, and Johan Olsen. "A Garbage Can Model of Organizational Choice." *Administrative Science Quarterly* 17 (1972):1–25.

Cornford, F. M. *Microcosmographia Academica*. 5th ed. Cambridge: Bowes and Bowes, 1954.

Dewey, John. *Democracy and Education: An Introduction to the Philosophy of Education*. 1916. New York: Free Press, 1944.

Douglas, Mary. *How Institutions Think*. Syracuse: Syracuse University Press, 1986.

D'Souza, Dinesh. *Illiberal Education: The Politics of Race and Sex on Campus*. New York: Random House, 1992.

Earnest, Ernest. *Academic Procession: An Informal History of the American College, 1636–1953*. New York: Bobbs, Merrill, 1953.

Ehrenreich, Barbara. "The Professional-Managerial Class Revisited." In Bruce Robbins, ed., *Intellectuals: Aesthetics, Politics, Academics*. Minneapolis: University of Minnesota Press, 1990, 173–185.

Erasmus, Desiderius. "Paracelsis: Or, An Exhortation." In *The Praise of Folly and Other Writings*. Edited and translated by Robert M. Adams. New York: W. W. Norton, 1989.

Flexner, Abraham. *Universities, American, English, German*. New York: Oxford University Press, 1930.

Frye, Northrop. *Anatomy of Criticism: Four Essays*. Princeton: Princeton University Press, 1957.

Gabelnick, Faith, Jean MacGregor, Roberta S. Matthews, and Barbara Leigh Smith. *Learning Communities: Creating Connections among Students, Faculty, and Disciplines*. San Francisco: Jossey-Bass, 1990.

Getman, Julius. *In the Company of Scholars: The Struggle for the Soul of Higher Education*. Austin: University of Texas Press, 1992.

Graff, Gerald. *Beyond the Culture Wars: How Teaching the Conflicts Can Revitalize American Education*. New York: W. W. Norton, 1992.

———*Professing Literature: An Institutional History*. Chicago: University of Chicago Press, 1987.

Graff, Gerald, and Reginald Gibbons, eds. *Criticism in the University*. Triquarterly Series on Criticism and Culture, no. 1. Evanston: Northwestern University Press, 1985.

Graff, Gerald, and Michael Warner, eds. *The Origins of Literary Studies in America: A Documentary Anthology*. New York: Routledge, 1989.

Gross, Edward. "Universities as Organizations: A Research Approach." *American Sociological Review* 33 (1968):518–544.

Halevi, Judah. *The Kuzari (Kitab al Khazari): An Argument for the Faith of Israel*. Translated by Hartwig Hirschfeld. New York: Schocken, 1964.

Hardy, Cynthia, Ann Langley, Henry Mintzberg, and Janet Rose. "Strategy Formation in the University Setting." In James L. Bess, ed., *College and University Organization: Insights from the Behavioral Sciences*. New York: New York University Press, 1984, 169–210.

Hardy, Thomas. *Jude the Obscure*. New York: New American Library, 1961.

Harrison, G. B. *Profession of English*. Garden City, N.Y.: Anchor Books, 1967.

Haskell, Thomas, ed. *The Authority of Experts: Studies in History and Theory*. Bloomington: Indiana University Press, 1984.

———*The Emergence of Professional Social Science: The American Social Science Association and the Nineteenth-Century Crisis of Authority*. Urbana: University of Illinois Press, 1977.

———"Professionalism *versus* Capitalism: R. H. Tawney, Emile Durkheim, and C. S. Peirce on the Disinterestedness of Professional Communities." In *The Authority of Experts*, 180–225.

Hirsch, E. D. *Cultural Literacy: What Every American Needs to Know*. New York: Random House, 1988.

Hodgkinson, Harold L. *Institutions in Transition: A Profile of Change in Higher Education (Incorporating the 1970 Statistical Report)*. New York: McGraw-Hill, 1971.

Horowitz, Helen Lefkowitz. *Campus Life: Undergraduate Cultures from the End of the Eighteenth Century to the Present*. Chicago: University of Chicago Press, 1987.

Ingalls, Daniel H. H., Jeffrey Moussaieff Masson, and M. V. Patwardhan. *The Dhvanyaloka of Anandavardhana with the Locana of Abhinavagupta*. Harvard Oriental Series 49. Cambridge, Mass.: Harvard University Press, 1990.

Jacks, Penelope, Daryl E. Chubin, Alan L. Porter, and Terry Connolly. "The ABCs of ABDs: A Study of Incomplete Doctorates." *Improving College and University Teaching* 31, no. 2 (1983):74–81.

Jacoby, Russell. *The Last Intellectuals: American Culture in the Age of Academe*. New York: Farrar, Straus and Giroux, 1987.

James, Henry. "An American Art-Scholar: Charles Eliot Norton." In *Notes on Novelists*. New York: Scribners, 1914, 412–423.

James, William. "The Ph.D. Octopus." *Harvard Monthly* 36 (1903):1–9.

Jaspers, J. M. F., and C. Frazer. "Attitudes and Social Representations." In S. Moscovici and R. Farr, eds., *Social Representations*. Cambridge: Cambridge University Press, 1981.

Jencks, Christopher, and David Riesman. *The Academic Revolution*. 3d ed. Foreword by Martin Trow. Chicago: University of Chicago Press, 1977.

Keller, George. *Academic Strategy: The Management Revolution in American Higher Education*. Baltimore: Johns Hopkins University Press, 1983.

Kerr, Clark. *The Great Transformation in Higher Education, 1960–1980*. Albany: State University of New York Press, 1991.

————*The Uses of the University*. 3d ed. Cambridge, Mass.: Harvard University Press, 1982.

Kierkegaard, Søren. *The Concept of Irony: With Constant Reference to Socrates*. Translated by Lee M. Capel. Bloomington: Indiana University Press, 1968.

Kimball, Roger. *Tenured Radicals: How Politics Has Corrupted Our Higher Education*. New York: HarperPerennial, 1991.

Lazarsfeld, Paul, and Sam Sieber. *Organizing Educational Research*. Englewood Cliffs, N.J.: Prentice-Hall, 1964.

Lentricchia, Frank. "On Behalf of Theory." In Gerald Graff and R. Gibbons, eds., *Criticism in the University*. Evanston: Northwestern University Press, 1985, 105–110.

Levine, Arthur. *Why Innovation Fails: The Institutionalization and Termination of Innovation in Higher Education*. Albany: State University of New York Press, 1980.

Light, Donald. "Surface Data and Deep Structure: Observing the Organization of Professional Training." *Administrative Science Quarterly* 24 (1979):551–559.

Lodge, David. *Small World*. New York: Warner Books, 1984.

Lutz, Frank W. "Tightening Up Loose Coupling in Organizations of Higher Education." *Administrative Science Quarterly* 27 (1982):653–669.

Mead, Margaret. "Conference Arrangements." In W. Warner Burke and Richard Beckhard, eds., *Conference Planning*. 2d ed. La Jolla: University Associates, 1976, 45–61.

Midrash on Psalms (Midrash Tehillim). Edited by William Braude. 2 vols. Yale Judaica Series 13. New Haven: Yale University Press, 1959.

Minnich, Elizabeth, Jean O'Barr, and Rachel Rosenfeld, eds. *Reconstructing the Acad-*

emy: Women's Education and Women's Studies. Chicago: University of Chicago Press, 1988.

Newman, John Henry. *The Idea of a University Defined and Illustrated.* Edited by I. T. Ker. Oxford: Clarendon, 1976.

Nietzsche, Friedrich. "We Scholars." Chapter 6 of *Beyond Good and Evil.* Translated by Helen Zimmern. In Willard Huntington Wright, ed., *The Philosophy of Nietzsche.* New York: Modern Library, 1954, 498–519.

Norton, Charles Eliot. "The Intellectual Life of America." *New Princeton Review* 6 (1888):312–324.

——"Some Aspects of Civilization in America." *The Forum,* Feb. 1896, 641–651.

The Norton Anthology of English Literature. Edited by M. H. Abrams et al. 6th ed. 2 vols. New York: W. W. Norton, 1993.

O'Toole, Simon. *Confessions of an American Scholar.* Minneapolis: University of Minnesota Press, 1970.

Pelikan, Jaroslav. *The Idea of the University: A Reexamination.* New Haven: Yale University Press, 1992.

Riesman, David. *On Higher Education: The Academic Enterprise in an Era of Rising Student Consumerism.* San Francisco: Jossey-Bass, 1980.

Robbins, Bruce, ed. *Intellectuals: Aesthetics, Politics, Academics.* Minneapolis: University of Minnesota Press, 1990.

——*The Phantom Public Sphere.* Minneapolis: University of Minnesota Press, 1993.

——*Secular Vocations: Intellectuals, Professionalism, Culture.* London: Verso, 1993.

Rosovsky, Henry. *The University: An Owner's Manual.* New York: W. W. Norton, 1990.

Ruscio, Kenneth P. "Many Sectors, Many Professions." In Burton R. Clark, ed., *The Academic Profession: National, Disciplinary, and Institutional Settings.* Berkeley: University of California Press, 1987, 331–368.

Santayana, George. *Persons and Places: Fragments of Autobiography.* Edited by William G. Holzberger and Herman J. Saetcamp, Jr. Cambridge, Mass.: MIT Press, 1986.

Silk, M. S., and J. P. Stern. *Nietzsche on Tragedy.* Cambridge: Cambridge University Press, 1981.

Slavin, Richard E. *Cooperative Learning.* New York: Longman, 1983.

Smith, Page. *Killing the Spirit: Higher Education in America.* New York: Penguin, 1991.

Snow, C. P. *The Two Cultures; and, A Second Look: An Expanded Version of "The Two Cultures and the Scientific Revolution."* London: Cambridge University Press, 1969.

Statistical Abstract of the United States. Washington, D.C.: Government Printing Office, 1991.

Sykes, Charles J. *Profscam: Professors and the Demise of Higher Education.* Washington, D.C.: Regnery Gateway, 1988.

Tannen, Deborah. *You Just Don't Understand: Women and Men in Conversation.* New York: Morrow, 1990.

Trilling, Lionel. "English Literature and American Education." *Sewanee Review* 66 (1958):364–381.

——*Sincerity and Authenticity*. The Charles Eliot Norton Lectures, 1969–1970. Cambridge, Mass.: Harvard University Press, 1972.

——"The Uncertain Future of the Humanistic Ideal." In *The Last Decade: Essays and Reviews, 1965–1975*. Edited by Diana Trilling. New York: Harcourt Brace Jovanovich, 1979, 160–176.

Urquhart, Brian. "Address by Sir Brian Urquhart . . . November 3, 1989." In Theodore R. Giuttari, ed., *Proceedings and Committee Reports of the American Branch of the International Law Association, 1989–1990*. New York: International Law Association, 1990, 45–49.

——*A Life in Peace and War*. New York: Harper & Row, 1987.

Urquhart, Brian, and Erskine Childers. *Towards a More Effective United Nations*. Uppsala: Dag Hammarskjöld Foundation, 1992.

Vanderbilt, Kermit. *Charles Eliot Norton: Apostle of Culture in a Democracy*. Cambridge, Mass.: Harvard University Press, 1959.

Van Maanen, John. "Doing New Things in Old Ways: The Chains of Socialization." In James L. Bess, ed., *College and University Organization: Insights from the Behavioral Sciences*. New York: New York University Press, 1984, 211–247.

Veblen, Thorstein. *The Higher Learning in America: A Memorandum on the Conduct of Universities*. New York: B. W. Huebsch, 1918.

Veysey, Laurence R. *The Emergence of the American University*. Chicago: University of Chicago Press, 1965.

Watkins, Evan. *Work Time: English Departments and the Circulation of Cultural Value*. Stanford: Stanford University Press, 1989.

Wax, Murray L. "Myth and Interrelationship in Social Science: Illustrated through Anthropology and Sociology." In Muzafer Sherif and Carolyn W. Sherif, eds., *Interdisciplinary Relationships in the Social Sciences*. Chicago: Aldine, 1969.

Weick, Karl. "Contradictions in a Community of Scholars: The Cohesion-Accuracy Tradeoff." In James L. Bess, ed., *College and University Organization: Insights from the Behavioral Sciences*. New York: New York University Press, 1984, 15–29.

——"Educational Organizations as Loosely Coupled Systems." *Administrative Science Quarterly* 21 (1976):1–19.

Wellek, René, and Austin Warren. *Theory of Literature*. 3d ed. New York: Harcourt, Brace & World, 1956.

Woolf, Virginia. *A Room of One's Own* (1928). New York: Harcourt Brace Jovanovich, 1957.

Ziolkowski, Theodore. "The Ph.D. Squid." *American Scholar* 59 (1990):177–195.

Index

God, Kids, & Us

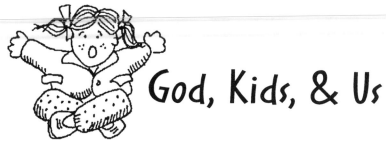

God, Kids, & Us

The growing edge of ministry with children and the people who care for them

Janet Marshall Eibner & Susan Graham Walker

MOREHOUSE PUBLISHING

Published 1996 by Anglican Book Centre, Toronto, and United Church Publishing House, Ontario

U.S./Episcopal edition published 1997 by

Morehouse Publishing
P.O. Box 1321
Harrisburg, PA 17105

Morehouse Publishing is a division of the Morehouse Group.

Cover illustration: Michael Engel
Design and spot illustrations: Saskia Rowley

Grateful acknowledgement is made for permission to reprint excerpts from the following copyrighted works:

DOONESBURY copyright 1994 G. B. Trudeau. Reprinted with permission of UNIVERSAL PRESS SYNDICATE. All rights reserved.

"Lebanese-Syrian Mass Bread," reprinted from *Living Bread: Recipes for Home-baked Breads for the Eucharist and for the Fellowship and Family Tables* by Christine Whitehorn Stugard © 1983 Forward Movement Publications, 412 Sycamore Street, Cincinnati, Ohio 45202 USA. Used with permission.

"Sunday School, Circa 1950" from REVOLUTIONARY PETUNIAS & OTHER POEMS, copyright © 1970 by Alice Walker, reprinted by permission of Harcourt Brace & Company.

"Lord it is night"; this copyrighted material is taken from *A New Zealand Prayer Book—He Karakia Mihinare o Aotearoa* and is used with permission.

"The Lutheran Baptismal Covenant," a portion of the Baptismal Covenant, is reprinted from LUTHERAN BOOK OF WORSHIP, copyright © 1978, by permission of Augsburg Fortress.

A catalog record for this book is available from the Library of Congress.

For

Paul, Caroline, and Mark

Ralph, Meghan, and Juliane

Contents

Acknowledgements

In February 1991 about a dozen members of the Diocese of Toronto Children's Unit drove north of Toronto to the Hockley Hills Mansfield Education Centre for a snowy weekend of writing, talking, and eating. One member brought four Macintosh computers from his school. After a party on the Friday evening, we set about writing a resource called *God, Kids, & Us*.

Members of the unit, past and present, had been asking for a manual for church school superintendents — or at least for a compilation of the resources brought to parish consultations and to the annual Children's Unit conference, God, Kids, & Us — and a working group had already outlined chapters. At that time Susan was job-sharing the position of Children's Ministry consultant with Cheryl Kristolaitis; but before the actual writing began, Cheryl assumed new responsibilities in another diocese and Janet replaced her.

The project was our initiation as a new team sharing the Children's Ministry consultant position.

We gathered groups of three or four people around the computers. Ideas were organized and fleshed out, questions were asked, helpful resources were named. We switched spots and made comments, added more information, or noted questions. Eventually everyone had read everything, commented on everything, and left everything on a disk for us to edit into the manual. At last, with the help of our assistant, Janet Taylor, the manual circulated. However, with each new project or consultation there was something to be added.

In the relatively few years we have been in this ministry, we have realized the legacy of generations of people deeply interested in sharing the unique story of God's love for us through Jesus Christ. The stories are told and retold, illustrated and highlighted in many ways. We are always searching for new ways to pass on the Good News. These ways often turn out to be old ways! This is a round-about manner of saying that *God, Kids, & Us* has grown. While we believe that the ideas as expressed in these pages are our own, we acknowledge that many have contributed to their formation — communities we have worshipped with, lived in, worked with, and colleagues in this ministry in our diocese and in the national network of those with a passion for the inclusion of children in the life of the church. Ideas are new to new people, and often the best ones are recycled and revitalized for a new generation of children and those who work with them.

Among the many enthusiasts we have worked with, we would like especially to acknowledge the invaluable contributions of Janet Metcalfe, Bruce Carmody, Marion Jenkins, Douglas Cowling, Gwynne Barker, and Saskia Rowley.

One last note: the stories in this book are true and come from our own experience in ministry with children — our own and others!

Janet Marshall Eibner
Susan Graham Walker
January 17, 1996

Introduction

How can we know God really exists?

Why, if God wants us to be good, is it so easy to be bad?

How come everything in church is always like kindergarten?

Welcome to *God, Kids, & Us*, a collection of thoughts, opinions, experiences, resources, work sheets, and stories gathered through our job-sharing partnership as program consultants in children's ministry for the Anglican Diocese of Toronto. Through our association with the diocese, we have been blessed by the many communities who have invited us to journey for a while with them as they explore, challenge, and create ministries for and with the children in their midst. This ministry has been enlivened by a small group of dedicated volunteers, the members of the Children's Unit, who have shared with us and with the diocese a passion for ministry with children and those who care for them.

Our work as program consultants falls into two broad categories. We respond to requests from congregations; small groups; and individuals, clergy and laity. In particular, we spend time with church school volunteers, parents, and children. We listen to their stories and hear about their experiences of seeking to provide meaningful Christian formation for children at church and at home. With them we help generate new ideas and develop, plan, support, and evaluate programs for learning, worship, and living out our baptismal ministry. This help includes reviewing curricula and models of church school organization; addressing the challenges of all-age worship and learning; planning with parishes for envisioning events which include children and young people; and wrestling with questions about family life and what faith has to do with it. Secondly, we offer educational and skill-building conferences, resource fairs, and workshops for church school volunteers, clergy, parents, and children. We train leaders in children's ministry to plan and produce large events focusing on our faith heritage and holy days. These events help children and adults mark, learn, and celebrate the role and life of the cathedral in the diocese, the major feasts and seasons of the liturgical year (such as All Saint's Day, Ash Wednesday, Ascension Day, Advent, Lent, patron saint's days), community celebrations of baptisms ... the list goes on and on. As consultants, we span the boundaries between congregations and communities. As we go from congregation to congregation, we gather ideas, experiences, stories, and insights; and we share what we have learned with others we meet along the way.

We are two people with a variety of life experiences, qualifications, and degrees; but of them all perhaps the most influential for our work have been the birth and baptismal certificates of our children, Caroline, Mark, Meghan, and Juliane. These young people are the stimuli for our theological education. They ask us difficult questions. They challenge us to explore and live out the daily experience of our baptismal ministry, to ask "So what does all this mean for our lives?" and to become intentional about our formation as Christians in an increasingly secular society where, for the most part, our contemporaries have rejected the church as a place to express their spirituality and explore their values. We have learned to work together in partnership, as sisters and colleagues with a shared vision, responsibilities, and tasks. To this partnership we bring different and distinct gifts that have made the ministry far richer than either of us alone could have imagined.

We come with the challenges from the dinner table and from the warm, dark talks before sleep. We come with the questions that wake us in the middle of the night, the mysteries of our inner life and that of those we love. We bring our hopes for an exciting journey together, a shared adventure, and a desire that somehow our children might experience through our model of Christian living something of what we are called to be as brothers and sisters in Christ. We bring our desire, shared with the church, that the children have "an inquiring and discerning heart."[1] We bring our quest for a rich familiarity with the story of the family of God, which we share with our partners, Paul and Ralph, with our families, our faith communities, and so many others.

These elements (our families, our partnership with the diocese, and our participation as lay people in the life of the church, including our own parishes) represent many relationships. These are the spheres of influence that we cherish, that inform who we are; through them we continue to discover who we are called to be.

God, Kids, & Us belongs to all these people.

Children's ministry —
Being the church with children

Children are part of the body of Christ. Through baptism, children become full members of Christ's community, the Church. As members, children can learn and teach, give and receive pastoral care, and participate in the mission, administration and ministry of the Church.

Mission statement of the Children's Unit, Diocese of Toronto[2]*

Children's ministry is being the church with children. We believe that we are called to enable, encourage, and celebrate with adults and children as they

- experience their baptism as a lifestyle rather than an event;
- share their faith pilgrimage;

---

* The United Church of Canada's Theological and Education stance of the Ministry with Children Working Unit is as follows: "We believe that children are part of the body of Christ—a community in relationship with God through the gift of Jesus Christ, a community in which all members are valued and contribute to the whole. Through baptism, children are recognized as members of the body of Christ, of the people of God, of the Christian church."

- learn, tell, celebrate, and live the gospel story in the eucharistic community, at home, at work, and at school;
- become intentional in the process of Christian formation;
- are supported in their roles as parents, church school volunteers, mentors, ministers;
- find meaningful membership in the life of the church — in worship, education, community life, and administration;
- are empowered to live as Christians in their own world.

This conviction implies fundamental assumptions and beliefs.
- Children are capable of meaningful religious experience.
- Children sense God's presence and respond to it.
- Children have deep relationships with God.
- Children should be active participants in the ministry of the church.

Our role as adults is to nurture and support children; to create positive experiences of faith community by including children in our worship, education, and administrative life; to help children *be*, with us, the Body of Christ.

> *I grew up in a large parish in the late 1950s and early 1960s. I remember being led out of church every Sunday to one of those Sunday schools everyone remembers (or hears about) — hundreds of children in a parish hall. Those brief moments at the beginning of the service were the only time I was ever in the church until at age nine or ten I joined the junior choir. Then, Sunday after Sunday, I was in the church service the whole time, trying to be quiet in the large stalls between the nave full of people and the sanctuary full of clergy. Other than going in and out and standing, kneeling, and sitting, we never moved from our spot. The service, except for the singing, was not for us. We didn't participate in the action of the eucharist. We gave what we were expected to give, our voices. At eleven, I was prepared for confirmation and looked forward both to understanding what all this was about and also to being free not to continue!*

Learners and worshippers

This story may have a familiar ring about it. For too long the church has taught, and taught well, that worship is for adults and education is for children. As children we also learned that for the central activities of the community — the worship, the eucharist, the planning, and the ministry — we were not welcome, and that even if we were there, our presence would have no effect, would make no difference. Most of us left as soon as we could, and never came back. Many have been lost. But we believe that it is a sign of the diligent work of the Holy Spirit in the world that some of us have found our way home. Moreover, when we have returned, we have wanted the experience of church to be different for ourselves and for our children; and we are challenging our faith communities to recognize this need for change.

However, many children today, like their parents before them, come to church only to be relegated week after week to the church school. Like their parents, these children are likely to fall away from the community before they have had any real experience of the work of the church (worship, fellowship, prayer, stewardship, outreach, evangelism, and decision making). Basement church schools and a "less is best" attitude to children in the nave and the sanctuary are now teaching another whole generation that what they are exploring in their educational programs has no meaning for the rest of the congregation, and that little of their experience of faith is of value to the community. Many children are still learning that they are in fact members of the future, rather than members today, and that while they are now more welcome at worship and at the eucharist, their presence should not make a difference to what is happening.

Meanwhile, parents returning to our congregations and seeking religious nurture for their children are the same people who left the community as adolescents. Their strongest memories of church are based on church hall and basement Sunday school experiences and on confirmation classes. We too often make the mistake of assuming that these adults, by virtue of their age, feel comfortable in worship and know what is expected of them in stewardship, administration, pastoral ministries, and outreach. We assume that people feel comfortable articulating and sharing their faith with others, especially children. In fact, for the most part, parents returning to the church feel truly inadequate to the task of raising their children as Christians, and look to communities of faith to do this for them. It is only by learning to look past assumptions and by recognizing the experience, desires, and needs that new and returning Christians bring, that congregations can respond effectively. Returning and new Christian families will learn that we are all learners and worshippers. With children, all are called to a journey of faith.

That last statement is particularly important. It is easy to invite people into our churches, but to include them on the journey means to allow, and even to encourage, them to have an impact on the community. The community will become different. It will change and grow.

The pursuit of genuine inclusion leads to some particular challenges. Ways must be found to acknowledge and respond to the needs of people of all ages to worship, to learn more about their faith, *and* to know that their presence at occasions for both worship and learning has meaning for the life of the community. We often ponder these things by asking

- how do we include children in the worship life of our community?
- how do we effectively include adults in the educational component of our community?
- how do we listen to what the children and their parents have to say about what they need to receive from, and give to, the church?
- how do we prepare for the full and meaningful inclusion of children and young people in the range of events and activities of congregational life: events such as congregational planning, retreats, quiet days; activities such as planning for worship, outreach into the community, discernment of ministry, and administration?
- how do we help congregations face the challenges and anxieties that change brings?

Two generations together

Our task today as Christian educators is to find ways of engaging and supporting two generations in learning about a faith and ministry which has implications for us both within the gathered faith community and in the scattered community of home, school, work, and social relationships. We are discovering that a creative environment for learning with children and those who care for them means...

Knowing that we are journeying together

Being grown-up does not mean that we are all confident about sharing our faith with others or that we have figured out what living our baptism means. This statement is especially true for the generation which has, by and large, left the church. If they do return (usually for the sake of their children), these people feel uncomfortable in a worship environment that is either new to them or has changed dramatically since their childhood. They do not feel confident in sharing the faith with their children. These parents return so that someone more capable can answer the difficult questions their children are beginning to ask. We need to offer opportunities for all ages to learn more about what faith means to their lives. We need to acknowledge that most adults feel ill-equipped to "teach" their children about faith, the Bible, religious questions, and values. This situation is especially true for parents entering the church for the sake of their children. We need to help parents, and other adults who volunteer to be with our children, to see that their role is to present God and religious issues in a loving and caring atmosphere — to begin a pilgrimage, best taken together, which leads into a wonderful adventure of learning about their relationship with God, with the Christian community, and with each other.

As we have watched and participated in this faith journey in our own lives and work, we recognize the mystery; we cannot know all there is to know about what we find along the way. Sometimes we can teach one another.

Was Jesus ever as bratty as my little sister?[3]

How can I know God can be everywhere, especially when sometimes I feel scared, like at night or in the school yard?

More often we will question and explore together and, perhaps, surmise what might be the case.

If God forgives us, why did God kick Adam and Eve out of Eden?

Is God a man or a woman?

If God knows how I feel, why do I need to pray?

Sometimes the process will be fun.

My dog died on Good Friday. Did my dog die for all dogs' sins?

Why can't God give me everything I ask for?

Sometimes it will be difficult.

Why did God make my brother die?

If there is a God, why doesn't Daddy believe in him?

At other times we may just need to recognize and accept the mystery. It is difficult and exhilarating to be on this pilgrimage together. We have learned, however, that a healthy environment for faith to grow is a place at church and at home where people, whatever their age, can ask and begin to find answers, with us, to the big questions in life. While children will pose questions in ways that are charming, disarming, and seemingly naive, they are, for the most part, the same questions that adults wrestle with. Our spiritual pilgrimages, as children or as adults, differ less than might be thought. Sometimes the right answer starts with

I don't know. Let's find out together.

I'm not sure, but let's suppose...

This experience in my life leads me to believe that...

Engaging in the faith journey with children is an opportunity less to instruct than to nurture a shared learning opportunity in which meaningful mentoring relationships can grow and new ways of exploring the meaning of faith in our lives can be opened. Here we will discover ways that children offer leadership. We will find ourselves being mentored — guided in our own spiritual growth — as we are mentoring. Children's natural inclination to explore, question, and celebrate their faith in ways that are relevant to their lives is a great and energizing contribution to any adult's faith development and learning. As we explore our role as mentors, we will find that we too need mentors. We will need to seek out those who are a little farther along on the pilgrimage to guide and direct us as we go. And so a web of relationships is built.

Our faith journey often leads us to new questions that will challenge our understanding of Christian community.

- Are there ways to worship, pray, and learn so that connections are made between what goes on in church and what goes on at home, school, and work; between what happens on Sunday and what happens on Wednesday; between what we profess to believe and the way we live? What are the joys and challenges in linking faith and daily living? Are there ways that groups of families could support one another on the journey and explore the questions together?

- Who else do we need to help us grow and learn along the way?

- What about church school and worship? How can our congregations be open to the challenges that these relationships will bring to how we learn and worship? How can we begin to model a different and more inclusive way of being together within the structures we have inherited?

Involving both experience and knowledge

An eight-year-old girl came to church one morning in Advent quite distressed. How could it be possible for Mary and Joseph to know that Jesus was going to be a boy when there was no amniocentesis?

Children, like adults, are capable of bringing and receiving both experience and knowledge. In this way children are ministers within the church.

If we centre our time with children on the content of our Bible stories and the words of our liturgy, without attachment to experience, ritual, symbol, and relationship, we run the risk that as our children begin to doubt and worry about the inconsistencies between the world-and-church they know and the world-and-church our Christian stories and traditions proclaim, we will lose them. We can offer lots of content, set up ways of measuring each child's success in taking in the information, and end up, as John Westerhoff warns, helping to create a generation of agnostics or, worse, atheists who are biblically literate.[4] Without the integration of meaningful experience and exploration of faith and spirituality through rituals, symbols, and relationships, we are nourishing only part of each child.

On the other hand, if we create learning and worship opportunities which are centred on the social and relationship-building aspects of the community without being grounded in the stories and traditions that make up who we are as the people of God, we run the risk of providing a faith without content. In this model, youth groups are nice places to hang out on Saturday night, but there are no points of entry into the worshipping community; children feel at home and welcomed in the sanctuary and nave, but no attempt is made to tell the stories or relate the rituals in ways that are instructive to them or in ways that enable them to play a meaningful role in planning or presenting.

The balance between experience and learning is a tension that is felt by many congregations. Communities must provide opportunities for children to experience faith *and* learn the stories and traditions *and* make connections between the faith and their daily lives. Learning is much more than a chance for adults to down-load all their biblical and theological knowledge into children before they celebrate their tenth birthday by deciding that enough is enough and leaving the church. There is always a tension between the desire to provide lots of measurable content in the church school program and the desire to focus on the development of meaningful, mentoring relationships between children and adults. This is a tension that is felt by almost every church school. There is so little time on Sunday mornings that it is quite natural to feel the pull towards making sure that children leave knowing something more about a favourite Bible story or having created some new piece of art work that expresses a deepened understanding of a key theme; but opportunities also need to be created that include children in the experience of faith and in the learning of its stories and traditions, making connections between all of it and its import for their lives today. The chances are good that as we begin to explore how we might resolve this tension better within the structures and systems of church school and worship we already have, we will learn that the balance we seek for our children is also a balance we need to find for ourselves.

Children's ministry — Being the church with children

Accepting each child as a full and complete member of the faith community

Are children members of the church? Are they the possessions of members? Or are they future members? What in the liturgy of baptism is conditional on chronological maturity? The answers to these questions have ramifications for how we behave with the children in our midst.

Not everyone in a congregation will have the same answers. If we believe that baptism is our full initiation into the Body of Christ, we acknowledge all baptized children as members of the church. It is vitally important for the health of our congregations today (and tomorrow) that we consider children's ministry in light of the fact that, for many people, their childhood experience of church will determine their approach to their life-long spiritual journey. We cannot just *play* at being the church with children; we must *be* the church — a community of people of all ages searching together for ways of ministering with the gifts the Creator has bestowed on us. Children's ministry, then, is the creation of positive, inclusive, community-building experiences for children who are full members of the community *today*.

This understanding means that we need to be advocates with, and on behalf of, children to ensure that they are valued and respected by the whole church community today and that they are included in the whole life of the congregation — worship, fellowship, planning, ministry, and decision making, as well as education. Every child deserves the love, care, acceptance, and, yes, sometimes even tolerance of the other members of the church family.

What's in a name?

What we call our time with children is problematic, especially if we are committed to moving away from school imagery. If "church school" or "Sunday school" is no longer appropriate, what is?

We have yet to hear a really great alternative. Whatever is used, let the name reflect the value of the experience we are sharing with children. Designations like "treasure island," "the treasure chest," or the "magic kingdom" evoke fun times but are somewhat condescending and do nothing to indicate the valuable learning of both children and adults during this time. Would we give other integral areas of ministry, such as outreach or stewardship groups, fantastic or playful names?

For purposes of this book, we refer to the time spent with children on Sunday morning as "church school." It's not great. It's not really what we mean. It's definitely not catchy. But it is the best we can come up with for now. Please keep trying to find something that works!

Take heart!

Children's ministry is so much more than church school. Basic program needs, along with a few assumptions about the role of children in the life of our community, bring us to the point of discovering an array of engaging and exciting possibilities and challenges. Take heart! The effective inclusion of children and adults in the worship and education life of a congregation is a tall order which challenges both clergy and lay people to explore their baptismal calling together. At its best, it is an energizing, nourishing, and transformational ministry shared by community members of all ages. We wish you well on your journey and hope that the ideas in *God, Kids, & Us* will help you along your way.

Children at worship —
Styles, models, and next steps

Thanksgiving dinner. This is one of the three occasions in a year when the family gathers. There are five brothers and sisters, their spouses and children — eleven children in all, aged six through seventeen, including nine boys. The table in the large dining room seats the adults and two girls. The boys are in the kitchen. Plates for the boys are filled with traditional fare. Grace is bellowed around the kitchen table. The other plates are filled; and before everyone has tucked into turkey, the kitchen is empty but for nine heaping dinner plates. The adults and two girls continue eating, but are soon interrupted by calls for parental intervention on the driveway basketball court. Reflecting on the event later, it seemed we had made a number of mistakes. We decided to do things differently the next time we met.

Christmas dinner. The same ten adults are there, plus an uncle and aunt and the same eleven children. The dining room and living room furniture has been moved, and tables and chairs borrowed, enough to make the room look like a UN conference. A seating plan has been devised (and fought over) to place children and adults together but not beside members of their own immediate families. Carols are sung as the plates are filled; and grace is offered with reverence. The meal continues amid chatter, laughter, and the popping of Christmas crackers. Only the youngest boy crawls from his chair to stick his head up in the space between the tables.

There were important lessons for me in these events. How are we to be a family together if we separate ourselves off so crudely — young males in the kitchen! We and they thus miss rare opportunities to learn what is important to us as a family: to speak with aunts and uncles, to hear those familiar family stories, to share accomplishments and concerns, to build ties and interests with one another, to appreciate the idiosyncrasies of the relatives! Eventually, we hope, the children will also learn to manage the utensils; to put the napkin on the lap, not the head; not to interrupt (or to interrupt appropriately); and to develop the skills to contribute to the conversation.

***

Julie is seven years old. Her picture, drawn during the sermon, shows happy people going into the church. A big yellow sun is shining in the sky. She is vigorously colouring a young man on roller-blades who is smiling a very broad smile, waving, and standing at the doorway into the church. When she's finished, Julie looks up and *announces: "Guess who this is? It's Jesus saying 'Hi' to everybody as they come in here!"*

How do churches live out this welcome that God extends to all without condition? How are children enabled to be the Body of Christ in our liturgies? Can a congregation call itself the Christian family without encouraging the participation and inclusion of the youngest members in its central celebration — the eucharist, the family meal?

Children are capable of understanding much about the experience of worship. Let us look at the Jesus Julie knows. She is clearly envisioning Jesus as someone who knows her, someone who likes and accepts her, someone who makes her feel comfortable, someone young. She has learned about this Jesus through her time spent in community — in worship, in education, and through the relationships she has found.

As Julie attends and takes part in the liturgy of this community, she will gradually assimilate more and more of its meaning and culture, and learn more and more of its language. As we too attend, gain experience, and take part, different aspects of the liturgy will speak to us more deeply. New and different meanings will evolve. No one's faith is static; both adults and children continually grow in understanding. Like Julie, all of us can experience Christ in our midst and worship God meaningfully through liturgy when the symbols, rituals, language, and relationships we find there are expressive of our lives and of our faith.

While a child colouring quietly in a pew or wandering from favourite spot to spot may not seem engaged in worship, she is both present and attentive. We confidently expect that one day Julie's parents will find her giving communion to her stuffed animals, baptizing her doll and saying all the correct words, showing off to her friends how fast she can recite the creed, or even arguing simple points of doctrine ("If everybody is welcome, why don't they come?").

As parents we know that it takes time to learn, and in our best moments we are willing to wait and to make allowances along the way. Instinctively we know that children are experiential learners, that they absorb lessons and adopt behaviours through active participation in family rituals. We do not

Children at worship — Styles, models, and next steps

make our children eat in the basement until they master the rules of etiquette, know our family's history and tradition, or understand the concept of nutrition.

At its best, worship is the place where the gathered community of faith can experience transcendence — the animating love of God, the reality of the reign of Christ in our lives — and glimpse the kingdom of God. We enable this experience by telling our family stories and sharing our traditions and culture. We make relationships; learn how to exercise our need to give and our need to receive; and together find nourishment, forgiveness, healing, strength, and renewal.

Families and congregations also face a common challenge. Each new generation needs to find its own place in the community. A family welcomes new members by marriage or birth. A community grows in similar ways. Most commonly, new members arrive through their own birth, followed by baptism. Others enter by marrying someone who attends church. Still others come as adults with their children, searching for values and meaning in their lives, asking questions about what it means to be part of the Christian pilgrimage. In growing, the community, whether family or congregation, will change. New generations will impact on etiquette and traditions. Not only musical and clothing styles, but how we are parents and what we expect from our children, will change significantly from previous generations. New generations will even redefine when it is important for the community to gather and which celebrations and events are central to its life.

If these new generations are not allowed to make a place for themselves and to work with the community to claim the church as their own, they will leave. If our congregations cannot find ways of both ministering to them and being open to their ministry to us, they will leave. If they cannot find a way to nurture their spirituality in our congregations, they will leave. If they and their children cannot feel comfortable and included, they will leave. This challenge is not easy. Ask anyone with a teenager. Ask any congregation working towards more engaging and inclusive liturgy for children. But the rewards are well worth the struggle. When our worship is truly God-centered, the presence of the children enhances our experience. Children can open us to new perspectives. Their enthusiasm can awaken a new awareness of God's presence in our own lives. Rather than being a distraction, children can be a blessing and resource for us.

Take a close look, from a child's perspective, at some of the moments in the routine of your congregation. There are many aspects you could choose: space arrangements, printed material, and so forth. For example, look at the first impression — the greeting.

- How are children welcomed into church?
- In general, how are children and their parents (or adults with them) helped to feel comfortable?
- Is the welcome child-centred for children and adult-centred for adults?
- Do greeters seek the comfort of the children as they try to make sense of an unfamiliar setting and unfamiliar activities?
- Is the service easy for children to follow?
- Are there printed materials for children (activity sheets, a child-friendly service bulletin, colouring materials)?
- How do they know when to do what during the service and after?

In one congregation the greeters at the door, specifically charged with welcoming newcomers, included whole families as part of the team. New children were attended to by the children of the welcoming family. They were shown around, told about the "interesting parts of the service" and what to do, taken to the church school, introduced to others in their age group, and taught the rituals of getting to the refreshments first at coffee hour.

In a truly welcoming community a certain atmosphere will prevail. People of all ages will have a friendly attitude towards each other; they will smile at each other; they will speak to each other. Children will feel free to sit near the front of the church where they can see what is going on. Often they will choose to sit with favourite people other than their parents. Music will be appealing to both children and adults, and different styles of music will complement worship. The language will be the best — the most beautiful and poetic — that can be offered to God, but it will also be language all can understand. The symbols used to express our experience of faith, celebration, and holiness will hold potent meaning for people of all ages.

Jesus welcomed little children even though his friends thought they would be a nuisance. As his followers, we will want to welcome children too. Little children may not remember every word that was spoken, but they will retain the experience of being a valued part of the community — of belonging, acceptance, enhanced self-worth, affection, and interdependence. In the church, as in our homes, children need to be included in the activities of the "family" in order to become incorporated into its life and norms. Welcoming children in church is the responsibility of the whole congregation. Not to do so risks losing yet another generation from the church.

Worship together

Many church school curricula assume that a congregation will have "all-age" or "intergenerational" worship services periodically throughout the liturgical year. Some curricula provide helpful suggestions for planning these services; others do not. Including children in worship that both is meaningful to them and maintains the integrity of the liturgy is a desirable ambition and one to which more and more congregations aspire. Clergy and lay people are looking for ways to plan all-age worship to suit their own situations and traditions.

As a church community begins to include children in the liturgy, it finds itself challenged to rethink some very basic and time-honoured assumptions about worship.

- Is worship a time of private prayer and reflection, or is it a time for the community to celebrate God's love for us? What is the place of silence? How can we learn to listen more?
- Is liturgy a performance, planned and performed by a few; or is it the work of the people?

- Is worship a time alone with God, or is it a time when the realities of daily life intersect with our quest for transcendence and community?

- Is worship mostly passive or mostly active?

- Is worship only meaningful for those of us who "understand" with our minds what is going on; or is it an experience that engages us, young and old, as much through our senses and bodies as through our intellects?

- Must worship with children necessarily be distracting, busy, or childish?

Worship for all ages will be more effective if decisions are made first about how to make it active, respectful, experiential, participatory, or celebratory — or all five.

If worship is the gathering of the community to participate in the liturgy — literally "the work of the people" — then we must develop ways of including children without alienating adults. We know that this vision can be challenging and can stir up both excitement and anxiety in a community, but making the journey towards the inclusion of children is well worth the effort and patience required. The church will become a place where children and adults know each other, where parents are relaxed, and where children behave as if this is their space too. Children will be found quietly exploring their favourite places in the worship area and feeling comfortable sitting (perhaps briefly, perhaps for longer) with a variety of favourite adult friends. Children will know the rhythm of liturgy and know what to expect and what is expected of them. Children and adults will be able to tell the story of worship, what they find there, and how their contribution is meaningful.

Models of worship

There are many ways to move towards more inclusive worship. Here are a few approaches. Each has advantages and challenges. Depending on the situation in your church now, each model can be an ideal, a resting point, or a place of beginning.

The children's service

> *Whenever a month has a fifth Sunday, Trinity Church has a Children's Service. Under the watchful guidance of their church school teachers, the children hand out bulletins, read a lesson, sing a song, and collect the offering. The sermon, a "children's talk," is short; "children's hymns" are sung; and after church the children help serve at coffee hour. The adults notice that the children do these tasks well, as capably as the adults. Some parents are beginning to realize that these Sundays are the only times that their young teens will come to church without a fuss.*

What does it look like?

In this model the children are occasionally offered the opportunity to perform specific tasks in the church on Sunday. The children might be greeters, read a lesson, take up the offering, or sing a song. Successful implementation involves careful planning and coordination with various church groups — readers, greeters, the choir — and preparation and rehearsal of the children for their new roles.

What are the benefits?

Usually the children respond favourably to the challenge and will have feelings of accomplishment and pride when they excel at tasks the congregation usually sees as adult responsibilities. These results can be especially true for adolescents who are ready and eager for meaningful tasks within the adult environment. If time is taken to prepare and rehearse, the adults are left with a good impression of the children and their abilities. The children are highly visible on these occasions, and they experience the full liturgy. Because they do not ordinarily stay for the full time, they will have many questions about what happens in the service; these occasions thus provide an educational opportunity.

What is missing?

Having all the tasks done by children is no more inclusive than having them all done by adults. Children rarely get to put their own creative contributions into the worship. If the children carry out prescribed tasks without having any effect on them, the message is clearly "You can be here but only if you do it our way, even if it doesn't make sense to you. Remember these are our jobs and our worship — not yours, yet." There is little meaningful interaction between the generations in the worship. The faces may become more familiar, but their owners will not know each other any better. These services often lack spontaneity unless there is a goof or ad lib made by a nervous or extroverted child, which the adults may find charming or humorous.

In the Children's Service model the emphasis for children as participants and performers is on their behaviour. They must meet norms both that are imposed by others and that may make no sense to the children.

> *Why do we sit still and quiet when the music is lively and energetic?*
>
> *Who says we can't change who we are sitting with?*
>
> *Why does the reading have to happen at the lectern?*

The liturgy, while including children, rarely incorporates any of their behavioural norms or needs (for movement, colour, hands-on activity). In essence, children are being invited to participate in a service that adults are hoping the next generation will grow into and perpetuate.

There is a danger that children will experience worship as a performance rather than as the work of the whole congregation built into a familiar

35

pattern, which varies according to the season, the readings, and the life of the community. For volunteers, the danger is that these "all-age" services will be seen as another part of the church school program to be organized, prepared for, and supported by church volunteers and avoided by other adults.

> *In a former parish, we had an annual visit from a young people's group called Article XXIV, specializing in contemporary rock settings of the eucharist. Lots of publicity (or warning, depending on your point of view) was given. While I found these occasions exciting, I was aware that many of the older members of the congregation were very uncomfortable. On one occasion an older member, who had avoided these events in the past, arrived. After some wrestling with herself, she decided to stay. As the service progressed, I noticed that she seemed more relaxed, even if she was not exactly moving with the beat. I asked her at coffee what she thought. She said, "This is not my kind of music or expression, but I could see that those young people really believed in what they were doing. They were not making fun of this. They were worshipping. That inspired me."*

Where might we go from here?

If this is your model of all-age worship, here are a few next steps to consider.

- Allow the children to select the jobs they would like to do from a range of opportunities, and then let them tailor the tasks.

- Invite greeters to prepare welcome cards or pew art, sermon notes or activity sheets, and a few crayons to give out to each family with children.

- Help readers choose from a variety of ways to tell the story — dance, artwork, drama or dramatic reading, music, and so on.

- Encourage the use of intercessions that reflect the life of the community. Leaders of the Prayers of the People can write petitions with a little guidance. Perhaps a family could prepare and offer the prayers together.

- Bake the bread for the eucharist. For faith communities with a tradition of communion wafers, children often remind us of the old joke: "I can believe it's Jesus, I just can't believe it's bread." Bread is a central and potent symbol connecting the divine with our everyday lives. Try using bread baked and presented by families in the congregation. There are plenty of recipes for communion bread; a good one is offered at the end of this chapter (Resource sheet 2, "Lebanese-Syrian mass bread," p. 51).

- Reinforce the significance of the offertory. Is money the only thing we have to offer? Is there something the children have made, a mural or banner, for example, which they would like to offer?

- Match participating children with adults in the congregation who usually do selected tasks, so that they might work together.

When adults who regularly exercise worship ministries (for example, greeters, in the chancel guild, readers, servers) are invited to help the children prepare for their parts in the service, learning and preparation are linked with relationship building. Children can observe adults performing their roles in worship, and adults will be challenged to express these activities in ways that engage and make sense to children. As relationships grow, the learning is guaranteed to go both ways!

Children's church

> St. Christopher's church school has a special corner. There is a small altar with a colourful frontal covered with painted handprints and children's names. Once a month the children, their volunteers, and Jim, the young assistant priest, gather around this altar to tell and act out stories, pray, sing, collect their offering, and have communion. They spend a little time each week preparing for this worship. Today Matt is accompanying one of the songs on his violin.

What does it look like?

This worship service takes place in the church school or children's chapel with a broad age range of children and volunteers present. Perhaps a member of the clergy celebrates the eucharist with them in the church school; or after the children have their own liturgy of the word, they join the adults for the eucharist in the sanctuary and nave. In places where the whole congregation is not open to having children in the worship space for any or all of the service, Children's Church might happen on Sundays designated as "intergenerational" by the church school curriculum.

What are the benefits?

Although children and adults not involved in church school do not worship together, this model does recognize that worship is an important aspect of a child's faith development. The format can be very creative because the boundaries of possibility are set by the imagination of the church school volunteers and the children themselves, rather than by the norms of the adult worshipping community. Worship can be prepared and enacted by the particular children involved. Without the encumbrance of pews or tradition, there can be freedom in the arrangement and use of space. Behavioural norms can be set by participants. Chances are a new and lively worshipping community may grow, parallel to the congregation in the sanctuary and nave.

What is missing?

Children and their volunteers are being segregated. This service is as exclusive as worship in the sanctuary and nave. If the experience is not shared by children, their parents, relatives, or other adults in the congregation, how can they learn from one another? This model is an expression of two separate worshipping cultures using one building.

The challenges presented by adolescents will remain. Will they have a place in the church school worship? Will they find ways of making the transition to the other worshipping community? Or will they be lost? If adolescents are incorporated into the sanctuary worship, will it be meaningful to them? Will their ideas and expectations, formed by the other worship experience, be heard?

Where might we go from here?

- Regularly invite a small group of adult guests to the children's worship. Do not forget to give them jobs! Try to make the newcomers feel as comfortable as possible, perhaps by making the celebration as instructive as you can.

- Include children of various ages in the planning of more and more elements of the service. These children will probably end up knowing a great deal about liturgy and sharing their learning with their parents or the other adults in the congregation. Once the children are confident and accomplished in their tasks, they might be invited to share their skills with the rest of the community by participating in the adult worship service.

- Do not be too hasty to move the service in time or space, even if more and more adults are drawn to a liturgy that is becoming a spirit-filled and popular alternative. Consider carefully the options for where and when the liturgy happens. Before you decide to move into the sanctuary and nave, recognize the advantages of flexible space. The ways in which people are able to gather together (including the arrangement of furniture and the position and posture of bodies) have a significance, especially for their experience of community. Also, make sure you have a critical mass of supporters (at least thirty committed adults) before moving to a new time.

Intentionally inclusive

After one planning meeting and an afternoon of rehearsal, we were ready to celebrate Palm Sunday. Children and adults processed through the church singing and waving hosanna banners. Even babies, as young as five and six months, were given brightly coloured rattles made out of palms to shake as they were carried along the road to Jerusalem. Instead of the normal gathering and liturgy of the word, story-tellers told us about the Last Supper, Gethsemane and the trials, Jesus' crucifixion, and the anticipation of Easter. With each story a symbol — a bowl and towel, a crown of thorns, a pall-covered cross, and a lily plant with its flowers still tightly shut — were placed in the church for all to see. In preparation for the story of Jesus' death, four children with honour and in solemnity processed down the centre aisle, carrying on their shoulders a plain, wooden, six-foot-long cross, which they then draped with the funeral pall. We felt the weight of that cross and all it means for us in a new way that day.

What does it look like?

In this model, worship is seen by the church's leadership as the work of all the people. Worship is an important ministry of the baptized and is carefully planned. A planning group first takes into consideration the age range within the congregation and the activities that are part of worship preparation, and then looks ahead for appropriate opportunities — based on the liturgical year, the lectionary, and the community life — to use the skills and talents of everyone to contribute to worship. Children and youth are respected as individuals (not necessarily always as part of a family group) along with people of other ages.

When worship is intentionally inclusive, all ages participate in the service whether or not the church school curriculum designates the day as an intergenerational worship Sunday. Appropriate pieces of preparation and presentation (readings, prayers, baking the bread, greeting, music, and so forth) will be undertaken by various groups of people according to their interests, gifts in ministry, and talents.

What are the benefits?

A planning team, which is essential in this model, provides an opportunity to be as inclusive as possible. A team that comprises children, youth, and adults (whether parents or not) enables those responsible for worship — clergy, worship committee, readers, intercessors, choir, and so on — to ensure that all the congregation is represented and engaged by the worship. Children can participate, discover their ministries, and become recognized as full members of the church today, as well as the church tomorrow. A clear connection is made between education and worship. There is an explicit recognition that the whole people of God have a deep desire to learn and grow in the faith and to worship God as creator, redeemer, and sustainer of our life together.

What is missing?

This model is not always efficient in terms of the amount of time needed to plan and prepare. Creating worship that fits the unique talents and gifts of a particular community requires time, discernment, and energy. Some predictability may be lost; tasks may not be quite the same week to week. Also, ministries are often closely linked to the skills and talents of particular persons and so may not be interchangeable without adaptation. Unless care is taken, seniors, empty-nesters, and single people may feel excluded by the emphasis on family, youth, and children. The element of surprise and spontaneity may be disquieting for some.

Where might we go from here?

- Remember to evaluate at regular intervals. Name the values and set goals for the liturgy planners, and check with other worshippers to see how you're doing. If you find yourself getting into a regular pattern, ask yourself whether it is indeed the most appropriate way for your community to worship, or whether you are getting tired or too exclusive.

- Be aware of new resources.
- Look for groups or individuals who are still at the edges of your community, and find ways of including them.
- Explore some new ministries — even for the adults!

Helping children and their parents feel comfortable in church

Recently a new family arrived at St. Paul's with twin boys aged three. The first Sunday the boys were tentative and shy, clinging closely to mom. The next week they began to range. They explored the sanctuary, chasing around the altar, climbing the pulpit stairs, swinging off the altar rail. Their mother, outnumbered two to one, was at a distinct disadvantage; but although she was clearly distracted and distressed, nothing really terrible happened. Nothing was broken, spilt, or set on fire.

While there were several dozen children under the age of six at the service, no one else joined the boys in tearing around the space. There was, of course, some background noise and some coming and going from the worship space into the hall and back again; but with the rest of the children knowing what to expect and how to behave, the presence of two newcomers did nothing to disturb the normal pattern of participation.

After the service the twins' mother was noticeably frazzled and apologetic, but the pastor and some of the other parents explained that there was no need for anxiety. During the coffee hour one family invited the twins back into the sanctuary and allowed them to touch the furniture and explore the altar, lectern, and pulpit from an adult's height, all the while explaining their importance and their parallel with special places at home.

If the twins regularly participate in worship in the future, they will follow the lead of others in the congregation. They will learn the

rhythm and rituals of the service and come to know what to expect.
Some weeks will be easier than others, but in time mom will see how
other parents deal with the issues and will hear the stories of parents
who have made it through this stage and survived, with the congrega-
tion, to tell the story.

Whether children are present for the whole service or for a part, it is important that congregations help young families feel comfortable at worship. Two of the most effective ways of doing this are by communicating clearly the community's expectations and by telling the stories of how other families have found their way (successfully and not) into the community's life. Most parents returning to church feel uncomfortable in worship because they have little previous experience of it. They were not often included in worship when they were children, even if they went to church school. They are watching carefully, eager to find some clues to tell them what is expected, especially if the culture seems different from one they experienced in the past.

There are many ways in which congregations can help families find a comfortable place in the worshipping community. Here are a few suggestions.

- Prepare a mission statement about children to present as a handout at the entrance of the church or as a regular paragraph in your bulletin. State clearly and simply how the role of children is understood by your congregation or church, and why. Here is an example:

  By virtue of their baptism, children are part of the Body of Christ.
  As full members of our congregation, they are welcome to worship
  and to receive the sacrament of communion.

- Develop some simple guidelines, based on the congregation's mission statement, that tell parents and children what the norms of the church are. The suggestions do not need to be complicated, as shown in the examples below.

Children at worship — Styles, models, and next steps

Please don't bother stalking your child. No one runs faster in the opposite direction than a toddler being pursued by a parent.

If you are concerned about the noise generated by small feet on our hard-wood floors, we suggest that your children wear soft-soled shoes to church — or take advantage of our supply of "church shoes" (slippers).

Have the guidelines available as a small handout at the back of the church. (See Resource sheet 3, "Guidelines for parents," p. 52).

- Have a corner where activity sheets, relating to the gospel story of the day or season, are available for children to pick up and work on in their places.

- Tell your stories — the good ones and the not-so-good. Children and parenting are great conversation starters. Let new families know what it was like for you when your children were that age. Surely we all have at least one story to tell of the time our two-year-old truly embarrassed us in church and everything turned out okay.

It was the second Sunday in Bill's first parish, a small rural church. The congregation was, for the most part, made up of a sea of grey hair, but a few younger people had come to see what a young pastor might be like. Having decided, for the sake of the young families who were checking them out, to model a more relaxed and accepting atti-tude towards children in church, Bill and his wife allowed their active toddler to roam around the church quietly exploring the space and the people during the service. To read the gospel, Bill came to stand among the congregation, halfway down the centre aisle. His son met him there and, while the reading was going on, climbed over and hugged him. When the reading ended, Bill returned to the chancel, while the child, on his way back to his mom, announced in his loudest two-year-old voice, "I touched my daddy! I touched my daddy's penis!"

At first there was deathly silence; then, one by one, snorts began, embarrassed chuckles, and finally gales of laughter. What was initially an extremely embarrassing situation became the opening of a conversation between young parents and seniors in the church about the differences in past and present child-rearing practices and about the meaning of the expectations, joys, and challenges of this new generation for a congregation wanting more young families in its midst.

The grumblers

Every congregation has them: the folk who will not accept the presence of children in worship. The grumblers can make life very uncomfortable for parents and other sympathetic adults, including the clergy. They make noises of disapproval and voice their discontent to any who will listen. They block the effective inclusion of children and their families. If grumblers are crippling your community's efforts to develop inclusive worship, take a good look around your congregation one Sunday. The fact is — the trend lines are correct, the data is hard — churches have been suffering from declining membership since the 1960s. Now all the mainline Christian churches are facing serious concerns about their survival into the next century. Is it right that a few people who cannot come to terms with change exert so much power and hold so many others hostage? Every congregation says it wants revitalization, renewal, young people, and young families; but if the long-time members really mean "but only on our terms," these things will never happen.

Here are some suggestions for dealing with the grumblers. However, we suspect that the issue is much deeper than noisy children. While we strive to walk with these folk and help them find a way to engage with and contribute to the changes that are evolving, we must also recognize that they are probably grieving the loss of traditions and stories that mean a great deal to their own faith journeys. You may not change minds, but any of these strategies, or others you come up with, should lower the tension level.

- Offer different services at different times, Saturday evening, for example. Newcomers will probably find it easier than the grumblers to accept new times to worship.

- Do not completely drop any special services of particular nostalgic significance that are part of your tradition, such as services of the word, choral evensong, or lessons and carols.

- Find ways to build relationships:

  A secret pal project (from *The Whole People of God* curriculum).[5]

  A lottery. Number the bulletins and draw numbers at the children's talk to see who will be guests of the church school this week. It is difficult for an elder of the congregation to refuse a beaming five-year-old holding out his hand.

  An "adopt a grandfriend" social event such as an "out at 5, home by 7" card/games night.

- Have a direct conversation. Ask for clarification: what is the real objection?

Many adults in our congregation were made uncomfortable and embarrassed by an older woman whose sounds of displeasure were quite loud each time a child fussed during the prayers. In a quiet corner during coffee hour, one of the church board members was elected to speak with her about her obvious disapproval of children in church. With some reluctance, the delegate approached her. We learned that although she was having great difficulty understanding why children would be allowed at worship, she was more disturbed by the painful impact of the pitch of small children's voices heard through her hearing aid.

A reflection

It is unfortunate that so much energy in worship is tied up in advocating small changes to redistribute tasks, or to get the current worshipping community to loosen up a little. As long as these activities remain the focus, we are perpetuating a liturgical life that exists to please those who are already attending and comfortable with what is being provided. Without some radical rethinking of who worship is for and how it is done, children will continue to be seen as a group separate from the main community. A vision of the full inclusion of children will be narrow. The inevitable results will be either a show-and-tell model of performance, worship that suffers from perpetual childishness and is unfulfilling for the adults in the community, or a virtually unchanged liturgy during which the children have learned to conceal their boredom and from which many others will stay away because the challenge to their attention span is too great.

There is much to learn about liturgy as the work of the community of faith. There exists a real challenge to help people think creatively about liturgy and move past a general misconception that adults and children cannot share a meaningful worship experience together. What would happen if we presumed that worship (yes, even the music) should be instructive and accessible to those outside our community, rather than just those inside? What would happen if we assumed that it is possible, and even a key value of liturgy planning, to engage people of all ages (yes, even toddlers) in worship at least once or twice during the service? Genuinely inclusive liturgy will mean significant change in and challenge to much of what we now recognize as worship.

Possibly the greatest challenge, should we really want to include children and their parents in worship, will be to our heavy reliance on all things verbal as the primary liturgical medium. Texts, readings, sermons, prayers — we rely most ardently on words. We trust them to convey meaning and instruction. However, children are good at reminding us that we are an embodied people with many ways of experiencing, learning about, and interacting with our environments. Their parents are good at reminding us, especially if they are new to worship, that the language of liturgy is

Children at worship — Styles, models, and next steps

often foreign and does not communicate what we, who are familiar and comfortable with it, intend.

This is certainly not to say that we need to throw away our books or texts (for some traditions this idea would be dangerously close to heresy); but as a first step, we need to take a critical look at worship to see what sensual riches it holds, or lacks. Unfortunately, for most worship we could as well check our bodies at the door of the church; but the more variety and richness there is in worship, the more experiential and instructive it will be for all members of the community, regardless of age. As we have learned from our experience of children receiving the food and drink of the eucharist, each of us can find ways of deep understanding and meaning through actions, symbols, and participation, even when our levels of intellectual comprehension are very different. The way that we perform the actions of liturgy teaches and communicates as much to the worshippers as do the words. There are times in worship that quite naturally lend themselves to a variety of media and action — ways of telling the stories, of praying, of singing, of gathering the community around the altar for the eucharist. There is still much scope for imagination and creativity.[6]

Starting the conversation on children at worship

Here is a short parable that we enjoy using as a discussion starter with groups in congregations, including families coming for baptism and new families in the church.

Peter and Penny go swimming
by Janet, Laurie, Jennie, and Victor Metcalfe

Soon after Peter and Penny were born, their parents began taking them to the local swimming pool every weekend. The parents were enthusiastic swimmers, and they hoped their children would be keen swimmers too.

Of course Peter and Penny were not allowed to go into the swimming pool itself; they were looked after in a little room right beside the pool. Sometimes they cried because they wanted to stay with their parents, but that wasn't allowed because they might disturb the adult swimmers. Besides, they were too young to understand swimming, and they wouldn't appreciate it fully.

When Peter and Penny were three years old, they were allowed to go to another room just down the hall from the swimming pool. There they heard stories from the Swimmer's Manual, and they coloured pictures of people swimming.

When they were six years old, Peter and Penny went to another big room — a big room with lots of children. Here they began to get really serious about swimming. For the first ten or fifteen minutes they were allowed to take off their shoes and socks and splash around in the wading pool. They then went to classes with other children their own age to learn more about swimming. They were taught by some very dedicated people who loved swimming, but who hardly ever swam themselves any more because they were busy with the children.

By the time Penny and Peter were thirteen, they had studied the Swimmer's Manual in even more detail and had learned the rules of the swimming pool off by heart: "You shall not run on the deck; you shall not bring flotation devices into the pool area..." They had also learned about the properties of water, the muscles used in swimming, and the various swimming strokes. They had studied great swimmers of the past, including Olympic medal winners. They had heard about Canadian swimmers who went to other countries such as Africa or India to teach swimming, and they had seen slides of groups of African or Indian swimmers standing beside their swimming pools.

On special occasions, Peter and Penny had been allowed to go with their parents into the pool as long as they didn't splash around too much and disturb the other swimmers or bother the life guard.

At last Penny and Peter finished swimming school and were allowed to accompany their parents into the swimming pool every week. They tried it a few times. Much to the disappointment of their parents, Peter and Penny had lost interest and preferred to watch television instead.

Questions for discussion with a congregational group or parents

- How do you think Peter and Penny interpret and feel about this experience?

- Have you ever had an experience of exclusion or a long initiation time in your life? How did it feel? What was its effect on you?

- In what ways do you see coming to church with your children to be like taking Peter and Penny to the swimming pool?

- How are we treating the children and young adolescents in our congregation?

- What are the risks involved in the way we treat the children in our congregation?

- What are we doing well? What might we do differently?

Here is a good recipe for communion bread for families to make together. This bread does not crumble.

Lebanese–Syrian mass bread

1 package	active dry yeast
3 1/2– 4 cups	sifted all-purpose flour
1 1/4 cups	warm water
2 tablespoons	cooking oil
1/2 teaspoon	sugar
1 teaspoon	salt

In a large bowl, combine the yeast and 1 1/2 cups of flour. Combine the warm water, oil, salt, and sugar. Add wet ingredients to dry ingredients and beat on low speed with an electric mixer for half a minute, scraping the sides of the bowl constantly. Beat 3 minutes at high speed. By hand, stir in enough of the remaining flour to make a moderately stiff dough. Turn out on a floured surface and knead until smooth and elastic — about 5 minutes. Cover and let rise 45 minutes. Punch down and divide into 12 equal portions. Shape into balls and let rise 10 minutes.

On a lightly floured surface, roll each ball into a 5 inch circle. Place 2 inches apart on ungreased baking sheets. Cover and let rise for 20 – 30 minutes. Bake in a 400 degree oven for 10 minutes or until puffed and lightly browned on the bottom. Remove from the baking sheet and immediately wrap in foil to cool.[7]

Resource sheet 3

Guidelines for parents of children at worship

This suggestion list for parents has had many manifestations. One congregation adapted it and handed it out, with pencils or crayons, to children on small sheets of paper. One side encouraged the children to draw what they heard or saw, and the other offered these suggestions to parents.

May we suggest —

Relax! God put the wiggle in children — don't feel you have to suppress it here in God's house.

Sit where you feel most comfortable — near the front to be able to see and hear; near the entrance to the narthex or the church hall.

Use a gentle touch — an arm around the shoulder or holding hands gives reassurance and appropriate attention.

Explain parts of the service. Help the children find their place in the bulletin and any books being used.

Sing the hymns, pray, voice the responses. Children learn liturgical behaviour by copying yours.

If your child needs to leave the service, please feel free to go with him or her, but please come back!

Always remember that the way we welcome children in the church directly affects their experience of faith and the church.

Pastoral care — Paying attention

One of the joys of ministry with children is that we are challenged to pay attention — attention to each child's individuality; to clues, beyond the verbal, that point to each child's inherent identity; to the distinctive gifts and needs that each child brings. Children reveal their unique natures in many ways, including their behaviour, their approaches to learning, their responses to other people and events, and the life experiences they bring to the faith community. To offer our full attention, and respond to what we learn in ways that help children to develop their full potential, is to provide pastoral care.

Learning styles

During coffee hour a group of the younger women in the congregation had plunged into lively conversation about the drabness of the sanctuary. All agreed that the worship space needed more colour. Lots of ideas were proposed — perhaps some seasonal or thematic banners placed over the pulpit, perhaps a generic symbol over the choir... The din grew as voices overlapped, each with a new idea about what was needed. Meghan, aged eleven, who had been paying rapt attention to the discussion, suddenly burst in. "No, this is what you need," she interjected; and grabbing a piece of scrap paper and pencil, she drew a design for the space that met all the requirements.

Even at age eleven, Meghan spends most of her time in the pew sketching. Sometimes she draws what can be seen around her; at other times, she makes a representation of what is being taught in the lessons or the sermon. She has been known to complain that the sermon was too short when it didn't allow her enough time to get a sketch just right.

Meghan is forever tying strings to her wrists to remind her to do something. Studying for tests requires a lot of paper, since really to learn something, she must write it down, over and over. A supply of Bible worksheets and puzzles will fend off her boredom in church school when there is a lot of discussion, or will provide a comfortable alternative when the activity is really boisterous and physical

***

Caroline often prefers to stay in church rather than go to church school. At ten years old she is one of the youngest of the regular readers. After filling in at the last minute for her mother, Caroline was asked by the woman who arranges for readers if she wanted to be put on the rotation. Though shy in social situations, Caroline agreed and now reads regularly and well — at almost the proper speed, with expression, with due acknowledgment of punctuation. While the rest of her family is busy in the service or in the church school, she sits with her stuffed animal, a little book and pencil, and another adult friend. During the sermon she plays with the animal on her lap and occasionally writes something in her book. These notes turn out to be questions about what she has heard in the readings or in the sermon.

In other settings Caroline is continually asking questions about what she has heard. In school she relies first on what she has heard, before referring to any notes she may have taken. What her teacher *has said is very important. It is easy for Caroline to retell the story line from a book, movie, or television show. In her bedroom the things that are tidiest and most organized, other than her many stuffed animals, are her radio and tape player. Music and stories, tapes from her singing lessons, or the pop radio station are playing whenever she is in the room.*

***

David owns a snake named Michelle. David is fascinated by snakes and likes the way they feel. He knows a lot about them, especially from caring for Michelle. He finds it hard to feed the frozen baby mice to Michelle, but he knows that it must be done. At church David has lots of opportunity to move around. He comes to the front for the music at the beginning, and he goes to his church school class. In the class his favourite activities are acting out Bible stories and using his body to show feelings. He also like to make things. When the children return to the liturgy, David shares the peace enthusiastically with many people throughout the church, giving warm hugs. Sometimes he helps take up the bread and wine or the collection. He also likes to stand next to one of his favourite adults to sing the hymns and songs.

More on learning styles

These are real children whom we know. Each learns differently. Meghan is a visual learner; Caroline, an auditory learner; and David, a tactile learner. Each experiences the world differently, takes in and absorbs information differently.

There are many ways of understanding how children and adults learn. One theory suggests that each of us, adult or child, learns in three ways. Although we can function in all of them, one of the three is our preferred method, the one we naturally turn to. We learn by

- hearing and speaking,
- seeing,
- moving and touching.

If we recognize from the beginning that no one approach will suit all children, then we can free ourselves to be creative with resource and curriculum material, evaluating and adapting it with the specific children in our community in mind. By accommodating different learning styles in our planning, we celebrate God's diversity in our midst.

> *If we put learning theory to use, we stop "covering" scripture and help students find meaning in scripture. We recognize that no single approach meets all students' needs. Standardizing our teaching methods is a real temptation in our culture, where we standardize everything from intelligence tests to premeasured packets of coffee. When we celebrate diversity, recognizing it as integral to God's unfolding plan, we use different methods for different students.*
>
> *Living the Good News* curriculum[8]

Think of the children in your group. You will probably be able to identify the tactile learner easily, but can you also discern the preferences of the others? Can you recognize your preferred learning style?

Now think of a typical church school session. Does each session have activities which appeal to each learning style? Do you tend to highlight the activity which appeals to your own learning style? Think of the curriculum and read it with fresh eyes.

A good curriculum will have activities, or options within activities, that correspond to the three learning styles. Use them. Make choices that will correspond with the needs of your group. Each activity is there to provide a learning opportunity for a particular learning style. Slavishly doing all the activities in the order suggested may not serve the needs of your learners. Keep them in mind and let the curriculum work for them. It is especially effective if the members of the group can select the activity which suits their style. Then, as guide, you might be able to help them risk choosing an activity that will challenge them to use another, less dominant style.

A different approach to discipline

Some children may find it difficult to engage in church school activities. There may be many reasons: perhaps the children have been forced to come, or they may have personal traits which get in the way of their ability to engage the material. We may think, for example, of the child with "ants in her pants" as a discipline problem, but another approach to her behaviour may better help her to be comfortable in church school.

Often the child considered to be challenging prefers to learn by moving and touching. She or he is not engaged by quiet listening and discussion of lesson plans. Indeed, such children are easily bored and frustrated by this kind of approach — as frustrated as the adults around them are by their behaviour. Often "behaviour problems" can be solved or avoided when program planning acknowledges the high activity needs of these children and incorporates some active tasks for them. Leaders can consider assigning more energetic children to gathering materials, carrying messages to other classes, being "it" in active games or songs, or acting in role plays. These activities build on active children's need to move, meet their learning style requirements, and nurture their self-esteem.

Most curricula offer common-sense approaches to dealing with inappropriate behaviour. The following suggestions may be helpful.

- Speak politely to the child, using his or her name and saying "please" and "thank you." It helps to speak at the child's level, both physically and intellectually.

- Keep the rules clear and simple. Post them on the walls, using picture symbols for small children. If they know what is expected of them and what will be happening, the children will be more cooperative.

- Acknowledge the child's feelings; then seek a solution to the problem together.

- Indicate the natural consequences of the inappropriate behaviour and the reasons for the appropriate behaviour.

Some congregations have created pastoral care teams to help children who do not seem to be interested in the program. These specially recruited adults (perhaps some who support the program but do not want to teach) float around the groups looking for the child whom some would describe as disruptive, distracted, or "out of sorts." A team member is able to deal personally with the child and, by taking him or her aside, may discover the cause of the behaviour. If so, strategies can be designed to engage this child's attention and participation.

Getting to know the child beyond the behaviour and reputation is essential — and takes time and care. Several strategies are possible.

Quiet area

Is there a place in your church that can be known as the quiet area — a corner set apart or a sitting-room or lounge, perhaps one normally off limits to children? Some children are not comfortable in groups and need a quiet space and quiet activities. Having such space available allows children to choose to move to this area. An adult may use this opportunity to inquire if there is anything the child would like to talk about. Often, talking may be difficult. To help give expression to deeper concerns, try working with the child through a game (speaking through puppets), art work (free drawing or drawing feelings or pictures of the problem), story-telling, or writing. The quiet area may also be used as a place where a child can safely "vent" and take time away — in the restorative, not the punitive sense.

Communication with other family members

It is helpful to know in advance if there is a child who will need special attention. Church school registration forms can include a section for parents to provide this information about their child. The form may ask such questions as

> *What do we need to know about your child?*
> *What are your child's favourite toys/games?*
> *What are your child's least favourite activities?*

Through the year, volunteers will find it helpful to share their experiences right away with the parents and to ask their advice. Parents know their child better than anyone does, and it is likely that they have developed helpful strategies for engaging their child.

While these strategies may temporarily "solve the problem" with the child, taking on such a program in even a moderately sized church school will lead to bigger questions and concerns. In any congregation today there may be children from homes facing crises: joblessness, illness, the death of someone close (including family pets), a family break-up, blended families, and the many other pressures of our age. How might we intentionally care for the effected children in our midst? Can we be a community that takes seriously the concerns that children bring, that addresses the needs of children as individuals as well as members of family groups? Can this model work with all members of the congregation, not just children? What might such a community look like?

> *I look to my faith community for support as a parent and family member. Here there are others, of different ages, who share a common story and values. I trust and admire many of these people. We have experienced their care and support in the past. My children, who are not yet adolescents, have many opportunities to get to know these adults and have begun to form relationships with them. I give thanks for this situation, because I know that some time in the future my children are going to need someone, other than me, to talk with and to help answer the questions they have. I also know that I have been such a person to at least one young person in our congregation. Chris is one of our regular baby-sitters as well as a member of the same congregation. Sometimes she experiences tension with her parents and sister. Nothing alarming, but Chris seems to need to share that with someone she trusts. I told her that she could call any time, just to talk. I said that what she told me was in confidence and I wouldn't share it with her family unless we agreed together that I could. She has called, or stayed for a chat after an evening of baby-sitting. I think she understands that I'm willing to listen but that I'm not her parent. This is one expression of real community.*

People in the congregation or church school can help support children in their growth, whether or not they are in what would be described as a crisis. These adults are mentors or models. (And frequently children model behaviour for us adults!) Mentoring begins with treating children as individuals with hopes, dreams, and fears. It begins with knowing the children by their personal, not just their family, names. It begins with speaking to them directly, not through their parents. It begins with asking the children how they are doing, and getting beyond the polite, "I'm okay." It means remembering what is going on in their lives ("How did the skating competition go?") and being truly interested in the answer. Mentoring includes being open to the children's concern for us, as well, and being honest when they ask us how we are ("Actually I'm feeling tired today. It's been a busy week.").

Special needs

Being inclusive also means being able to accommodate children with "special needs." Every child has special needs; some children, however, have identifiable physical and psychological challenges:

- physical challenges,
- emotional challenges,
- learning disabilities,
- health-related problems.

Until recently, segregated education was considered the most appropriate way to meet the needs of disabled children. This view has now given way to a conviction that the needs of all children should be met within regular community settings.

The church, however, has not always been seen as a welcoming place for families with a member with special needs. At best this situation is very sad. At worst it is a violation of all that the gospel says about the way Jesus responds to the challenges faced by the human community. If church is still a place where the upright and well-dressed worship in quiet decorum, a cerebral palsied person who cannot control his or her limbs and vocal cords may be seen as an embarrassment.

If, on the other hand, a congregation opens its arms to the wider community, shows that it is inclusive by being physically accessible, and pronounces clearly that it welcomes all, no matter what their gifts, the vision of living authentically as the children of God — of serving as God asks — is more nearly attained. How can congregations genuinely include people with a variety of physical and developmental needs when concepts of faith development are linked with cognitive and verbal ability and when criteria for participation are rooted in physical and economic capacity?

Inclusion enables the disabled child to develop self-esteem and a sense of belonging to the community. The special advantage that a church school setting provides is a loving, safe environment for individual development. Access to such an environment should not depend on one's physical, cognitive, or emotional development.

Moreover, if disabled persons are excluded, intentionally or unintentionally, from the faith community, other members of the congregation are prevented from interacting with their disabled peers and the centuries-old discomfort that people feel with those who appear "different" is perpetuated. Such exclusion also prevents normal and natural curiosity about physical and mental differences from being explored and satisfied.

Including those children who are able to achieve and develop within the regular church school program, regardless of the severity of their condition, provides an invaluable learning experience for the whole community. The process, while demanding, will be rewarding in the long term.

Facilitating inclusion

The first step towards integrating the disabled child into the church school setting is to communicate with the child's parents or guardians about his or her specific needs. Questions can be asked on the registration form.

> *Are there any special needs or learning disabilities which we should be aware of?*

If yes, may we speak with you about your child's needs so as to be able to make him/her as comfortable as possible?

Church school volunteers will need to know of needs and be part of discussions with the child and family.

It is important to help the church school group, children and volunteers, feel comfortable in the presence of the disabled child. Leaders might consider inviting the child's parents to an open discussion with the church school children about the disability and special needs. This kind of session should take place only with the permission of the child. In such a setting, children would be able to discuss the common disabilities we all live with. Community building activities can be designed to provide a non-threatening environment.

Leaders will also want to consider ways of making it possible for these children to participate, so that all may enjoy the experience. Inclusion in the community is modeled when leaders

- make the classroom and church accessible to the disabled child;
- ask for a volunteer partner to assist when needed;
- avoid babying or treating the child with unnecessary attention;
- encourage everyone to offer supportive comments about contributions;
- provide resources to match individual skills.

Many congregations might find it worthwhile to hold a training event or consultation on meeting the needs of children with physical or learning disabilities in their community. Special education teachers in the congregation or members of support groups in the community might be invited to act as resource persons.

Children and death

At some time in the life of any faith community, it is likely that children will be confronted with death, whether that of a friend or family member, the result of a tragedy in the community, or the loss of a family pet. Adults often have trouble dealing with death and may wish to protect children from the ending of life, but it is important to address the issue when it arises. Children need the opportunity to grieve just as adults do.

In a small town, a thirteen-year-old boy died very suddenly of meningitis on the Saturday of Thanksgiving weekend. Three generations of his family were active in the parish, and the faith community was devastated. After the initial shock and the funeral, attended by many children and young people, families were faced with questions about why and how. They also wanted to know what to do and what to say to the boy's sisters, parents, and grandmother. Any word or gesture seemed inadequate. It seemed easier to do nothing, but that wasn't right either.

Resources were available, in this case from Bereaved Families of Ontario. The advice was practical in approach and format. It was distributed to everyone in the congregation and assisted many to approach the family with care and compassion.

***

I was called to be present as a consultant with the church school the week after one of their clergy collapsed and died of a heart attack while celebrating the Sunday eucharist. The children, and many adults who chose to join us, talked of what they had seen and heard. They spoke of their feelings, their fears, their sense of vulnerability, and their desire somehow to express their shock, disbelief, and grief to the priest's young family. They said they needed to do something; so we decided to make cards of condolence and sympathy. These cards were created during church school time, then brought into church during the offertory and presented to the priest's widow and child as the church school's expression of sorrow and compassion.

Children need to be encouraged to express their feelings about death — to know that it is all right to ask questions about it and to feel bad and cry. Our role can be to share the devastation and to encourage a response with questions.

What have you heard about...?

How do you feel about...?

I wonder how John feels about his Granddad's death?

How would you feel if a member of your family died?

What might we say to John the next time we see him?

Children also need to know that it is all right to

- cry and be sad,
- feel frightened,
- feel confused,
- not know what to say,
- touch or hug their bereaved friends,
- say the name of the deceased person and talk about him/her.

In fact this last response is to be encouraged. Often the worst aspect of losing a family member is when people act as if the person had never existed.

It is also a good idea to decide how children might show a grieving friend how much they care. They can make a card, write a letter, gather for a special lunch, make a gift... It is especially important that children closest to the bereaved child have the opportunity to share their feelings in a tangible way. Our task in a church school setting can be to enable the children to find their way of showing their feelings.

Children have many questions about death. Some can be answered easily; many do not have simple answers. However, the child needs to know that the question is worth asking. A definitive answer is not what is needed. An adult can acknowledge the question and search with the child for a response that might fit the moment. It is perfectly all right to say, "I don't know about the answer to that; let's see if we can find out together." Clergy, bereavement groups, or those who have suffered loss can provide very helpful resources to individuals and communities experiencing the pain of death.

Pastoral care — Paying attention

The realities of family life

Family life is significantly different now than in the mythical "good old days" of full church schools and a single model of the family. As a result, we need to be aware that each family defines itself differently. Its members are those whom *they* recognize as family. A narrow definition will limit our ability to minister to those who might come to us. In the past two decades, separated, divorced, and blended families have become more common. Church members are not immune to these trends. Indeed, such wrenching events draw people to the faith community for support. The chances are good that in any community there are children who are members of a family that is not composed of husband, wife, and biological siblings. Christian educators need to be aware of the possible effects of such circumstances on the lives of those who join their learning groups. Children also need to discover from the Christian community, in loving and constructive ways, that laying blame and fault is not helpful or constructive, but that exploring their feelings can be.

Even if not living within new definitions of the family, people come to the church with many stresses and challenges at this point in the late twentieth century. No doubt we can all name them: the pace of change, shifts in the job market, the impact of technology, job loss, caring for aging family members, career demands, economic hardship, recovering from past pain, parenting early adolescents and teenagers. Our communities need to find ways of addressing these family life issues within a Christian context.

The reality is that many families will be facing circumstances that do not allow weekly attendance at church. In some cases absence is a matter of choice; in the case of custody arrangements in separation and divorce, it probably isn't. It is especially important in planning church school lessons to realize that attendance will probably be sporadic for the children in these family situations. Try to make each lesson stand on its own so that no child is put in a position of feeling uncomfortable, or even guilty, about not knowing what happened in previous weeks. Many children have enough to cope with without feeling "behind" in church school lessons.

Other disclosures are more disturbing and by law require immediate action on the part of anyone who hears them. Child physical or sexual abuse and any actions which endanger the life of a child must be addressed. We urge you to learn the policy for your church and community. Plan a response to such disclosure before it happens and be sure that volunteers know what they should do. Clergy and any other staff should have information and clear instructions about what to do should a child, or adult, disclose abuse.[9]

Church school — Getting organized

Sunday School Circa 1950

"Who made you?" was always
The question
The answer was always
"God."
Well, there we stood
Three feet high
Heads bowed
Leaning into
Bosoms.

Now
I no longer recall
The Catechism
Or brood on the Genesis
Of life
No.

I ponder the exchange
Itself
And salvage mostly
The leaning.

Alice Walker[10]

How do I know what works for our church school?
How else can church school be organized?
What about a curriculum?

Church school volunteers usually have lots of questions and face many challenges. We are confronted with a variety of tasks, including choosing and evaluating curriculum, allocating and organizing available space, designing and implementing program sessions, recruiting and supporting additional volunteers, providing pastoral care, managing supplies, and passing on the faith to children. Moreover, most of us have to create our programs in some of the least attractive parts of the church building. Sent away from the gathered community and its space filled with interesting windows, flowers, and expensive furniture, we find ourselves in dimly lit basements and large, musty old halls, which are often not dedicated to the exclusive use of the church school. As one volunteer noted, "Our church school is held in a room in the basement next to the furnace where every Sunday is Ash Wednesday." It is easy to understand why children and the adults who care for them in church schools have often felt dispirited.

We in the church schools have inherited so much: the space provided for our activities, the organization of classes, the expectations about being teachers and instructing children in the faith, and the venerable stories of the good old days when there were hundreds of children filling the church school. These are important stories of our churches' past. For most of us, however, these accounts no longer have bearing on our reality. Nor are the expectations and hopes we bring for our experience of church and church school the same as those of the 1950s and 1960s. As parents, educators, volunteers, and children, we are a very different group living in a very different world. Perhaps it is time to take a good look at the structures and systems the church is offering us and make them our own!

Start with evaluation

Evaluation is a word that makes us nervous. We tend to overlook this task, and we pay for doing so. When it becomes part of what we do — a discipline, if you like — evaluation can save us many headaches and much time.

There are more models of church school organization than we can keep up with, and each comes with a bundle of good news stories and a bunch of not-so-good news stories or challenges. The success of a program, structure, or recruitment strategy depends only in part on choosing the option that matches the gifts, skills, and quests of the volunteers and the learning needs of the children. The real success stories come from groups of children and adults who adjust, create, recreate, amend, and transform programs and structures to make the church school experience their own special opportunity to explore their faith together.

Any one church school is probably organized to accommodate a set of circumstances, some of which are unique to the community in and for which it operates. The physical setting, liturgical tradition, and demographics of the whole congregation all play an important role in shaping the program. It may well suit the needs of the children and adults perfectly. Or perhaps the structure suited a time gone by, a set of circumstances no longer relevant, and really does not work well any more. If an evaluation has not been made recently, how is anyone to know?

It is not unusual to find a situation where volunteer burn-out is high, recruitment has become a major headache, the children are complaining of boredom, and there is no energy for meeting together for social or learning events. If this scenario sounds familiar, look at the way the church school is organized. You may be working with a set of expectations and responsibilities that do not match the gifts and skills the current volunteer corps has to offer.

Take time *now* to examine the organization of the congregation's church school. Consider the questions outlined in Work sheet 1, "Taking a look at the church school program," beginning on page 81. Gather a group of people to discuss them and agree on some actions. This gathering might include the pastor, members of the board or some other decision-making group, church school volunteers, parents and children. Determine together what aspects of the organization of the church school are fixed, by tradition or by other factors beyond your control. Then discern the opportunities for change to meet the unique and present needs of your community. Identify the key challenges for your work with children. Where is your congregation's "growing edge" of ministry with children? *Remember, evaluation and adaptability are keys to success!*

Children themselves can contribute a great deal to these discussions, because church school is the major part of their church experience and the place they are likely to feel the strongest sense of ownership. This is especially important for children in grades 4 and up. The congregation that is not meeting their needs for meaningful inclusion risks losing these children as they approach adolescence. Church school teachers, volunteers, and coordinators have the ability to make children feel important, valued, welcomed, and needed by including them in discussions regarding their church and church school experience; helping them to plan, carry out and evaluate their church school program; and being responsive to their interests and opinions.

Hold a consultation

Why not begin a church school season by holding a consultation with all those who have an interest in the Christian formation of children in your congregation? Think of everyone who might have an interest: parents, former teachers, clergy, youth group, junior choir leaders, and so on. Assure at least some of these people that you want them to bring their wisdom and that they are *not* being asked to volunteer. The questions suggested for evaluation in Work sheet 1 could form the basis of the conversation, or a design such as the one found in Work sheet 2, "Children's ministry gathering," on page 85, might be used. The purpose of the "Children's ministry gathering" Work sheet is to establish a statement of purpose for the program and to determine a series of actions based on it. The advantage for the church school or children's ministry coordinator is that overall responsibility for Christian formation of children is shared with others in the congregation. A consultation can highlight the importance of *a ministry of formation for children* to the life of the congregation and to the lives of all the baptized.

There are many effective ways of collecting ideas from a group of adults and children. The four described below may be helpful.

Brainstorming

Explain that the purpose of brainstorming is to generate as many ideas as possible, whether or not they seem reasonable or achievable, and that evaluation and decision making will come later in the process. Invite the group to offer their ideas on the topic (for example, "How can we recognize the volunteers this year?"). Encourage everyone to contribute their suggestions. Accept them *all;* write them down. Discourage any discussion or critique (the hardest part of the process to effect) until all ideas have been shared. When the list seems as complete as possible, the group can begin to evaluate the practicality of the suggestions and develop an actual plan.

Anonymous plans

Give each participant a pencil and an identical (in size and colour) piece of paper. Ask everyone to write out their ideas on the topic, ("The purpose of our church school is ...."). Collect the papers, shuffle the pile, and invite one person to read them aloud or compile them for discussion.

Taking stock

Develop a specific evaluation sheet. Ask questions carefully. Be sure you are prepared to respond to what you receive. Gather the responses, and use them to determine what the next steps are for your group.

The many whys

Name a problem or situation that needs fixing (for example, volunteer recruitment). Write this topic on a piece of paper and post it high on a large blank wall. Invite people to list all the possible reasons (one per sheet of paper) why the topic is a problem. Post the papers on the wall. The only rule is to phrase the reasons without naming individuals (for example, "people do" or "someone could"). Read out all the possible reasons. Ask the group to come up with reasons for the reasons. Once again ask, "Why?" Keep going until you find that one or two reasons generate a lot of comment. These are the real reasons for the issue, and here is where change may be welcome.

Just talking about change does not make it happen. If change is needed, the change needs to be planned. Good planning answers three questions: Whom will it help? What will they do? When will they have it done?

Models of organization

Church schools come in all shapes and sizes. Here is a "mix and match" list of the more common organizational styles. No one model will be any congregation's perfect fit. However, knowing what others are using can help us to evaluate the kind of educational environment currently being provided for our children and can also point to other possibilities.

When is church school?

Exploring the theme

The children and adults begin together in the church where they gather and pray and where the theme for the liturgy is set, usually by the priest or minister, in the children's focus or talk. The children then go to church school to explore this theme through reading and stories, music, crafts, drama, and other experiential activities. If the liturgy is the eucharist, the children return to the church at the peace or the offertory hymn and stay until the dismissal.

Liturgy of the word

A separate, but fairly complete liturgy of the word happens in the church school. Children and adults begin the liturgy in different places, or if they begin together in church, the children leave the worship space shortly after the gathering time. Church school time will include a gathering, activity, music, prayer, readings, and theme setting. Then, together or in groups, children begin an activity to explore the theme. If the liturgy is the eucharist, the children return to the church at the peace or the offertory hymn and stay until the dismissal.

Junior church

In this model, the children's educational and liturgical experience takes place almost entirely in the church school. They may enter the church to receive communion, but only after the eucharistic prayer is complete; and if so, they go immediately back to the church school once they have received communion. In these types of church schools, the agenda tends to be primarily educational; however, increasingly a time of worship, even the eucharist, is included. At their best, these services involve children, youth, and adults sharing leadership and can develop into a new liturgical expression for the congregation.

Christian education — but not during worship time

This method offers an opportunity for both children and adults to gather for learning. The program might take place immediately before or after worship (adults and children worship together). In other cases, it takes place on a weekday after school or in the evening, perhaps with a potluck dinner. These programs are also used as a supplement to Sunday morning church school.

> *At various moments in the church year, we hold a "family event" to which the whole congregation is invited. On the Saturday before Advent Sunday, on Palm Saturday, or before a baptism, we gather for some group learning and an activity which will help families celebrate the season, concluding with a potluck meal. We begin at*

4:30 to 5:00 p.m. and introduce the theme with an activity in which we all can participate. We then work on a family project: making an advent wreath, building an Easter garden, creating banners for the Palm Sunday parade, baking bread for the eucharist at the baptism, and so on. Then we eat together. It is amazing what a community building event this is. It gets beyond the superficialities, and people begin to talk about important questions in their lives with others.

Where do we gather for church school?

Dedicated space

Some churches have space that is "the church school." It is used primarily by the church school, and anyone else who wants to use the space asks the permission of the church school coordinators or teachers. Wall space is available for displays and art work, which is supplied and changed by the church school participants. There may be a special gathering area marked by a table, cross, or even an altar. There may be classrooms assigned by grade or age groups with either temporary or permanent walls dividing the spaces.

Created space

In a growing number of churches, space is shared by other groups — church and secular groups — who rent the space during the week. It is a challenge to create the church school each week. There may be a designated cupboard or trunk for materials. It is difficult to maintain any wall space; and room dividers, tables, and chairs must be put out and cleared away each week. The good news about not having a space of your own is that it is very difficult to look like a "school."

One-room church school

Creating the space week-by-week lends itself well to a model of church school that is growing in popularity by choice and by necessity — the one-room church school. Many churches now have only a few children on any given Sunday. Either attendance is not predictable enough to group the children by age or grade, or a small group encompasses a wide age range.

Some congregations with larger church schools are trying a one-room activity centre model, because it offers a really creative approach to Christian education. Each week the children select the way they will explore the story or theme from a variety of activities available (perhaps chosen from a curriculum at various age levels) according to their own learning needs and moods.

Choosing a curriculum

A curriculum is a framework for teaching the faith. Purchasing curriculum is not the only way of approaching a Christian education program, but it is the method most commonly used in North American church schools. Writers of curricula have in mind a market which determines the parameters of the content they present. No purchased curriculum will ever be a perfect fit for any church school. The "group" envisioned by curriculum writers will always be different from the unique group of children in each individual community.

Curricula come in a wide variety of packages, from bright and glossy to simple reproducible newsprint sheets. They can ask very different things of the volunteers and expect very different things from the children. A good program provides a framework for two or three generations of Christians to share their experiences, their questions, and their hopes — to travel together for a while as pilgrims of faith. It will help lead children and adults from *learning about faith* to *action because of faith* in some very powerful ways.

While no curriculum will ever be a perfect match, there will be some that fit the theology, ministry, and mission of the congregation better than others. There will also be some that fit the church school's resources better than others. When choosing a curriculum for the church school, look carefully at the story, the educational style, the assumptions it makes about the users, and the opportunities it presents to share faith beyond church school. If you are changing from one curriculum from another, what is it about the former curriculum that directs you to change? Does it fail to engage the children in the group? Do you want something fresh? These are valid reasons. It is important to acknowledge them. When considering a curriculum, read the catalogue and sample lessons.

Symbols and rituals

Symbols are objects, occasions, and activities that are richly meaningful and help us experience our relationship with God through all our senses. Rituals are repetitive actions or activities that say something important about how we experience and respond to God. Young children, in particular, need rituals (just try to change the bedtime routine or shorten a favourite story!). Young adolescents also need ritual; although they will occasionally resist, it does provide them with familiar and stable territory at a time when so much else in their lives is changing. In evaluating a curriculum, look for the ways in which it uses symbols and rituals. Does it find ways to connect God and faith with symbols from everyday life? (For example, one of the most positive and powerful symbols for young people today is the reduce-reuse-recycle triangle. How might this symbol be "baptized" to teach about God?) Are there rituals that will appeal to the children and reinforce their learning in positive ways?

Learning styles

No one lesson will ever provide the perfect learning activities for each child in the church school class. We need to recognize this and let ourselves off the hook a bit. However, we also need to make sure that over a period of time many different activities are provided to engage as many of the children as possible. It is quite unfair to expect an active child to engage in week after week of colouring, cutting, and pasting. Too many quiet crafts are a sure recipe for what is commonly called "discipline problems" and bored children. Look for a wide variety of activities — drama, role play, crafts, short discussions or brainstorming sessions, interesting stories. These help create an environment that provides plenty of variety.

Relationships

More than anything else, church school is a place where meaningful, mentoring relationships can grow between children and adults who are not related but who share a faith. Successful curricula recognize that the most memorable part of church school are the relationships. The way we behave when we are with the children is much more powerful and influential than the content of what we are teaching.

Resources for the home

Many families are seeking ways of living out their faith at home. Look for take-home materials that suggest activities, prayers, and conversation starters that can be incorporated into meal and bed times. Remember, however, that just handing the material out will not work. The paper will end up where all other paper ends up — on a counter or in the waste basket. Use of the material will take a bit of teaching (demonstrating the opportunities to enhance family dinner conversation, for example). Introduce it at a parent event early in the church school year, and use it at other events during the year to reinforce it.

There are other questions to be asked when choosing a curriculum. Work sheet 3, "Choosing a curriculum," which begins on page 95, offers some areas for reflection.

Using the curriculum

No curriculum can be followed without some change and adaptation. No curriculum will ever be just right for any church school. Choosing a curriculum means deciding which resource will be the cornerstone of the church school program. It is by no means the only resource at hand, nor is it the only way for children or adults to grow in faith. The gift, skills, and interests of the volunteers, parents, other adults in the community, and of the kids themselves, are all important assets for the program. Incorporate these and play with the curriculum, making the program suit the community's own structure, time frame, and personnel.

The key to the effective use of any curriculum is *adapt, adapt, adapt!*

Writing your own

It is appropriate for you to create your own program for a day or a unit. This will allow you to do some teaching about issues and events important to the congregation: your patron saint, eucharistic preparation, a social ministry day, what being a Christian means in your community. The curriculum lesson plans provided by many of the published curricula are helpful models to use to provide the framework for your content. (*The Whole People of God*, for example, uses a plan of opening, theme, exploration of the theme, integration of the theme, and closing.)

Small church schools are realizing that programs, especially curricula, must suit their size and multi-age grouping. All-aged and small church schools are becoming a very common model of program, but most curricula still assume age- or grade-specific groups with enough children to form each class. There is a real need for programs written specifically for the small church schools. While it is hard work to develop your own program, the learning opportunities are endless.

Work sheet 1

Taking a look at the church school program

Taking a look at the church school program

Work through the following questions, preferably with a group of people who are interested in and knowledgeable about children's ministry in the congregation. The results will provide a clear picture of the role and structure of the church school and will help leaders identify strengths to build on and challenges to address in the coming year.

• Vision

Is there a clear mandate for the Christian formation of all baptized members of the community? In what ways is the church school part of this mandate?

• Purpose

Why is there a church school? Is there a clearly stated mission? Is it the right mission statement for your church school today? Are there other purposes for the church school that are understood but not stated?

The mission statement does not need to be elaborate; a clear and concise phrase or two is preferable. A statement of your goals lets your community know why the ministry is important. It also helps volunteers and potential volunteers know how they might contribute to an important ministry within the church.

• The Participants

Who are the children?

How many are there? How old are they? What are their favourite activities? Is there a cultural mix you need to be attentive to? Are there any special needs? What is the attendance pattern? What factors contribute to this pattern (ski season, divorced parents, and so on)? Chances are good that the cut-and-paste curriculum that charmed last year's group of nine-year-old girls will drive this year's bulge of seven-year-old boys crazy, and their teacher too. Is there a cultural mix you need to be attentive to? Are there any special needs — physical, developmental, or emotional — that should be taken into consideration?

Who are the volunteers?

Are they veterans, new recruits, parents, teenagers? What are their training or volunteer development needs? What are their spiritual and learning needs? Why do they participate? Are you a team, a cooperative, a collection of individuals? What do you expect of each other? Are there clear and up-to-date job descriptions for all the volunteer roles in the church school?

• Administration and finance

What is the relationship of the church school coordinator (superintendent) with the ordained leadership and governing bodies of the congregation? Do you have representation on any advisory or decision-making groups in the church? Do you raise your budget? Do you have a budget? Do you control how the budget is spent?

• Congregational planning

How is planning carried out in the congregation? Is the focus week-to-week, the liturgical season (Advent, Christmas, Epiphany, Lent, Easter, and so on), or the civil calendar (start-up in September and January, finish in June)? Or is some other calendar the basis for planning (planting and harvest seasons)? How do non-Sunday church school events (teacher training, special events for families, the celebration of holy days) fit in?

• Worship and church school

What has been successful in the past? Is it still satisfactory? Do the children regularly worship with the rest of the community? How much time do you usually have with the children? Does this differ from week to week? What

Worksheet 1

do the differences depend on? Do different preachers have an effect on the church school timing? If this is the case, do you have access to the preaching schedule so that volunteers can plan accordingly? Is the rotation of services (eucharist, morning prayer, special celebration) known and predictable?

• Church school space

Where does the church school meet? What are the challenges and opportunities of the space? Is the space dedicated to the church school, or is it shared with other groups or organizations? Is it too large or too small for the number of children? Is it warm, comfortable, and inviting? Are there symbols marking the space, and are they meaningful to the children? If your space is shared with other groups, what do their decorations, art work, posters, and colours mean to the children?

• The model

Is your model that of a school, a junior church, an alternative liturgy of the word? How would the teachers, parents, and children describe it? Ask them.

Work sheet 2
Children's ministry gathering

Children's ministry gathering

Purpose:

To assess the needs of the church school at this time.

To develop a common purpose for the program.

To determine the steps necessary to achieving the purpose.

To (according to your specific needs).

Beginning

30 minutes

Opening welcome.

Review the purpose of the gathering.

Invite the participants to introduce themselves by giving their names and reasons for responding to the invitation to be at the gathering. (Write these statements on flip chart paper for later reference.)

Say together a prayer. Some prayers with special meaning for church school volunteers are provided on pages 88 and 89.

Middle

60 minutes

Brainstorm:

What is the purpose of the church school in our congregation?

(Write *all* responses on the flip chart paper.)

Once all the ideas have been gathered, ask people to indicate the one or two (no more) most important ideas. Allow each person to "vote" by placing a coloured dot or check mark beside their favourite ideas, so that all have indicated their priority.

or

Test the ideas listed against the promises made in the Baptismal Covenant from *The Book of Common Prayer* (U.S.) (provided on pages 90–91).

How do they relate?

Ask a pair of participants to write a purpose statement guided by the weighted ideas or the discussions:

"The church school at _____ is..."

Invite the rest of the group to discuss the impact of having such a purpose statement. What needs to happen for it to be "owned'" by the church school and the congregation? How do we bring it to life?

- Who needs to do what by when?
- What would be the action steps — teacher training, spiritual growth opportunities for teachers and families, more space, and so on?
- What can we do? Who do we need to have help us?
- How will we know when it has been done?

What will we do with the purpose statement? Present it to the governing body of the community? Publish it in the literature produced by the church school committee? Include it in a newsletter article or a banner in the church or parish hall?

Ending

15 minutes

Where do we go from here?

Closing prayers.

Opening prayer

God our creator and redeemer,
thank you for the gift of these children
entrusted to our care for a time.
May we be patient and understanding,
ready to guide and forgive,
that in our love these children may know your love,
and learn to love your world
and the whole family of your children;
through Jesus Christ our Lord. Amen.[11]

Closing prayers

Almighty God, who has committed to thy holy church the care and nurture of
thy children: enlighten with thy wisdom those who teach and those who learn;
that, rejoicing in the knowledge of thy truth, they may worship thee and serve thee
all the days of their life; through Jesus Christ our Lord. Amen.[12]

or

Glory to God,
whose power, working in us,
can do infinitely more
than we can ask or imagine.
Glory to God from generation to generation
in the church and in Christ Jesus,
for ever and ever. Amen[13]

or

Lord,
it is night.

The night is for stillness.
    Let us be still in the presence of God.

It is night after a long day.
    What has been done has been done;
    what has not been done has not been done;
    let it be.

The night is dark.
    Let our fears of darkness of the world and of our own
    rest in you.

The night is quiet.
    Let the quietness of your peace enfold us,
    all dear to us,
    and all who have no peace.

The night heralds the dawn.
    Let us look expectantly to a new day,
    new joys,
    new possibilities.

In your name we pray.
Amen.[14]

Work sheet 2

The Episcopal Baptismal Covenant[15]

Do you believe in God the Father?
I believe in God,
the Father almighty,
creator of heaven and earth.

Do you believe in Jesus Christ, the Son of God?
I believe in Jesus Christ,
his only Son, our Lord.
He was conceived by the power of the Holy Spirit
and born of the Virgin Mary.
He suffered under Pontius Pilate,
was crucified, died, and was buried.
He descended to the dead.
On the third day he rose again.
He ascended into heaven,
and is seated at the right hand of the Father.
He will come again
to judge the living and the dead.

Do you believe in God the Holy Spirit?
I believe in the Holy Spirit,
the holy catholic Church,
the communion of saints,
the forgiveness of sins,
the resurrection of the body,
and the life everlasting.

Will you continue in the apostles' teaching and fellowship, in the
breaking of bread, and in the prayers?
I will, with God's help.

Will you persevere in resisting evil, and, whenever you fall into sin, repent and return to the Lord?
I will, with God's help.

Will you proclaim by word and example the Good News of God in Christ?
I will, with God's help.

Will you seek and serve Christ in all persons, loving your neighbor as yourself?
I will, with God's help.

Will you strive for justice and peace among all people, and respect the dignity of every human being?
I will, with God's help.

The United Church of Canada Baptismal Covenant[16]

Profession of Faith

Questions are asked of the candidates or their parents, using one from each pair of the following:

1.

Desiring the freedom of new life in Christ do you promise to resist evil and to live in love and justice?

or   In the presence of this community of faith, do you commit yourself to follow the way of Christ in your public and private life?

    I do, by the grace of God.   **I do.**

2.

Do you believe in God, Source of love, in Jesus Christ, love incarnate, and in the Holy Spirit, love's power?

or   Do you profess your faith in one God, Creator, Christ, and Spirit?

    I do, by the grace of God.   **I do.**

3.

Will you join with your brothers sisters in the mission and ministry of Christ's Church?

or   Will you support the life and and work of Christ's church?

    I will, God being my helper.   **I will.**

To the parents:

Will you share with your *child* the Christian life, and seek to grow with *him/her* in faith, hope and love?

or   Will you nurture your *child*, and together grow in faith?

    I will, God being my helper.   **I will.**

Congregational Commitment

The people may stand to pledge their support, using one of the following sets of words.

to the congregation:

Let us pledge to these persons
our support and care.

As a baptized and baptizing church,
we commit ourselves
to support and uphold you
within the community of faith

**May God grant us all
the grace to live our baptism.**

to the parents and candidates:

By your presence and witness
the Body of Christ is renewed.

to the congregation:

As a baptized and baptizing
church, do you commit
yourselves anew to the
nurture and support of the
renewed community in Christ?

We do, with God's help.

The Lutheran Baptismal Covenant[17]

The minister addresses the baptismal group and the congregation.

P: I ask you to profess your faith in Christ Jesus, reject sin, and confess the faith of the Church, the faith in which we baptize.

P: Do you renounce all the forces of evil, the devil, and all his empty promises?

R: I do.

P: Do you believe in God the Father?

C: **I believe in God, the Father almighty,**
     creator of heaven and earth.

P: Do you believe in Jesus Christ, the Son of God?

C: **I believe in Jesus Christ, his only Son, our Lord.**
     He was conceived by the power of the Holy Spirit
         and born of the virgin Mary.
     He suffered under Pontius Pilate,
         was crucified, died, and was buried.
     He descended into hell.
     On the third day he rose again.
     He ascended into heaven,
         and is seated at the right hand of the Father.
     He will come again to judge the living and the dead.

P: Do you believe in God the Holy Spirit?

C: **I believe in the Holy Spirit,**
     the holy catholic Church,
     the communion of saints,
     the forgiveness of sins,
     the resurrection of the body,
     and the life everlasting. Amen

Work sheet 3

Choosing a curriculum

Choosing a curriculum

These questions will help children's ministry leaders evaluate curricula for use in the church school program.

• Assumptions

What are the assumptions within the curriculum you use?

Does the curriculum assume two hours preparation time? Does it make assumptions about the congregation? Does it assume a particular culture — national, denominational? Does it assume that children are all of the same ethnic origin? Do these assumptions fit with your situation? Are you prepared to ignore, override, or adapt those which do not fit?

• Appearance

How does it look?

Is it attractive and appealing to the eye for children and adults where appropriate? Does the style assist the reader in preparing for the lesson?

• Story and vision

What story does this curriculum tell?

According to the curriculum...

What is its vision of God and church? Who is God? Jesus? The Holy Spirit? Who and what is the church?

What is the role of the scriptures? Does the curriculum follow a lectionary so that the whole of the congregation is exploring the same readings?

What is the purpose of Christian life? How does it present the rest of the world?

Does the vision of God and church portrayed by the curriculum match that taught and lived by the rest of the worshipping community? Does it match the mission of the congregation's education program, or that of your church school?

• Symbols

Is there a good use of symbols?

Are there a variety of symbols from both our Christian tradition as well as from everyday life? Are these symbols congruent with those upheld by the rest of the congregation?

• Rituals

Are there rituals? Look for program pieces that happen in each lesson, that involve the children, and that represent something important about the relationship between God, kids, and us.

• Approach to learning

Is there a good assortment of activities to choose from so that church school planners can select lessons that will meet the different learning needs of children in the group (things to touch, read, hear, see, do)? Are the activities appropriate to the specific age group?

• Christian living

Does the curriculum ask the "so what does it mean for us" question? If the love of Christ doesn't make a difference to our lives, why should we care? It's good to learn the Bible stories, but this is only half the task. In order to live our baptism as a lifestyle, we also need to explore what the scriptures mean for our daily lives and our lives within the Christian community.

• Relationships

How does the curriculum nurture relationships between adults and children? Can it be adapted to encourage and build relationships with others in the congregation? How will it lead adults into learning?

• Practicality

Is the curriculum possible for us? In what ways does it fit the space, equipment, amount of time, and number of volunteers our church school has now? In what ways will it challenge us to do something differently? Who else would we need?

What else would we need? How clear are the instructions? Is it easily adaptable? How long will it take to prepare for the lessons?

• Volunteer support

Does the curriculum give the volunteers some opportunity to learn and grow in their faith at their level?

• Take-home resources

Does the curriculum offer supplementary resources? Does it provide ways of helping children take what they are learning home with them? Are there suggestions for activities, prayers, and conversation starters that can be incorporated into meal and bed times?

• Other events

Does the curriculum include ideas for other celebrations and events which are part of your church's life, concern, and ministry? Often these resources will come from places outside of the curriculum, for example, from local or national church offices.

Volunteer ministry — Rethinking recruitment

Not me! I've done my time.

I spend all week with my kids, Sunday morning is for me.

Once I say "yes," will it be forever?

I don't know about religion; I came for you to take care of that.

Recruiting volunteers for the church school is a task that strikes panic into the heart of clergy and church school coordinators each spring or fall. Traditionally, church schools have been run, implicitly or explicitly, on the cooperative model. Parents or relatives who wish to have their children participate are expected to take on some teaching responsibilities.

Some church schools have very creative ways of enlisting parents. Every September one church puts the church school sign-up sheet in the foyer of the building. Parents are invited to enroll their children by placing their names on the sheet; but, for every five children, an adult volunteer must be added to the list. There is much jockeying for position — if your child is number six, you are in a bind. Do you add your name as a volunteer? Do you recruit someone else for the task? Or do you hang around and wait for someone else to fill the spot? This method certainly spreads the recruitment anxiety around, but does it do justice to the children and their need for a quality program? There is a pretty good chance that the children pick up the stress and reluctance experienced by the adults as they scheme to get to the sheet at a time when they will not feel the need to volunteer. This model also ignores the pool of potential non-parent volunteers in the rest of the congregation and denies them participation in a worthwhile ministry.

Church schools are now paying for some long-standing assumptions that make it difficult for today's adults to find their place and make a contribution. The old assumptions make it virtually impossible to move beyond the holy baby-sitting attitude into a new way of being with the children in our midst. Unless they are identified, examined, and addressed, these assumptions will undermine efforts to raise the profile of Christian education ministry.

Some unhelpful assumptions of well-intentioned church schools

- Any warm body will do.
- If you are a parent, you have a vested interest in having a church school.
- The only possible contribution is to be a "teacher" in a class.
- You have to know the subject matter and then you have to teach it — all by yourself. *But:*
- You do not necessarily need to know the material very well.
- Being a church school volunteer is reward enough in itself.

Expanding the vision

Being with children in the church school is a crucial ministry for the faith community — a calling to mentor children in the faith. When we think back on our own childhood and adolescence, we remember adults who made a real difference for us. These were adults who, somewhere along the way, took us seriously, scolded us appropriately, expected more than we thought we could give, and then guided us as we stretched and grew. These special people in our lives probably never knew that they played this role. They may never know how much they mean to us.

By volunteering in the church school, we offer ourselves to be such special people with the children of our congregations. We may not know when we achieve such status — it may be that right now a seven-year-old is looking forward to seeing you this Sunday because you always say "hello"; or some eleven-year-old may be hanging on your every word because you are an interesting adult (not her parent). For these young people some important formative impressions of church, Christian character, and community will be based on the time we spend together.

Discerning the people who have a ministry with children is more than guessing who is least likely to say "no." Rather, we should consider who we want sharing their time, themselves, and their faith with our children. Who seems to have rapport with young people? Who really listens to children with interest? Who includes children in their conversation? (How many times do parents receive compliments meant for their children even when the child is standing right there?) Who are our story-tellers or musicians? Who has a special skill or talent that could be shared? Who are the congregation's living saints? These are people who are able to make the connections between the gospel and their weekday lives. Who are the community's holy people? These women and men are hard to describe; but we immediately recognize their faith, spirit, and character. Who are the adults who are eagerly learning about their own faith, who acknowledge that they don't have all the answers, but who want to spend time exploring the questions? Often the most dedicated volunteers are involved because of something they want to learn.

Do we believe in God?

Will Grandma know me when I get to heaven too?

Does God really hear me? I prayed that Grandpa wouldn't die, but he did.

Many young families returning to church, or coming to church for the first time in their lives, have little or no experience of faith. They come looking for something, first for their children, but also for themselves. A crisis or a challenge is likely to have brought them. It may be a family struggle or a tragedy. It may be that a child has started to ask difficult questions. It may be that they are finding the world's offerings to be spiritually sterile and are looking for a community of people with whom to share some common values.

For these folk, the church school can be the agency for Christian education of two generations together. The church is also one of the few places left in our society where we can expect to experience a community of all generations, from the very young to the very old, who can together share their wisdom, learn about our great and formative stories, explore their values, and nurture a growing faith.

The children's program can, and should, involve many adults. They can participate in roles other than that of "teacher." It is important to have some volunteers who are confident in sharing their faith with children and adults, but also of value are adults who see themselves more as learners than teachers. A children's ministry is greatly enriched by a group of volunteers who may have very different gifts of time, energy, and talent to offer but who share a common interest in the faith development of children. Some people will be able to give weekly volunteer time. Some will offer a particular skill or service for shorter periods of time. Still others will be regular guests, volunteering once a month or so.

The inclusion of many adults in a variety of ways will provide a rich educational and relational environment for everyone involved. It may also alleviate some of the generational tensions found in congregations. There are probably many adults who do not have a clue what the church school is about and who may have ambivalent feelings about the presence of children in any aspect of church life. Fostering personal relationships between children and the more senior members of a congregation can do much to promote community harmony. And it will not hurt to have a few fans on the congregation's management or advisory board at budget time. Raising the profile of children's ministry is a big part of an ongoing recruitment strategy.

Identifying the qualities

Enlarging the vision of who might be involved in the church school program is the first step in good recruitment. The next step involves explaining to prospective volunteers the reasons *they* have been chosen to be invited to participate.

- *I have noticed that the children really like to sit with you and your family in church. You seem to have a good rapport with them...*

- *I heard you speak about how your faith nourishes and strengthens you in your work. I wish the kids in the church school could spend some time with you...*

- *You mean a lot to me. I listen to you speak about your faith and your love of God, and I wish the children in the church school could hear what you have to say...*

- *I admire the way you are so open to exploring and learning about your faith. The children in the church school could benefit from someone with your energy to learn...*

- *You have a lot of good questions. Spending time with us in the church school would be a great way to search for some answers...*

When we tell people what it is about them that has led us to invite their involvement, we are actually letting them know that we have paid attention to them. We have listened, noticed, and now responded to their particular cares, interests, and gifts. Already, in the earliest stages of recruitment, we will have shown care and support of our volunteers.

Defining the task

Identifying the people to recruit and the reasons for those choices are key components of good recruitment practice. Also it is important to be very clear about what the potential volunteers are being asked to do. People should know what they will have to take on, in role and in task.

One habit of church school organizers has been to try to create a school environment. This approach makes some sense when we realize that in many, many congregations, educational programming means church school. For most of us, in fact, education means school. Children are organized by grade or age and put into classes, and in larger churches, even into classrooms. Volunteers are called teachers, whether or not they have had any teaching experience or training. Things are made even worse by the ascription to church school "teachers" of lots of expertise, when the structures, time-frame, resources, and even intent of the church school program inhibit volunteers from functioning as educators. (For example, many curricula now value and emphasize the relationship between children and adult volunteers. They provide a program that sees us all as learners together. At the other end of the spectrum, there are "cut and paste" curricula which require little or no preparation or thought on the part of the volunteer. The adult is superfluous to whatever learning goals the curricula writers have.)

Finally, many people tend to assume that the best volunteers are professional teachers. For people who are teachers in their weekday lives, teaching yet one more day is seldom a glad gift. Often professional teachers can be excellent resources for the church school as consultants on learning or behavioural issues. In this way children's ministry can profit from professional educators' wisdom and experience while respecting their need to do something different with their volunteer time.

Many volunteers doing a variety of jobs will enrich the children's programs. Some possible roles include

- coordinator;
- organizer — of meetings, of recruitment strategies, of evaluations;

- teacher — another way of thinking about this role is "being on first" with a group or class;

- apprentice — working with a more experienced volunteer;

- pastoral care person — to spend time in another space with a child who is not being engaged by a group activity, or to spend time with a group that needs some extra grown-up help;

- last-minute leader — to take a class if someone doesn't show up, and do something unexpected with the kids;

- arts and crafts coordinator — to look after the supplies and to organize and facilitate a special project every now and then;

- musician;

- story-teller — such as a senior who visits the church school a few times each year to tell favourite Bible stories or stories about the history of the congregation;

- drama coach — for pageants and other times when the curriculum suggests role plays or dramas;

- dancer.

The list goes on and on and depends only on the imagination and the talents and skills of the congregation. This approach offers people lots of different volunteer opportunities in the children's program and enables them to find ways of participating by negotiating the kind of job that fits their unique talents and energy.

Sharing the leadership — The team approach

Developing a list of people with different roles, skills, and gifts to share with the church school is only the beginning of sound staffing. A shared leadership approach offers many benefits to the participants: no one volunteer must carry the full weight of responsibility for a group of children; tasks can better be allocated according to interests and abilities; and the children have opportunities to form relationships with more of the adults in the faith community. There are several ways of sharing the leadership of a church school class among a group of volunteers.

Week by week in pairs

In this model, volunteers meet at the start of each term to negotiate the schedule. Children's groups are led by pairs of volunteers who choose Sundays based on their schedules and the lesson requirements. The pairs may be fixed — a married couple may choose always to teach together — or they may be flexible. Since there will be a different set of adults in the church school each week, it is a good idea for all the volunteers to come together to the church school two or three times during the year so that the children know all their faces and names.

Through the year with a larger team

Teams of three to six volunteers take responsibility for a particular group in the church school for the year. Each team organizes its teaching roster. The children get to know their team. Arranging several opportunities for the team to meet the children, not necessarily in church school time, may help them to recognize that the rotation of leaders is planned, not happenstance. The team may gather periodically to discuss the children and plan the classes.

For a unit with a team

Leaders serve for a block of no more than seven or eight weeks of the year. This system allows enough time for the volunteers to get to know the children well and frees them for other activities for the rest of the year. Leaders can shape the time they have together. They may follow the curriculum or supplement it with an ongoing project: building an Easter garden through Lent; learning a skill, like navigating through the Bible or prayer book; rehearsing a play; and so on.

Occasional appearances as guests

Some volunteers may participate in the program less often than group leaders. People with specific gifts may choose to visit once in the year, once a term, or even once a month to share their talents and enrich the program. These people can work with an adult who is familiar with the children in the group to develop a workable project or event. After the event, the children can find a way to thank the guest for his or her contribution. These "guest appearances" are key opportunities to introduce potential volunteers and supporters to the church school and the children.

Determining time commitments

Volunteers need to know more than what is being asked of them and why. They need to know how much time they will need to contribute. To be fair to the volunteers, and honestly supportive, recruiters should be accurate in assessing and communicating the time commitment that is expected or that the job requires. An invitation to participate in the church school program should include a specific indication of both the desired activity and the required time.

- *I've noticed the beautiful crafts you made for the bazaar. Would you consider coming to the church school once a term to show the children how to make something?*

- *I hear you play the (piano/guitar/flute). Would you give one Sunday a month to the children's program to help us learn some new music?*

- *Your speech at last week's advisory board meeting was really moving. You speak very well. Would you come to the church school one Sunday next month to tell the children the story of...?*

- *Would you consider taking responsibility, along with three other people, for the nine- to eleven-year-old group for this coming year?*

Compiling the answers to the *who, why, what for,* and *how long* questions completes the second step on the road to good volunteer recruitment.

Supporting volunteers

The most committed and successful volunteers are often people who see that their contribution will offer them new learning and experience. Too often volunteers are handed the curriculum and their class list and sent off to do the remainder themselves. This situation is unjust as well as very likely to fail. Volunteers who do not really know what they are supposed to be doing, and who often feel insecure in their knowledge and abilities, cannot be expected to maintain their enthusiasm and enjoy a sense of making a contribution. If we care about nurturing our children's faith, we must recognize that grown-ups are also growing spiritually and that they too need to learn, grow, and develop in their faith. The church school may be the only place in our churches, as they are organized right now, where two generations can learn together what it means to live their baptisms.

Supporting and training volunteers is key to the success of children's ministry. Hold a couple of sessions of volunteer training each year, and explain that their participation in these is a condition of volunteering. Make these sessions fun: include group building, fellowship, learning, and food. Gather the volunteers together every month or six weeks to prepare the lessons together, reflecting on the scripture and themes for the weeks ahead, choosing activities, and recruiting appropriate volunteers. Allow for time to hear concerns about preparation time and insecurities about "teaching the faith." Find ways of recognizing that the primary role of the church school volunteer is to model a loving and caring relationship with children.

Professional teachers and early childhood educators in your congregation may not want to volunteer regularly in the church school, but they may be delighted to be asked to share some of their experience and knowledge about learning styles and development in training events.

At their best, support and training sessions can give rise to a delightful and very nurturing side-effect. Successful, ongoing small groups develop where adults take their involvement with children as an opportunity to explore and nurture their own spirituality. The gatherings become a time to reflect, pray, and learn together and to offer friendship and pastoral care to one another. A community of faithful people grows, able to attend to each other as much as to the children in their care.

Job descriptions

As clear, concise statements of tasks, roles, and time frames, job descriptions summarize the results of the recruitment steps described above and are simple, commonsense, but vastly under-used, tools of volunteer recruitment. It is risky for people to accept a job without a clear understanding of what they are being asked to do. Church school volunteers are so often expected to commit to vaguely described tasks with unspecified time limits that it is no wonder so many people say no. Providing job descriptions shows respect for volunteers and demonstrates that they are valued, that their contributions will be taken seriously, and that they will be supported in their tasks. A job description does not have to be fancy, but it does need to describe the job, the expectations, and the benefits. (See Work sheet 6, "Job description form," on page 117).

Showing appreciation

Volunteer contributions of time and energy are seldom adequately recognized. Sometimes we even make the mistake of asking for a new commitment as we thank someone for his or her past efforts. "Thanks, and oh, by the way, the eleven-year-old group needs a leader next year." Most volunteers are people who are already busy. Suitable appreciation is crucial. If people are not nurtured in their volunteer commitments, they will find other ways of spending their time.

When was the last time your congregation honoured the hard-working people from the church school? When was the work done by the church school participants and their leaders acknowledged as being as important as contributions made by other adults in the community? It is vital that congregations find intentional ways to celebrate the commitment of children's ministry volunteers and to honour their contributions. The following suggestions may help generate ideas.

- Ask the volunteers to evaluate their experience. After people have donated time and energy, find out what the experience was like for them. This attention will let them know that their opinions and ideas matter.

- Remember the church school in the prayers during worship. This recognition could also include remembering to pray for the occasions, joys, and stresses of the folk most often found in church school: new terms or units, school exams, illnesses, preparations for events such as pageants or holy day celebrations, and so forth.

- Create a special time to appreciate the volunteers in your congregation during a service or a social event.

- Ask church school volunteers how their experience with the children is going. Show some interest at coffee hour. Go into the church school area and see what it looks like and what the children are working on.

- Spontaneously offer to take a class for a week and let the regular teacher have a Sunday to hear the sermon.

- When appropriate, have the work of the children in the church school presented with the other gifts of the community at the offertory.

- Display with pride and prominence the banners, gardens, and murals made by the church school.

- Express appreciation with a simple gift, such as a good book or a gift certificate to a Christian bookstore, pots of thyme and sage representing volunteers' donations of time and wisdom, or a night of free baby-sitting.

All of these elements together — planning, recruitment, orientation and training, support, and evaluation — give us P. R.O.S.E., a volunteer management cycle that allows us to treat each other with respect and with due appreciation.[18]

Work sheet 4

Recruitment — Who and why

Recruitment: Who and why

1. Make a list of all the adults and teens in the congregation whom you would like to involve in the church school program.

2. List what you would like them to give to the program. What particular gifts and skills would you like them to contribute?

3. List why you think they would find ministry with children rewarding. Be prepared to answer the "Why me?" question.

Who	What	Why

Work sheet 5

Teacher training through the year

Teacher training through the year

This outline will help children's ministry leaders prepare an agenda for training and supporting the volunteers in their children's program. Planners should add details to fit their own situation.

Why? (Purpose)

- To help volunteers feel more comfortable and confident in the task of being with the children.
- To provide an opportunity for volunteers to explore their faith and their feelings about sharing their faith experience with children.
- To talk about and evaluate the joys and challenges of your church school experience and make any adaptations necessary.
- To problem-solve and build skills.
- To coordinate the logistics of the program: craft activities and resources needed, special events and celebrations, teacher schedules...

When?

Probably at least four times a year:

- in August or September to get started;
- before the beginning of a new unit or season in the curriculum;
- in June to evaluate the year and start planning and recruiting for next fall.

What?

During each teacher's training meeting...

- Begin with Bible study on the scripture passages to be covered in the next unit of lessons. Explore what volunteers think and feel about the themes of the lessons or unit.

  Some good questions to focus a discussion:

  a. How do you think a child would hear and understand these readings?

  b. What symbol or symbols — visual images, objects, sounds — are evoked by these readings? Why?

  c. Where would a child's personal experience meet with the theme of the readings?

- Do a week-by-week review of the lessons coming up in the next unit.

  a. What adaptations are needed?

  b. What special resources or preparation would be helpful?

  c. Who could help?

- Identify the special events your parish or congregation will be celebrating during this unit.

  a. Where will the children be in these events?

  b. Will there be an all-age worship service?

- Consider including some skill building in your teacher training. Perhaps there could be a discussion or workshop on faith development, learning styles, prayer with children, or some other topic.

Other resources

- Does the curricula include teacher training supplements which provide ideas for teacher training events?

- Are consultants or resource people in children's ministry available through your diocese, presbytery, or conference?

- Is there a neighbouring church with a program worth knowing more about?

- Are there other opportunities for training and support through conferences, resource fairs, and workshops offered outside of the congregation by a diocese, conference, or ecumenical gathering?

Work sheet 6

Job description form

Job description form

- ## Job title

  What is this job to be called? What is the purpose of the job?

  Why does this job need to be done? How does it contribute to the mission of the church school? How does it contribute to the wider mission of the church?

- ## Responsibilities

  What are all the duties that this job entails? Break them down into reasonably sized tasks.

- ## Time commitment

  How long will this responsibility last? How long will preparation take?

- ## Criteria for selection

  What skills are needed or would be useful? To what interests might the job appeal? Are there personality traits that would be an asset in doing this job?

- ## Training

  How will the volunteer be supported?

- ## Relationships/accountability

  Who else will be involved? What is the extent of the volunteer's accountability?

- ## Benefits

  Why would the volunteer want to be involved? What benefits would they get?

An evaluation process — Hearing and responding

Evaluation is the best tool we have to help us celebrate our successes and assess where adjustments are needed to fit a particular set of circumstances. The following is a model of an evaluation that looks at most aspects of a congregation's ministry with children. While it was designed for a diocese-wide evaluation for all congregations using *The Whole People of God* curriculum, it could be used to evaluate *any* curriculum. It was intended to generate an evaluation for us in the diocesan Children's Unit about how *The Whole People of God* was working in Anglican parishes. We received hundreds of responses. The wealth of information and stories we received was incredible. While it was not our original plan, we felt that the material was so valuable that contributing congregations needed to keep their evaluations. So, once we had gathered as much information as we could, we sent each parish's responses back to them to use in their program planning and teacher training.

The design

The evaluation has several purposes. First, it helps church school volunteers, parents, and clergy get an idea about what the children actually think about church school and church. If you use the material, you will get an impression of how the children feel while they are there and some helpful data on what they like and do not like about the program. You will learn something about whether the basic message of the curriculum is actually being heard. Also, you will gain some insight into how the children are relating their church experience to their own "real" life (for example, *because of what I learned at church school ... I talk to my friends about church/church school*).

Second, the evaluation process gives parents, volunteers, and clergy an opportunity to think about how the program is working and what else they might like to try. Does the program match their expectations? Do parents and clergy know what the children are doing on Sunday mornings? What are the challenges in offering the gospel to children? Engaging in evaluation is also a great opportunity to include parents and clergy in the program. It happens, and it is a shame, that often parents and clergy do not even know which curriculum the church school is using.

Using the work sheets

At the end of this chapter, on pages 123 to 149, you will find a series of Work sheets to use for an evaluation. We tried to make the design fun. So grab some coloured pencils and give it a try!

Photocopy each questionnaire on a different colour of paper to make the results easy to sort. There are three children's sheets (kindergarten to grade 2, grade 3 to grade 5, grade 6 and up); one for parents (not church school volunteers); one for church school volunteers; and one for clergy.

The evaluation is best done right after church. Ask the parents and children to take some time during or just after coffee hour to fill in the forms. At that time church and church school are fresh in everyone's minds, and you are likely to get most of the forms back. If you are working with a multi-age school group, just give each child the evaluation sheet that fits their grade in school and collate all the answers together. (Most questions are similar enough across age categories that they can be gathered together.) The youngest children will need an adult or an older child helper to do some of the reading. Try not to direct the children too much. Remember, what is important is what they think they have done, whether or not it was part of the lesson plan.

The results

Once you have a stack of wonderfully colourful evaluations, how do you interpret the responses?

Our favourite kind of information is in narrative style and is very anecdotal. For our diocesan evaluation, we collated the responses, question by question. For each type of questionnaire, we gathered the responses to each question into a list, noting when a particular idea or suggestion came up more than once. While this procedure was time consuming, the resulting charts of responses taught us much more than we expected about what children and adults were thinking about church and church school, and about where the strengths and weaknesses lie in our ministry with children.

Collect the responses by question. For the first question you can make a list of the activities on the questionnaire. Each time a child names a favourite activity, place a check mark beside it on the list. Each time something is named as a "don't like," place an "X" beside it. You will soon see what is working for your groups and what is not. Do the same for each question. Make lists of what the children say in response to each question. You will find that there are probably themes that emerge.

With the adult forms you are bound to have much more narrative. Summarize the content, looking for consistencies and themes. You will probably also gather new information — things that surprise you or that you never thought of before.

Watch for the emergence of issues or opportunities to which you should pay attention. Does the curriculum actually match the expectations of the children, volunteers, parents, and clergy? Are there educational opportunities or needs for children, parents, volunteers, or clergy that should be addressed? Is it time for a meeting about children's ministry in the life of the community? (If so, see Work sheet 2 on page 85).

An evaluation process — Hearing and responding

Where do we go from here?

Inevitably, the evaluation will provide a wealth of useful material that will inform the church school committee and aid in program planning for the next year. Decisions can be made about the types and balance of activities chosen. Similarly, elements which are not going smoothly can be adapted for a better fit, possibly using suggestions which come from the children themselves.

You might want to write to the people who produced your curriculum and let them know what you have learned. They should be happy to receive constructive consumer feed-back. Who knows, you might provide them with some key information for their writers' own process of evaluation and adaptation.

Finally, display the children's pictures and questionnaires (with their permission). Write up a report of the major findings from the evaluation to publish in the congregation's newsletter, bulletin, or to hand out to parents and other interested people. There will probably be messages in the questionnaires that everybody in the congregation needs to hear. Share the news that you care about ministry with children — that you are listening and responding to the successes and challenges in order to create a faithful and nurturing religious education experience for the children and those who volunteer to guide them.

An evaluation process
Hearing and responding

Questionnaire
for church school volunteers

I volunteer in the church school because ....

....

....

What is the average number of children in your group? ....

What is the attendance pattern? ....

....

I feel I know the children in my class very well (circle the number that best fits your view).

1	2	3	4	5	6	7	8	9	10
strongly agree									strongly disagree

I feel the children are comfortable with me (circle the number that best fits your view).

1	2	3	4	5	6	7	8	9	10
strongly agree									strongly disagree

The curriculum

The following questions refer to the most recent lesson you taught.

One thing I learned from this lesson was ....

....

....

What parts of the session did the children respond to best? Why? ....

....

....

Was there any time when you felt you were losing the children's attention?
Why? ....

....

....

What would you have done differently? ....

....

....

In general

How much time do you spend in preparation? ....

....

Do you have enough materials to choose from? Too much? ....

....

Do you find the lesson and activity ideas appropriate for your age group? If
not, are they generally too advanced or too simple? ....

....

What would you like to add to the curriculum? ....

....

Questionnaire for church school volunteers

Heritage

Does the curriculum provide opportunities for the children to learn about their denominational heritage?...

....

....

How would you incorporate more specific denominational teaching into the curriculum? ....

....

....

Space

Briefly describe your meeting space ....

....

What about the space works well? ....

....

What is challenging? ....

....

All in all

The three things I find most challenging about volunteering in the church school are:

....

....

....

The three things I find most rewarding about volunteering in the church school are:

....

....

....

Volunteering in the church school offers me a chance to learn more about my faith (circle the number that best fits your view).

1	2	3	4	5	6	7	8	9	10

strongly agree   strongly disagree

My favourite story from volunteering with the church school is:

....

....

....

....

....

....

Questionnaire for church school volunteers

Questionnaire
for children in kindergarten to grade 2

At church school we:

(circle as many as you want with blue or yellow)

ACT

sing

talk about important things

LISTEN TO STORIES

cut & paste

pray

dance

read

learn about God

draw

NOW — add any activities we've missed!

NOW — draw a big red box around the ones you like best!

NOW — make a big black **X** through the ones you don't like!

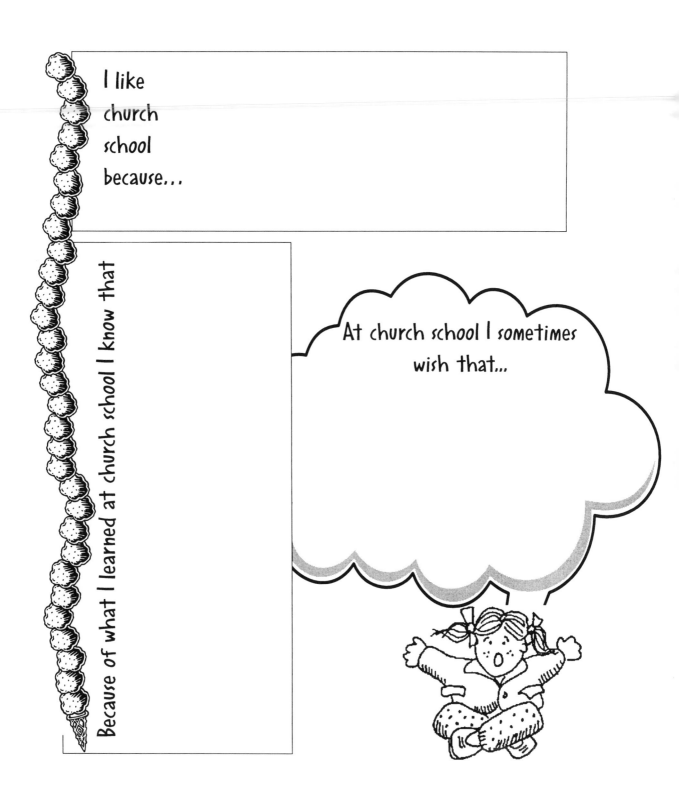

I like church school because...

Because of what I learned at church school I know that

At church school I sometimes wish that...

Questionnaire for children in kindergarten to grade 1

This is me at church school

Because of what I
learned at church
school I...

I feel _____
when I'm at church school.

I feel _____

when I'm in church.

Name: _____

Age: _____   Grade in school: _____

Questionnaire for children in kindergarten to grade 1

Questionnaire
for children in grade 3 to grade 5

At church school we:

(circle as many as you want with blue or yellow)

ACT

sing

talk about
important
things

LISTEN TO
STORIES

cut & paste

pray

dance

read

learn
about
God

draw

NOW — add any activities we've missed!

NOW — draw a big red box around the ones you like best!

NOW — make a big black X through the ones you don't like!

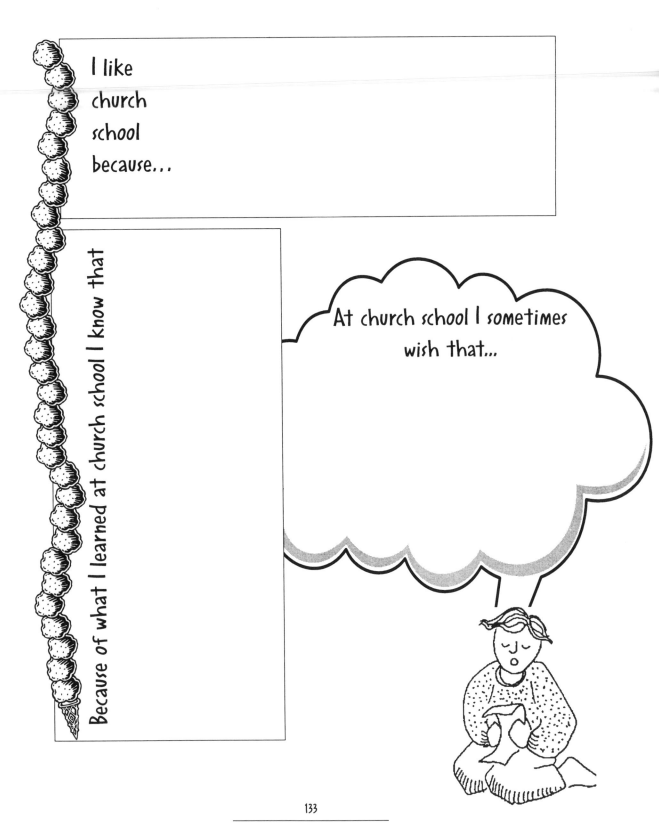

I like church school because...

Because of what I learned at church school I know that

At church school I sometimes wish that...

133

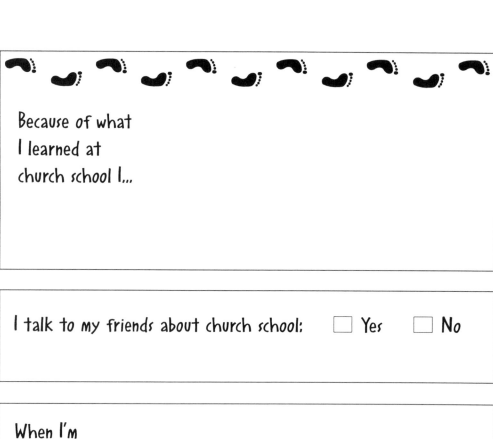

Because of what
I learned at
church school I...

I talk to my friends about church school: ☐ Yes ☐ No

When I'm
in church
school I
feel like...

because...

If I were in charge of next week's church school lesson, I WOULD	
	•
	•
	•
	•
	•
	•
	•
	•

Quertionnaire for children in grade 3 to grade 5

When I think about church I feel...

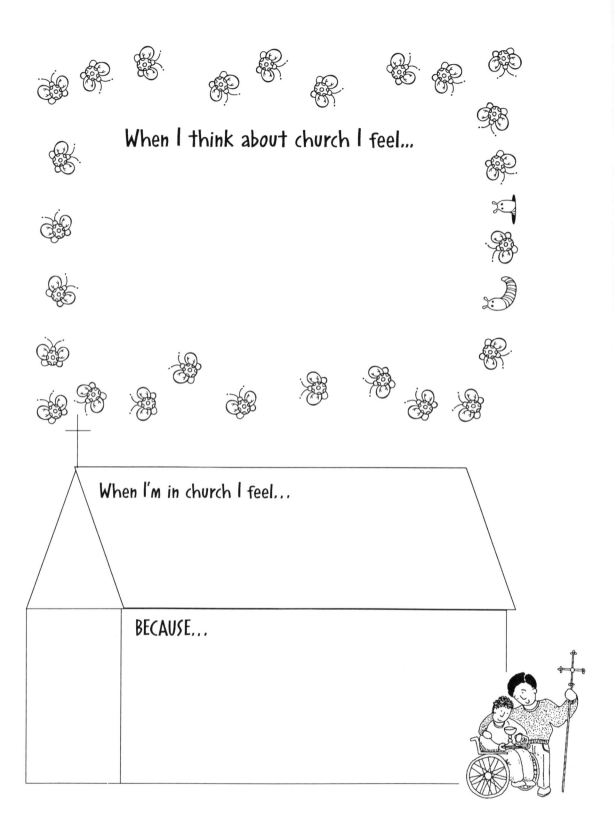

When I'm in church I feel...

BECAUSE...

MY friends go to church school because...

I love it!

Make a mark on the line to show how much you like CHURCH SCHOOL

I hate it!

My friends DON'T go to church school because...

Name: _____

Age: _____   Grade in school: _____

Questionnaire for children in grade 3 to grade 5

Questionnaire
for children in grade 6 and up

As the oldest children in church school, your opinions are valuable to us. You have first-hand (and, perhaps, long-term) experience of learning from the curriculum, and you are old enough to express your opinions in a way we will find very useful. Please complete this questionnaire for us.

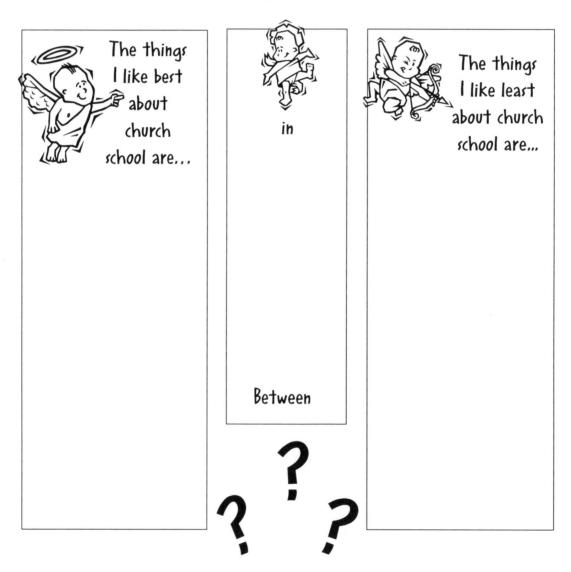

The things I like best about church school are...

in

Between

The things I like least about church school are...

Just an Idea

I talk to my friends about church school:
☐ Yes ☐ No

WRITE SMALL!

BECAUSE...

When I'm in church school I feel...

139

When I think about church I feel...

When I'm in church I feel...

BECAUSE...

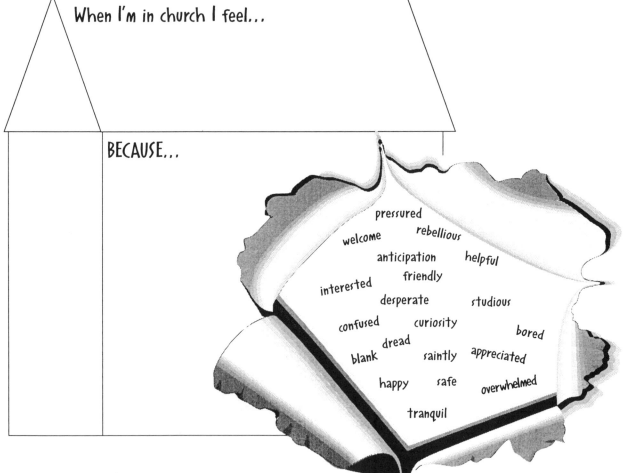

pressured

welcome   rebellious

anticipation   helpful

friendly

interested   studious

desperate

confused   curiosity   bored

dread

blank   saintly   appreciated

happy   safe   overwhelmed

tranquil

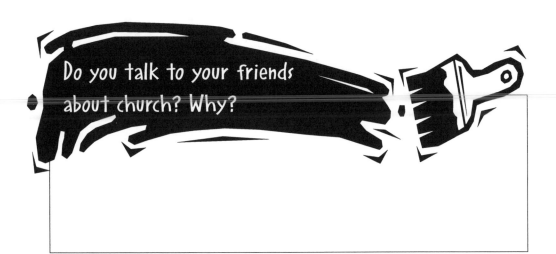

Do you talk to your friends about church? Why?

Church school would be more fun if we had...

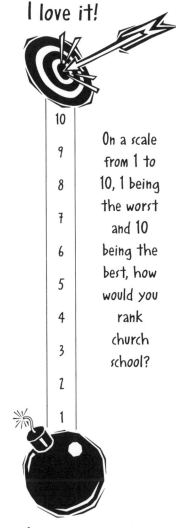

I love it!

10
9
8
7
6
5
4
3
2
1

On a scale from 1 to 10, 1 being the worst and 10 being the best, how would you rank church school?

I hate it!

Questionnaire for children in grade 6 and up

If I were in charge of next week's church school lesson, I WOULD

-
-
-
-
-
-
-
-

MY friends go to church school
because…

Because of what I learned at church
school I…

Because of what I learned at church
school I know that…

My friends DON'T go to church
school because…

Name: _____

Age: _____   Grade in school: _____

Questionnaire for children in grade 6 and up

Questionnaire for parents

What do you want for your children from a church school curriculum? ....

....

....

Does the church school's curriculum meet your needs? ....

Explain: ....

....

....

Are take-home materials available to you? ....

Do you use them? ....

How do you use them? ....

....

Do your children enjoy church school? ....

How do you know? ....

....

....

Do your children talk about the church school lesson without prompting?

....

From what each of your children says about the lesson, can you recognise the reading or the theme of the day? ....

....

Rank these aspects of church school in order of importance.
(5=most, 1=least)

Being with peers: 1 ☐   2 ☐   3 ☐   4 ☐   5 ☐

Bible stories: 1 ☐   2 ☐   3 ☐   4 ☐   5 ☐

Relation of faith to
  daily living: 1 ☐   2 ☐   3 ☐   4 ☐   5 ☐

Teacher/Child relationships: 1 ☐   2 ☐   3 ☐   4 ☐   5 ☐

What are some of the tough religious questions your children have asked? ...

....

....

Other comments on the curriculum: ....

....

....

Comments on the church service: ....

....

....

....

Name ....

Questionnaire for clergy

What are some of the tough religious questions children have asked you?

....

....

....

....

What do you want for children from a church school curriculum?

....

....

....

Rank these aspects of church school in order of importance.
(5=most, 1=least)

Being with peers:	1 ☐	2 ☐	3 ☐	4 ☐	5 ☐
Bible stories:	1 ☐	2 ☐	3 ☐	4 ☐	5 ☐
Relation of faith to daily living:	1 ☐	2 ☐	3 ☐	4 ☐	5 ☐
Teacher/Child relationships:	1 ☐	2 ☐	3 ☐	4 ☐	5 ☐

Does the church school's curriculum meet your needs? ....

....

Explain: ....

....

....

What comments do you hear from church school teachers on the curriculum and church school? ....

....

....

....

What comments do you hear from parents on the curriculum and church school? ....

....

....

....

What would you like to add to the curriculum? ....

....

....

Other comments on the curriculum: ....

....

Comments on the church service: ....

....

Heritage

Does the material help the children learn about their denominational heritage? ....

In what way? ....

....

How would you incorporate more specific denominational teaching into the curriculum? ....

....

....

....

Worship

Have you used worship resources provided by the curriculum? ....

....

Were they intergenerational? ....

Were they adaptable to the congregation's worship? ....

Have you any other comments or observations? ....

....

....

....

Recommended reading — Our favourite books

Ministry with children and the people who care for them is rich and challenging. To meet the challenge and to keep ourselves refreshed and energized it is important that we can touch base with others who share our passion for this ministry. One of our favorite ways of doing this is through reading. Here are a few of the books which we return to over and over for inspiration, hope, challenge, and nurture.

Cavalletti, Sofia. *The Religious Potential of the Child: Experiencing Scripture and Liturgy with Young Children.* Chicago, Ill.: Liturgy Training Publications, 1992.

Covin Juengst, Sara. *Sharing Faith with Children: Rethinking the Children's Sermon.* Louisville, Ky.: Westminster/John Knox Press, 1994.

Daley, Shannon P. et al. *Welcome the Child: A Child Advocacy Guide for Churches.* Friendship Press, 1994 (Section V: Chapters 1–3).

Harris, Maria. *Teaching & Religious Imagination: An Essay in the Theology of Teaching.* San Francisco, Calif.: HarperSanFrancisco, 1987.

Kimes, Barbara, et al. *Engaging in Transcendence: The Church's Ministry and Covenant with Young Children.* Pilgrim Press, 1992 (pp. 105–124).

MacLean, Paul, and Douglas Cowling. *Sharing the Banquet: Liturgical Renewal in Your Parish.* Toronto, Ont.: Anglican Book Centre, 1993.

Mueller Nelson, Gertrud. *To Dance With God: Family Ritual and Community Celebration.* Mahwah, N.J.: Paulist Press, 1986.

Ng, David, and Virginia Thomas. *Children in the Worshipping Community.* John Knox, 1981 (pp. 52–80).

Oppenheimer, Helen. *Helping Children Find God: A Book for Parents, Teachers and Clergy.* Harrisburg: Morehouse Publishing, 1995.

Roof, Wade Clark. *A Generation of Seekers: The Spiritual Journey of the Baby Boom Generation.* San Francisco, Calif.: HarperSanFrancisco, 1993.

Westerhoff, John H. III. *Spiritual Life: The Foundation for Preaching and Teaching.* Louisville, Ky.: Westminster/John Knox Press, 1994.

Westerhoff, John H. III. *Will Our Children Have Faith?* Toronto, Ont.: Anglican Book Centre, 1979.

Wolff Pritchard, Gretchen. *Offering the Gospel to Children.* Cambridge, Mass.: Cowley Publications, 1992.

We hope you find these as insightful and nourishing as we do.

In the Child's Best Interest: A Primer on the U.N. Convention on the Rights of the Child. Foster Parents Plan International and Defense for Children International, 1988.

Notes

1. From the service of Holy Baptism, the prayer over the newly baptized, in *The Book of Common Prayer*, According to the use of The Episcopal Church, p. 308.

2. Other denominations and national churches have similar statements expressing their mission regarding ministry with children. You might want to find out if your denomination has a similar statement to help guide your ministry. For a more thorough reading of The United Church of Canada's work on being the church with children, we recommend *A Place for You, Toward the Integration of Children into the Life of the Church* (Division of Mission in Canada, The United Church of Canada, 1989).

    The Office of Children's Ministries for the Episcopal Church and twelve dioceses have developed a document called *Towards Models for Children's Ministries in the Episcopal Church*. Their statement and goals are as follows:

    Dioceses and Congregations Affirmed the Following Statement and Goals.

    -   There is a place for each child in God's creation.

    -   Christian formation begins in the earliest stages of childhood.

    -   Children are continually being formed and transformed through the power of Christ. Children are Christ's representatives in the world. Children are ministers of the Gospel who bear witness to Christ.

    -   An important ministry of adult Christians is to honor children and to provide a safe and loving environment where adults and children together relate to God, share in Christ's teaching and fellowship, seek and serve Christ in all persons, and are partners in building God's Reign.

- Therefore, our task is to assist dioceses, congregations, and schools in the spiritual formation of children: honoring and receiving the gifts children offer, removing barriers for witness and ministry through experience and instruction in community.

Goals

- Help parents, members of the fellowship of faith and the church, recognize, honor and accept children as members and full participants of the Eucharistic community, and to nurture children's spirituality.
- Identify ways for the church to equip children for ministries in and with the Church and in a pluralistic world.
- Identify ways to help families nurture children in their Christian formation.
- Organize and support instructional activities for children so that they may fully participate in the Christian way of life as described in the Baptismal covenant.
- Urge Episcopalians to make their relationship, churches, schools and homes hospitable and safe for children.
- Urge our congregations to be advocates for the integrity of childhood and the dignity of all children.
- Make available to the Episcopal church, through the Office of Children's Ministries, all resources developed in the TREASURE Kids! Project.

Copies of this document and other resources are available through the Office of Children's Ministries, Episcopal Church Centre, 815 Second Avenue, New York, N. Y., 10017.

3. In 1993 we undertook an evaluation of the curriculum, *The Whole People of God* (Winfield, B.C.: Wood Lake Books). One of the questions we asked clergy, teachers, and parents was, "What are some of the tough religious questions your children have asked?" These questions come from the responses we received.

4. John H. Westerhoff III, *Spiritual Life: The Foundation for Preaching and Teaching* (Louisville, Ky.: Westminster/John Knox Press, 1994), 17.

5. *The Whole People of God.*

6. For a rich discussion of liturgical renewal for congregations with full inclusion of children and those who care for them, see Paul MacLean and Douglas Cowling, *Sharing the Banquet* (Toronto, Ont.: Anglican Book Centre, 1993).

7. Christine Whitehorn Stugard, *Living Bread: Recipes for Home-Baked Breads for the Eucharist and for the Fellowship and Family Tables* (Cincinnati, Ohio: Forward Movement Publications, 1983), 14.

8. *Leading the Way: An Educator's Handbook* from the *Living the Good News* curriculum (Denver, Col.: Living the Good News Inc., 1991).

9. For an example of a good sexual abuse policy for churches, see *The Diocesan Sexual Abuse Policy* (Anglican Diocese of Toronto, Canada, 1992).

10. John Westerhoff has often quoted this poem by Alice Walker, and most recently in his book *Spiritual Life*, cited above. The poem is from a collection of poetry called *Revolutionary Petunias & Other Poems* (New York: Harcourt Brace & Company, 1970), 11.

11. From the service of thanksgiving for the birth of a child, in *The Book of Alternative Services*, 612.

12. The Anglican Church of Canada, *The Book of Common Prayer* (Toronto, Ont.: Anglican Book Centre, 1962), 47.

13. *The Book of Alternative Services*, 214; The Book of Common Prayer (U.S.), 126.

14. The Church of the Province of New Zealand, *A New Zealand Prayer Book* (Auckland: Collins, 1989), 214.

15. *The Book of Common Prayer*, (U.S.), 304–305.

16. From *The United Church of Canada*, liturgical resources to be presented at the 1997 General Council.

17. From the *Lutheran Book of Worship* (Minneapolis, Minn.: Augsburg Fortress, 1978), 123.

18. Diocese of Toronto Logos Institute, Toronto, Canada.

Notes

Appendix

A CHILDREN'S CHARTER FOR THE CHURCH

Nurture of the Child:

Children are a heritage from the LORD, and the fruit of the womb is a gift. (Psalm 127:4)

The Church is called

• to receive, nuture and treasure each child as a gift from God;

• to proclaim the Gospel to children, in ways that empower them to receive and respond to God's love;

• to give high priority to the quality of planning for children and the preparation and support of those who minister with them;

• to include children, in fulfillment of the Baptismal Covenant, as members and full participants in the Eucharistic community and in the church's common life of prayer, witness and service.

Ministry to the Child:

Then Jesus took the children in his arms, placed his hands on each of them and blessed them. (Mark 10:16)

The Church is called

•to love, shelter, protect and defend children within its own community and in the world, especially those who are abused, neglected or in danger;

• to nuture and support families in caring for their children, acting in their children's best interest, and recognizing and fostering their children's spirituality and unique gifts;

• to embrace children who seek Christian nurture independently of their parents' participation in the church;

• to advocate for the integrity of childhood and the dignity of all children at every level of our religious, civic and political structures.

Ministry to the Child:

A little child shall lead them. (Isaiah 11:6)

The Church is called

• to receive children's special gifts as signs of the Reign of God;

• to foster community beyond the family unit, in which children, youth and adults know each other by name, minister to each other, and are partners together in serving Christ in the world;

• to appreciate children's abilities and readiness to represent Christ and his church, to bear witness to him wherever they may be, and according to the gifts given them, to carry on Christ's work of reconciliation in the world, and to take their place in the life, worship and governance of the church (from *Ministry of the Laity*, BCP p.855).

IMPLEMENTING A CHILDREN'S CHARTER FOR THE CHURCH

A Study Guide For Congregations

A Children's Charter for The Church is a call to the church to respond in new and intentional ways to Christ's mandate to care for, respect, and bring all children to Him.

This study guide is designed to help us understand more thoroughly the meaning and implications of that mandate. It may be used in many ways: a Sunday morning adult forum, a special advent or lenten series, or a vestry or leadership retreat are but a few possibilities.

The diocesan leaders who have developed it hope that the Children's Charter will help you and your congregation reaffirm your commitment to the children in your midst and intensify your advocacy on behalf of them and all children.

SESSION 1. NURTURE OF THE CHILD

Prominently display the scripture, Psalm 127:4, BCP. (see the *Charter.*) Have copies of A CHILDREN'S CHARTER FOR THE CHURCH to distribute.

Objectives:

• To affirm our identity as the people of God

• To compare our nurture as children in the church with that of children today

• To identify ways that we are currently nurturing children and possible changes

• To explore ways of enhancing worship and Christian education for children

1. Who are we? Remembering Our Baptism.

Distribute the Baptismal Liturgy (90–91). Depending on the size of the group, organize into smaller, intimate groups which can gather about a table. Each table should have access to a small pitcher of water and a fairly large shell or a bowl shaped like a shell.

The designated leader reads the scripture aloud (Mark 1:4–11) and allows a few moments for silent reflection, recalling memories of their own baptisms, or of others'. Ask each person to pour water from the pitcher into the shell as the memory is shared.

2. Stories of Being Nurtured.

• Read aloud the section of the charter, "Nurture of the Child."

• Ask participants to recall their earliest memory of church or of being aware of God. Select a word or phrase which describes this memory to share with the group. Record on newsprint.

• What would you like children in our congregation to remember about their experiences here? Using words or phrases, list on newsprint.

3. Helping Children Worship and Come To Know God.

• Identify how, where, and with whom children presently worship. Are those services "child friendly" and accessible to children?

• How do we identify, prepare and support those who teach and lead worship for children?

• How do we help parents prepare children for worship and receiving communion?

• In the Sunday School or Children's Chapel, do children come to "know God" or do they learn "about God"? What is the difference?

• From these discussions, identify what is being done to foster children's worship and experience of God's love within the congregation. Record on newsprint.

• What things need to be changed or initiated to bring present worship practices into harmony with the Charter's vision? Record.

• Save this and other newsprint.

4. Fulfilling Our Congregational Vision.

• Compare what is already being done with the new ideas for an expanded ministry.

• What things would need to be changed or initiated in order to enhance our ministry with children? Record as "Moving On."

Close with prayer.

SESSION 2. MINISTRY TO THE CHILD

Prominently display the scripture, Mark 10:16. (see the *Charter*.)

Objectives:

• To remember our Baptismal Covenant

• To examine how we fulfill our obligation as a congregation to the children we baptize and their families

• To assess our outreach and advocacy for all children in the community, especially those at risk

1. Remembering our Baptismal Covenant.

• Provide copies of the Covenant and the Welcome to the newly baptized for the group, (pp. 304-5; 308, bottom of page, *BCP*, U.S.) Read together, picturing children as members of the baptized community.

• Discuss what it means for children to be full members of the Eucharistic community.

2. Ministries to children and their families.

• Read aloud the section "Ministry to the Child" from the Children's Charter.

• As a group/s consider specific ways the covenant calls us to assist the newly baptized children and their families. What are we presently doing well? Record.

• What more could be done? List specific ideas. What is required to carry out the things we could/should be doing? Identify leaders in the parish who could help make it happen.

3. Reaching Out.

• Identify the "unjust and adverse circumstances" of children in the community.

• How are these different from our childhood experiences? List. What are we doing to identify and assist children who are at risk? What more could we be doing? Record these ideas.

• Are we reaching out to children in the community who are not experiencing Christ's love in a church setting? How could we do that? Record.

• What is required to be a Christian advocate for children? Do we consider advocacy part of our mission? Identify ways in which we could become better advocates for all children, e.g., agencies, organizations with whom we could cooperate. Record.

• Summarize what we have learned about our congregation's ministry to children — through its support of families, its reaching out into the community and its role as advocate. Summarize those areas and actions which have been identified as new initiatives for ministry to children. Record and save.

Closing Prayer.

Into your hands, O God, we place ourselves, the guardians of your children. Support and strengthen us as we seek to make the world a more welcoming place for them. Unify us in our concern and respect for them.

Into your hands also we place the children of our homes, our cities, and the world. Support them in their joys and sorrows, strengthen their families, enlighten their governments, shelter them from evil. Through your guidance, may we respond to their needs that they may discover the joy of your creation and know the bounty of your unending love. All this we ask in your name. *Amen.*

(From "Recognizing and Celebrating Children," Congregations Concerned for Children, Minneapolis. Reprinted in *Welcome the Child, A Child Advocacy Guide for Churches.* Shannon P. Daley and Kathleen A. Guy, Friendship Press and Children's Defense Fund, p. 22)

SESSION 3. MINISTRY OF THE CHILD

Prominently display the scripture, Isaiah 11:6. (see the *Charter.*)

Objectives:

• To understand the gifts children bring to the church

• To examine how the congregation presently supports children in their ministry within the church

• To explore new ways of receiving the gifts of children and encouraging and enabling them to live out their baptismal covenant

1. Children's Gifts.

• Read "Ministry of the Child" aloud. Invite members of the group to think of a time when a child has ministered to them. Describe the special gifts of children. What are some of the gifts you discern in the children in the congregation?

2. Children as Ministers.

• Discuss how the congregation accepts children in its midst. Are efforts being made to reconcile those who prefer that children are not present in the service and those who believe children belong in the service?

• Are children taken seriously as lay leaders? Identify, on newsprint, the roles children have in the liturgy; at parish events such as festive dinners, work days, outreach, pastoral care. Do adults and children participate together in these activities?

• Do children have opportunities to offer their gifts in ministry to adults? Do adults and children know each other's names? To what extent is the parish an extended family? What opportunities are being missed by our failure to expand the roles of children? Brainstorm new ways of helping children participate more fully in parish life as both givers and receivers of ministry. Record these comments and ideas as desired.

• What will be required to bring this about? Identify present parish leaders in all aspects of ministry who can help bring this new vision about.

3. Review from sessions 1, 2 and 3.

• What is already being done in children's ministries?

• Review the lists of possible new initiatives for children's ministries.

• Identify three to five ideas/goals which seem to be more important or energizing for enhanced children's ministries.

• Discuss how to begin the process of working on these goals; a timeline may be helpful.

• Plan how to invite others in the congregation to become involved in implementing the goals.

Concluding Collects:

Almighty and everliving God, ruler of all things in heaven and earth, hear our prayers for this parish family. Strengthen the faithful, arouse the careless, and restore the penitent. Grant us all things necessary for our common life, and bring us all to be of one heart and mind within your holy Church, through Jesus Christ our Lord. *Amen.*

Almighty God, heavenly Father, you have blessed us with the joy and care of children. Give us calm strength and patient wisdom as we bring them up, that we may teach them to love whatever is just and true and good, following the example of our Savior Jesus Christ. *Amen.*